THE MEDIATED MIND

The Mediated Mind

Affect, Ephemera, and Consumerism in the Nineteenth Century

Susan Zieger

FORDHAM UNIVERSITY PRESS

New York 2018

Fordham University Press has no responsibility for the persistence or accuracy of URLs for external or third-party Internet websites referred to in this publication and does not guarantee that any content on such websites is, or will remain, accurate or appropriate.

Fordham University Press also publishes its books in a variety of electronic formats. Some content that appears in print may not be available in electronic books.

Visit us online at www.fordhampress.com.

Library of Congress Cataloging-in-Publication Data available online at https://catalog.loc.gov.

Printed in the United States of America
20 19 18   5 4 3 2 1
First edition

CONTENTS

From Paper to Pixel

Ephemera

Imagine you are holding a cigarette card. A small, rectangular piece of flexible cardboard, it fits easily in your palm. A colorful image adorns the front, and tiny text fills the back. You could gaze at it or read it. You could pocket it for later, or devour it now. Over a century ago, this card protected your cigarettes from getting crushed. Maybe you saved it in an album, or maybe you threw it away. Perhaps you absorbed it while you smoked, in the minutes of a work break, or after a meal. Look more closely at the image. It shows a man on a beach, the ocean and palm trees behind him, staring at a footprint. He is wearing a pointed fur cap and looks surprised. The caption tells you this is Robinson Crusoe, and that the card is made by Player's Cigarettes. You turn it over. Two paragraphs let you know that this is Number 17 of 25 "Characters from Fiction," that *The Life and Strange Surprizing Adventures of Robinson Crusoe* was written by Daniel Defoe in 1719, that Defoe heard the story from the castaway Alexander Selkirk in Bristol, and other facts. This information creates nested worlds for you: the worlds of history, fiction, characters from fiction, Defoe's works, and the novel *Robinson Crusoe*, a work you may never have heard of or read. There are other sets of worlds: You could easily be contemplating a card about a freshwater fish, a recent boxing champion, or a king of Britain. If you didn't possess such information before, you may feel as though you've acquired some facts or culture. Equally, the card may also send you on a flight of fancy or a reverie, or engage your imagination in a fleeting, unproductive way. It may feed mental habits that do not exactly amount to learning, or consolidate your brand loyalty to Player's. It may evoke physical urgings, emotions, or affects. You may forget it entirely, or it may stay with you, shaping you in small ways you cannot measure or predict.

Cigarette cards were the first ephemera designed to be collected. Trivial, disposable things that have somehow endured, they appear now in a large online secondary market, as well as in library and museum collections. They encapsulate self-conscious experiences of mass media at the end of the nineteenth century, and in turn, help us reflect on our own mass media consumption and the embodied states of mind and affects through which it takes place. Ephemera, like the winged insects that share its Greek root, lasts through the day; in the nineteenth century, its basis was cheap paper. The adoption of the steam-powered rotary press, which could print about a thousand sheets per hour, generated the trivial printed documents and objects of everyday life, from bus tickets, bookmarks, and business cards to more consumable, yet still disposable, items: newspapers, illustrated magazines, advertising tokens, and giveaways.[1] Like our own screens, printed paper and imprinted objects touched every region of social life. Massive and anonymous, ephemera nonetheless intimately reconnected people to themselves, their families, and their social circles in ways they had never imagined. Temperance societies gave away medals, ribbons, and pledge cards to their members; families and friends circulated photographic cartes de visite and collected them in albums; postcards memorialized holiday travel; pornographic cards and peep shows shifted sexual practices; advertisements leaped to the eye from newly available surfaces.[2] As people engaged the medium, making it their own, a mass culture of social customs popped up around it: Literate and illiterate audiences listened to newspapers read aloud in public houses; husbands handed volumes of triple-decker novels off to their wives; lone puzzlers worked through crosswords and brainteasers to pass the time. This book unapologetically elevates such trivial ephemera to critical attention because it illuminates neglected facets of nineteenth-century experience. As David Vincent has shown, mass print called forth a range and variety of literacies, not limited to fluent, solitary, focused reading.[3] Visual perception, digital dexterity, and organizational ability were just a few of the habits that the new medium retrained. If this phenomenon sounds familiar, it is because ubiquitous computing has effected a similar sea change in twenty-first-century everyday life.

Yet our digital moment, of smart phones, social media, and unprecedented access to enormous amounts of information, is not merely analogous to the burgeoning of print in the nineteenth century. This book shows how the earlier period established entwined affective, psychological, social, and cultural habits of media consumption that we still experience, even as pixels supersede paper. Turning to the nineteenth century to think about the twenty-first may seem counterintuitive; it is certainly indirect. But establishing a longer, broader genealogy of media consumption is a matter of some urgency, to illuminate the ideological investments and epistemological conditions driving our present-day practices and discourses. How did we arrive at our contemporary consumer media economy? Revealing earlier nodes in the history of our own moment offers a valuable counterweight to the reflexive assumption that new media lack a past. Both futurist enthusiasm and conservative pessimism often react to innovations in consumer technology as if they were utterly new; in this way, they perform technological determinism. By contrast, media histories such as Lisa Gitelman's *Paper Knowledge: Toward a Media History of Documents* (2014) assemble genealogies of cultural forms; in that book, linking the late-nineteenth-century jobbing press to today's portable document format (PDF) file extension. Likewise, this book uses nineteenth-century printed ephemera as a springboard to reflect on our own digital saturation. I bring temperance medals, cigarette cards, inkblots, and cartoons to your attention because they form part of our own history. This move productively reimagines such material, drawing it out of its narrow orbit, bringing it into proximity with other media forms, and using it to analyze cultural politics. Thinking of print, paper, and imprinted objects not as trivial ephemera, but as facilitators of ephemerality, releases their theoretical and political potential. Attending to discourses of ephemeral media consumption departs from quantitative approaches, allowing us to imagine its scenes of consumption rather than rehearse its statistics.

Five of these scenes of ephemeral media consumption animate my inquiry in this book. The first is a special relationship between print media and the first modern, mass live events. Beginning with print, media constantly attempt, and fail, to capture and represent presence, especially the unique affects of mass events, but that very failure also helped create their ritualistic aura. Beginning in the early nineteenth century, mass live events held out the promise of an unmediated body politic, but proleptic and belated print media—whether in the form of advertisements, posters, journalistic reportage, reviews, or tokens and giveaways—created the promise itself. Reading about it before or afterward, or collecting memorabilia from it, stoked powerful yearnings to join the unmediated mass and feel with other people. To share beliefs and opinions with a large community, to unite with others below the threshold of consciousness, reflected a dream of wholeness through public affect and thought characteristic of the reform politics of the first half of the century. Similar fantasies also appear in Romantic formations of universal mind and shared spirituality, and in late-century parapsychological research into telepathic communication. Printed ephemera showed how the temporary suspension of a highly individualistic self could afford new possibilities for intersubjectivity, public feeling, and shared affect—just as twenty-first-century digital technologies and social media have done.

A second abiding relationship to mass media consumption is the tendency to conceive of it metaphorically as an addiction. Addiction operates on the irony that the commodity that you have chosen for your use turns the tables, changing you from a rational, purposive consumer into a pitiably dependent user. This book shows how the abiding language of media addiction, while it marks the moment when a new medium saturates a culture, also obscures the complex affective, psychological, and cultural transactions taking place beneath its surface. I begin by reframing the long-standing diagnosis of women's addictive reading of the suspenseful, sensational, transgressive narratives contained in novels.[4] First emerging in the eighteenth century, when novels such as *Pamela* (1740) helped create a new "media culture"—albeit on a much smaller, simpler scale than the nineteenth-century ones that I describe—this long-lived discourse typically attacked women's absorptive novel-reading as sick, trivial, narcissistic, and delusive.[5] Late-twentieth-century feminist and Marxist critics emphasized the evident political investments in such diagnoses.[6] But what happens if we look beyond the novel, to a wider variety of print media objects? Nineteenth-century middle- and working-class men and women habitually and voraciously consumed a great many genres, literary forms, and print forms besides sensation novels. They sought information, solace, simulated sociability, humor, and a host of other desirable objectives. From this wide range of activity, I isolate a new formation, an obsessive consumption of print in a quest for information as cultural mastery. Strategically invoking the figure of the "information addict," I show how it first emerged in the 1890s, prefiguring our own seeming "addiction" to the personal devices that feed us a steady diet of constantly updated, cheap information.

Once consumed, where does information reside in the mind? A third enduring figuration of ephemeral media consumption is the unconscious as media storage. In the nineteenth century, the question of what to keep and what to throw away first confronted consumers daily—especially with respect to cheap print. This phenomenon generated a paradox that is still with us: Although mass media items are meant to be disposable, we can't resist keeping them. James Mussell argues for the uncanniness of both printed and digital ephemera: It is that which a culture intends, and fails, to forget.[7] As printed material overwhelmed readers' ability to consume it all, fantasies of infinite mental retention emerged, relieving them of the burden of constant discrimination. As the late-Romantic writer Thomas De Quincey put it, "There is no such thing as forgetting possible to the mind."[8] In the 1860s, Forbes Winslow was just one psychologist to elaborate the idea, extolling "the tonic, permanent, and indestructible character of the impressions made upon the cerebrum" from infancy through adulthood.[9] Nineteenth-century writers often conflated memory and the unconscious by imagining a hidden storage site for experiences too numerous to keep present to the mind. When experiences are stored in memory, they acquire the character of both media files and information. Rather than theorizing a mental structure that purged disposable records from the mind, nineteenth-century writers imagined the capacity to keep them all. Although it had many more contours that complicate the analogy, memory began to be reconceived as media storage. Here are the origins of our own moment, in which technophilic ideologies of new media "arrest memory and its degenerative possibilities in order to support dreams of superhuman digital programmability," according to Wendy Hui Kyong Chun.[10] The illogical but eminently human solution to the overwhelming size of the archive was to continue extending it while hoping, somehow, to obtain mastery over it. In the psychic push and pull of nineteenth-century mass print culture, our own media fantasy of the mind's infinite memory first arose.

One feature of the mastery over mass print culture and its information overload was playback, the ability not merely to store experiences as information, but to reproduce them at will, transcending ordinary memory. Playback became a reality with the appearance of the phonograph in the 1870s, though it was a cultural fantasy before and after, responsive as much to print and visual media as to the archive of sound. In such fantasies, subjects achieved the mastery over experience and memory required for playback by developing extraordinary powers and prostheses. Such self-extension, to borrow a descriptive phrase from Marshall McLuhan, immersed the subject so far down in mediated deeps that scholars have described it as a form of embodiment: "The essence of nineteenth-century Britain might indeed be defined as a move towards a society's 'Being-in-Print.'"[11] Andrew Piper has shown how the idea of "dreaming in books" redefined the imagination at the period's beginning, but it was not confined to the book format.[12] Being in print was key to nineteenth-century middle-class life. Our own similar moment could be described as "being-onscreen," because we continually consume images and words on screens, and spread ourselves through the social interactions they permit. As an earlier such moment, being-in-print unleashed delightful fantasies of self-elaboration and expansion. A countertradition to a more familiar, critical ennui and nausea with mediated life, attended by its own fantasies of extricating oneself from the media mire, the discourse of playback drew on the technophilic imagination, leading subjects farther into mediated and simulated worlds.

Being-in-print generated the paradox that mass media, as our second nature, seems to afford individual expression, although it is mass produced, systemic, and anonymous. This paradox simultaneously generates fears that mass culture's nameless address homogenizes its consumers, reshaping them into a faceless, destructive mob or crowd, and creates desires for self-styling and social belonging that can be obtained only through mediation.[13] The nineteenth century was the first period in which consumers began daily to consider which parts of mass-produced culture they would incorporate into their psyches and which they would reject.[14] Our digital version of this practice is now so intensive and pervasive, it almost goes without saying; that is why its history is all the more important to analyze. Such self-fashioning through mass print generated a critical anxiety about influence on the one hand, and on the other, creative material practices of making, remaking, collecting, and curating.[15] The hyperrationalism and even paranoia of the anxiety was balanced by less rigid, more embodied states of mind, such as reverie, daydreaming, distraction, and enchantment. Accounts of nineteenth-century self-making suggest the wide array of psychological affordances of mass print, as its consumers compared, adjusted themselves to, incorporated, and rejected mass cultural norms. So too, collecting and arranging printed ephemera count as modes of literacy; they permit us to broaden our scope from paper to include imprinted objects and commodities such as medals and ribbons.[16] This broadening gesture helps us acknowledge the value of a wide array of human experience, breaking free from the common critical dismissal of mass culture as mindless or absurd. It helps us describe the everyday alchemy by which we find, lose, and rediscover ourselves in our interfaces with mass media.[17]

This argument matters because only by taking users' experiences seriously enough to recognize their history can we hope to understand the way our own media revolution is reconfiguring social life. The five abiding cultural formations I just described—the mediated desire for unmediated mass affect, information "addiction," the unconscious as media and information storage, playback, and self-fashioning via mass media—together articulate some of the major ambivalences we still feel about mass-mediated life. The angst surrounding media technologies, as described by Brenton J. Malin, is that their ostensible improvement of human life accompanies their apparent harm through overstimulation and information bombardment.[18] Ambivalence is a scene of heightened affect, a psychic tearing between two alternatives. The desire to keep and control mass-produced material that is meant to be discarded indicates how ephemeral commodities become expressive objects. The compulsive reliance on media technologies describes a desperate distress about disconnection from one's own cultural environment—and a compensatory longing to be free of it. The dread of losing oneself within the mass competes with a desire to merge with it.

Although I have separated these ambivalences to better understand their operation, they are complexly intertwined. Noting their commonalities reveals the significance of my central argument that nineteenth-century habits of mass print consumption prefigure our own digital moments: The concept of the mass media remains so fraught because it thrives on an irreconcilable tension between a highly individualized self, and the shared affect and collective agency that constitute the social. To understand this tension, I describe and analyze the varied, unpredictable psychology of ephemeral consumption, which loosened liberal individualistic assumptions of subjective constancy and unity. As Jonathan Crary has argued, modern mass culture was continuous with "states of distraction, reverie, dissociation, and trance."[19] Ephemera reflected the way attention inevitably disintegrates, and fragmented attention reliably reconsolidates. Whether bingeing on printed appeals, fending them off, or drifting away from and back to them, consumers established new mental and material habits, and became self-conscious of them. In the times and spaces of such quotidian habits, the self's edges became porous, admitting the mass. As I now demonstrate, a useful optic for glimpsing such transformations is affect.

Affect and Mass Culture

Perhaps the biggest paradox of mass culture, understood as the lived relation to mass-produced media, is that it simultaneously constitutes an implicitly rational public sphere and prevents that sphere's realization.[20] This paradox constantly vexes its relationship to theories of mind, and to the public sphere that is understood as their expression. Jürgen Habermas offered an account of the public sphere's historical emergence at the turn of the nineteenth century, which stressed the rational uses of print media in settings such as coffeehouses—and then lamented its degeneration into consumer entertainment and relaxation to fulfill "psychological" needs.[21] Michael Warner revised the concept with his influential notion of oppositional, multiple "counter-publics," or groups that "seek to transform fundamental styles of embodiment, identity, and social relations—including their unconscious manifestations."[22] Warner helpfully deconstructed Habermasian rationalism, gesturing toward the less predictable, embodied mental life of mass subjects. I too attend to the ways that gendered, raced, and classed subjects do not possess the privilege of approximating ideals of public reason that are really the effects of social distinction. But I focus on the spaces of overlap between mass media and embodied mental life, where social identifications and political alliances might but don't necessarily form. In this way, my study builds in part from Lauren Berlant's elaboration of the "intimate public sphere" as a kind of "culture of circulation." Participants in such a consumer market "*feel* as though it expresses what is common among them."[23] Such feeling makes visible an array of positions, habitable by people of different classes, genders, ages, and sexualities: the mass live audience member, the enchanted viewer, the information "addict," the self-fashioner, the collector, and the re-player of experience, to name a few. I describe the way mass-mediated material began to dwell in the mind—less so the rational mind taken up with egoistic cognition than the embodied mind of daydreaming, reverie, and feeling. Acknowledging the mediated mind obliges us to give up the illusory association between individual sovereignty, reason, and agency; but it repays us with new critical discoveries—of intersubjectivity, collective agency, and shared affect.

To show how consumers incorporate mass culture, remaking it and themselves, in practices that are both psychological and physical, I leverage the recent surge of interest in affect. In this book, *affect* refers to a dynamic quality of human mind and body that links emotion to cognition, self to other, and self to environment.[24] Affect and ephemera are complementary topics. As José Esteban Muñoz observed, they are both material without being "solid," in the sense of conventional scholarly proof, and are thus amenable to alternative modes of critique.[25] Kathleen Stewart describes "ordinary affects" as "the varied, surging capacities to affect and be affected that give everyday life the quality of a continual motion of relations, scenes, contingencies, and emergencies. They're things that happen."[26] Depending on your perspective, such an expansive description may seem refreshing, frustratingly tautological, or a bit of both.[27] Rather than reproduce Stewart's method, I borrow its useful gesture of neutral description and scene-setting, which cuts through older, more deeply entrenched politics of popular and mass culture. Stewart and I follow Eve Sedgwick's lead in *Touching Feeling* (2003), refusing paranoid readings that quickly explain away affective phenomena with grand narratives.[28] Additionally, I undertake analysis mindful of Teresa Brennan's argument that affect's transmission between people—for example, the kind that alters the atmosphere of a crowded room—resists the Eurocentric tenet that it arises and subsides only within individuals.[29] Observing affect is an appropriate method for studying the late nineteenth century, because that is when it arose as a motif within an emergent phenomenological body, in competition with named emotions.[30] Unnameable but palpable and real, affect appeared in conjunction with, but without being determined by, mass culture. Affect opens up nineteenth-century psychological experience as embodied, material, and situated, while avoiding rigid Victorian, Freudian, and Lacanian psychological structures and categories.[31] Avoiding "an easy psychologism," my account gives more space to everyday accounts of affective and other mental states than to nineteenth-century texts of psychological theory.[32] I invoke the language of affect to identify key scenes of apparently passive or absent print media consumption and show how they perform significant cultural work. The reverie that overtakes a reader whose eyes have momentarily lifted from the page, the pleasure of removing a cigarette card from one's pocket to gaze at its colorful imagery, the well-being felt in the presence of temperate friends and recalled later, alone, as one turned a coin-sized medal over in one's fingers—these are some of the ordinary nineteenth-century experiences that affect permits us to consider.

Such varied everyday experiences require a term other than "reading," with its connotation of highly individualized, intellectual decoding of texts. Consider Charles Dickens's description of a character in *Our Mutual Friend* (1865): "He glanced at the backs of the books, with an awakened curiosity that went below the binding. No one who can read ever looks at a book, even unopened on a shelf, like one who cannot."[33] On the one hand, Dickens describes an affective encounter with a media form—a moment of apperception that reveals a new consumer habit. On the other, the observation develops into a too-easy judgment—either one can read or one can't—that doesn't do justice to the multiple modes of literacy, attention, and affects that media objects elicit. In this book, I use the term "media consumption," because it connotes the whole range of visual, tactile, collective, affective, and aesthetic experiences that helped materialize print. "Media consumption" also plainly acknowledges the modern industrial economy in which these exchanges take place, but which does not completely determine them. Formerly, calling someone a consumer connoted mindlessness, but it no longer does. Richard Altick's classic *The English Common Reader* (1957), the monument in the history of reading for its quantitative evidence and descriptive overview of the emergence of mass print culture, often used the term "reader" disparagingly, in this old vein of "consumer." Like Dickens, Altick offered appealingly detailed glimpses of the social life of Victorian readers—"the cook in the kitchen let the joint burn as she pored over the *Family Herald*, the mill-hand sat on his doorstep of a Sunday morning, smoking his pipe and reviewing the week's outrages in the *Illustrated Police News*"—but he also judged such reading to be facile and mindless.[34] Far more recently, Leah Price's important *Doing Things with Books in Victorian Britain* (2011) dramatized two poles of its titular designation, the ostensibly serious bourgeois reading of novels and the mundane, excessively material uses of print, such as for wrapping food.[35] Price's prescient book marks out two ends of a field in which my own analysis dwells. At one end, an intensive reading abstracts reader and book alike; at the other, deeply materialized, nonsymbolic activities of nonreading take place. Between them lies the uneven terrain I intend to survey. Skimming light literature while daydreaming, rereading and rebinding one's favorite novel, collecting temperance medals or cigarette cards, and interpreting inkblots were just a few ways that media consumers interacted with print's materials and objects. In this way, I give media consumption a face— something that quantitative studies, however meticulously they re-create the politics of mass print production, regulation, and distribution, do not.[36]

Walter Benjamin's histories and theories of nineteenth- and early twentieth-century mass consumption, refracted through affect, offer touchstones for this project. Benjamin consistently asks how media technologies such as photography, panoramas, feuilletons, comics, radio broadcasts, and films subtly change their human subjects and objects—and how they might be used to energize the masses for progressive rather than fascist politics. In his unfinished magnum opus *The Arcades Project*, he described the psychological effects of material culture and assembled a vast trove of insights into the states of mind in which consumers related to the stuff of the nineteenth century—iron and glass, toys and plush, crinolines and bicycles.[37] A Marxist, Benjamin tends to imply that capitalism's machine technologies had eroded an authentic, spontaneous, and vital human creativity.[38] His most famous idea, that an artwork's unique "aura" declines as it is reproduced by mass media, is beguiling—and imperfect.[39] So is his quest for "collective innervation," a kind of psychic unity that might propel audiences toward revolutionary action.[40] To better describe nineteenth-century psychic engagements with printed objects and material, I briefly invoke and occasionally adjust some of Benjamin's terms and ideas. I find that the language of affect, and its capacity to reflect public feelings, gives realistic description to the elusive and often mystical states of being Benjamin evokes. For example, chapter 1 reinterprets the aura not as the trace of the artifact's ancient ritual status, but as a widening of collective affect into public feeling through a new kind of ritualization, the live mass event. Chapter 4 describes Benjamin's Freudian conceptualization of psychic insulation from shock to delineate a countertradition of self-exposure that converts experience into information. In such ways, I put Benjamin into dialogue with recent theorists of affect and mass culture.

Just as this book reminds literary critics that novels are media objects, it demonstrates to media historians that print is a media technology. Media historians and archaeologists often dwell on the telegraph, the camera, and motion picture projection, showing how their symbolic logic and technical processes shaped human culture.[41] Such devices trained people to consume ephemeral media in the nineteenth century. Yet I aim to show how consumers interacted with materials of print like ink, metal, paper, and cardboard, in ways that also count as technological. My critical narrative thus corrects Friedrich Kittler's account in *Gramophone Film Typewriter* (1999). Keen to identify a mechanical, depersonalized media subject emerging around 1900, Kittler schematically linked his titular devices to Jacques Lacan's real, imaginary, and symbolic unconscious domains.[42] Yet he virtually ignored the dominant medium of the nineteenth century, and ephemeral states of mind escaped his rigid categories. What happens when we seriously consider print as a consumer medium, predisposed neither to ludic mayhem nor to McLuhan's mechanical order? Like Kittler, I draw attention to "affordances" or usable features; unlike him, I let them breathe and speak over the voice of Lacanian psychoanalysis. William Gibson coined the term "affordances" in *The Ecological Approach to Visual Perception*

(1979); although it has become common in media studies, it is less so in nineteenth-century studies. In Gibson's account of how animals, including humans, intuitively interact with their settings, "affordances" means the "possibilities or opportunities" that the environment "affords" its inhabitants.[43] Media studies typically uses the term to describe how the surfaces of media objects suggest possible uses to their consumers. Asking after the affordances of print forms requires attention to their size, shape, and pages; the look of their text or images; their portability and other aspects of their circulation and materiality. Describing print-human interfaces, I acknowledge print's status as a technology at the site of its consumption. Where relevant, I analyze how its affordances emerged in relation to more familiar media technologies. For example, ink-gazing and ink games recalled phantasmagoria and dissolving views; fantasies of memory as a kind of media storage were inspired by the phonograph's introduction of playback into culture in the 1870s and 1880s. In every case, human minds and bodies provide the scale and lead the analysis.

Seeking to renovate banal and even irrational states of mind, I directly challenge the image of the mindless mass cultural consumer made notorious by Theodor Adorno and Max Horkheimer in *Dialectic of Enlightenment* (1947).[44] I see their critique as heir to a nineteenth-century discourse, in which S. T. Coleridge lamented the new circulating libraries, John Stuart Mill decried the manufacture of mass public opinion through newspapers, and Gabriel Tarde redefined society itself as imitation through mass media consumption.[45] Brennan cogently dispatches with such theories of group mind when she notes that they assume that affect is transmitted, without accounting for its mechanisms; group mind is assumed to be a given, but the procedure for investigating it is "essentially Romantic."[46] Another flaw of the theory of group mind is that its totalizing perspective fails to capture fugitive responses to mass culture. The term "mass" also better describes my intervention than "popular" because in accounts influenced by Marxist cultural studies, "popular" often connotes an idealized, lost premodernity, whereas modern mass communication "is the essence of inauthenticity."[47] Stuart Hall described the mid-nineteenth century in Britain as the historical point when political freedom was reframed as the freedom to consume print media, which seemed to reflect working people's interests, but no longer stood as their authentic voice.[48] As Martin Conboy eloquently describes the result of this mismatch, "There is a hole at the heart of popular culture, we might say: the hole is the absence of real people."[49] That absence, however, is the effect of an older model of Marxist cultural studies, usefully corrected by turning to a more speculative and descriptive attention to affect. Although Conboy eloquently describes alienated affect within mass culture, he also maintains the critical impasse that disparages all engagements with mass culture as vacant and valueless merely because they are indirect and complicated.

The critical criterion of "realness" tacitly promoted by Conboy and others fails to account not only for nineteenth-century experiences, but for populist politics—for example, of the temperance movement—that do not neatly match the Marxist grand narrative. Similarly, many well-intentioned progressive literary critics find themselves caught in various double binds, attempting to read cultural subversion into elite literary materials, conducting elaborate close readings of popular novels that their original readers were unlikely to have performed, and failing to study the ephemeral materials that truly meant something to millions of people. The problem has its roots in the well-described split between intellectuals and masses at the end of the nineteenth century.[50] The postmodern retheorization of culture that dismantled this high-low distinction left intact the structural situation in which elite literary criticism weakly performs its interest in, but also condescends to, the mass. As Raymond Williams limned this insidious logic, "The mass is other people."[51] To avoid this bad faith, I use the term "mass" and ask my readers to acknowledge their participation in it. Attention to scenes of everyday affect encourages this leveling and acknowledgment.

Our own expansive mediated moments have exposed the limitations of older approaches to mass culture. I am referring to the spread of cheap internet-related technologies over the turn of the twenty-first century, which has upended conventional business models in music, film, television, and publishing industries. The demise of monolithic broadcast radio and television and the ascendance of fragmented and niche media markets expose the mind-control interpretation of mass media as a Cold War relic. The resulting participatory culture has been described by Henry Jenkins as "convergence culture" in which media companies accelerate media flows across different delivery channels, and media consumers learn "how to use these different media technologies to bring the flow of media more fully under their control and to interact with other consumers."[52] I invoke Jenkins ambivalently here. On the one hand, his work relegates Marxist laments of alienation, and Adorno and Horkheimer's excoriation of zombified pseudo-individuals, to the vanishing era of broadcast. On the other, his gesture of engaging and reforming large media companies equally risks overlooking the way they profit from users' free labor. And it sometimes seems to valorize any creative interactivity with mass media, however puerile.[53]

Scholars concerned with media habits, affective labor, and the erosion of work and play have begun to supply this deficiency.[54] Thus, though flawed, Jenkins's focus on the participatory aspects of mass culture invites us to reinvent conventional Marxist narratives, and the attention of theorists of recent media to the affective forms and modes of interactivity gives us models for rethinking nineteenth-century media consumption.

Mass Print Consumption in the Long, Wide Nineteenth Century

Calling print the first mass medium may sound jarring to readers who would reserve that distinction for twentieth-century broadcast technologies such as radio and television, and to scholars who pinpoint the emergence of mass media in the 1890s, with the New Journalism and the skyrocketing of newspaper readership.[55] The 1890s is certainly the pivotal decade in this history, both quantitatively and discursively, and several chapters of this book treat it. That is when increased literacy rates generated new markets for leisure reading, and when the language of "the mass" converged with older discourses of "the mob" and "the reading crowd."[56] But other moments throughout the long nineteenth century also play powerful roles in this history. Romanticists, historians of the book, and historians of reading have proposed 1780–1800 as the critical period when print became ubiquitous enough to alter culture and society. By the 1780s, Reinhard Wittmann writes, "The desire for daily news, for journalistic information about topical political and ecclesiastical, literary and economic events, spread far beyond the bourgeois classes."[57] And William St. Clair contends that "by the turn of the nineteenth century, virtually everyone read books, magazines, and newspapers on a regular basis."[58] Yet 1800 differs significantly from 1840, a rough marker of when religious and reform movements on both sides of the Atlantic had established the financial and distribution networks to disseminate millions of cheap tracts, making printed ephemera even more ubiquitous.[59] This is also the point at which "broadcasting" becomes an agricultural metaphor for mass media distribution, as reformers imagine "sowing the seed" of inspired words.[60] Print expands again around 1860, after the lifting of newspaper taxes proliferated even more periodicals, and created new forms and genres linking working- and middle-class markets.[61] Critics such as Nicholas Daly also identify the decade as marking the emergence of modern mass commodity culture, of which print is a key component.[62] They are all correct. Rather than lay claim to a specific decade or decisive event, we need a capacious view of a long nineteenth century in which print became ever cheaper and more integrated into everyday life. From this perspective, we can begin to historicize its affects, material practices, and cultural discourses.

Histories and theories of media and psychology typically preoccupy themselves with Germany, France, and the United States, but focusing on printed ephemera and its accompanying states of mind allows me to draw Britain into this conversation. Britain's fast development of networks of print, and technical and aesthetic theories of mind such as the novel, earns it a place in these broader histories and theories. My depiction of nineteenth-century media consumers departs from those proposed in influential accounts that tend to ignore Britain's global and transatlantic connections.[63] Mass print media reflected Britain's cultural porosity—internally, in relation to continental influences, in its common linguistic basis with the United States, and in its formal and informal imperial networks.[64] For example, the temperance movement, which I identify as a neglected origin of mass culture, was a transatlantic phenomenon; the fantastic visual vocabulary of German Romanticism that would decisively shape later theories of the unconscious also beguiled English readers in Thomas Carlyle's tremendously popular translations of E. T. A. Hoffmann. The literary texts I analyze that represent different modes of media consumption, such as Wilkie Collins's *The Moonstone* (1868), George Du Maurier's *Peter Ibbetson* (1891), and Oscar Wilde's *The Picture of Dorian Gray* (1891), all defy interpretation along strict national lines. Their constitutive influences, authorship, circulation, and scenes and communities of consumption were too diffuse to be characterized as authentically or profoundly British. Following mass media and mediated states of mind where they lead, this book travels across the Atlantic, the channel, and the Irish Sea, and to the Middle East.

What does the temperance movement, which tried to limit or eliminate the consumption of alcohol, have to do with mass culture? Chapter 1 identifies it as a significant, if unlikely, origin of mass printing and distribution, mass rallies and festivities, and the dynamic relation between them. Traveling booksellers or "colporteurs" opened new distribution networks throughout Britain and the United States, pointing consumers toward sober spaces and "experience" meetings in which reformed drunkards told their stories. The movement's most successful activity, the administration of a pledge not to drink, recruited thousands—sometimes tens of thousands—at a time. Every pledge-taker received a card resembling a modern diploma, or a medal or printed ribbon, to memorialize his or her commitment. Charged with affect, this type of ephemera memorialized the live event, resurrecting its intensive collective feeling in moments of later struggle. These tiny, ephemeral tokens became powerful enough to provoke mainstream ire, and they were attacked as symbols of hypocrisy and crutches for the weak-willed. To the movement's adherents, temperance ephemera retrospectively and prospectively constructed auratic rituals of fellowship. The same is true of the performances of the transatlantic celebrity temperance orator, John B. Gough, famous for his ability to generate intense feeling in his mass audiences, which resonated long after the curtain fell. Print media often described Gough as a machine who reliably performed the operation of producing mass affect, moving his audience to tears, laughter, and rapt suspense. Temperance tracts, medals, and performances used ephemeral forms to obtain an ongoing commitment to sobriety from its members, a mass media strategy that would long outlast the movement's political aims.

Chapter 2 turns to the neglected archive of tobacco ephemera, the smoke-room booklets, cigarette cards, and other printed morsels meant to be consumed by men while smoking, because they begin to mediate the imagination, linking it to the mass. I show how tobacco-related poems, pictures, and print forms produced a self-referential discourse that compared smoking to consuming print, through puns on "leaves," "volumes," and "puffs" of speech preserved in paper. During the century, smoking transformed from a markedly social activity to a personal habit, like the media consumption it reflected; as it did so, its affect shifted from conviviality to relaxation and even sedation. I sketch the scene of the smoker's mediated reverie by turning to perhaps the most famous nineteenth-century literary smoker, Arthur Conan Doyle's fictional detective Sherlock Holmes. In him, I find a new development of the media consumer-as-smoker: More than cocaine, Holmes's tobacco pipe signifies his dependency on print media for solving his cases. When Holmes seems to be smoking and thinking over a case, such as in "The Man with the Twisted Lip" and "The Red-Headed League," he is instead mentally cross-referencing all the printed information he has consumed. His media "addiction"—really a reliance on trivial information—reflects readers' desire for encyclopedic knowledge. Such desires for cultural mastery drove the popularity of cigarette cards, which featured trivia, and became a staple of working- and middle-class life from their invention in the 1890s. Reframing Holmes as the first "information addict," I build the back story of our current intensified appetite for information in a knowledge economy governed by mass media.

From temperance and tobacco ephemera, I turn to an ephemeral material of mass print, ink, because its nineteenth-century cultural history reveals a mystified model of the unconscious as media storage that still has currency today. When viewers consumed text and image, ink normally went unseen; but when tens of millions learned to write, ink emerged as a flawed technology for cleanly communicating thoughts and feelings. Ink accidents caused blots and splashes, transforming ink from ground to figure, and signifying the chaos of unreason. At the same time, gazing at pooled ink to see remote events or the future became a well-known pastime and cultural referent; from an older model of divination, it emerged as a kind of psychological performance. Later in the century, deliberately spilling and spattering ink to make random forms became a social, aesthetic, and scientific practice. Inkblot games, art, and psychological tests formalized and standardized the quotidian ink accident; ink began to materialize the unconscious. Collins, in his novel *The Moonstone*, represented ink-gazing as a nascent figuration of the unconscious—not the deep, Freudian subjectivity of hidden, conflicting drives, but as information stored and hidden out of sight. Contiguous with conscious motives and affects, this "rational unconscious" produced an unvariegated affect in his literary characters. In tracing the nineteenth-century history of spilled, pooled, and blotted ink practices and discourses, this chapter shows how, along the way to the Freudian unconscious, the awkward technology of ink materialized a diverse array of minor affects and states of mind, from frustration and rage to flashes of genius, automatism, zaniness, clairvoyant information transmission, intoxicated absorption, and enchantment. Although Rorschach's inkblot dominated twentieth-century psychoanalytic understandings of the unconscious, ink's earlier history limns a counter-tradition that we still use to understand the darkness of the mind.

Chapter 4 explores the phenomenon of "playback," which was emerging into culture in the media technology of the phonograph in the 1880s, as a fantasy of a wider consumer and personal mastery. This fantasy had deep roots from earlier in the century, in the idea of the mind as palimpsest and later, as a photograph, recording every single perception and experience. Coleridge had suggested that "all thoughts in themselves are imperishable"; and in *The Gay Science*, E. S. Dallas contended that the mind's retentive properties were "absolute as a photograph."[65] The idea set up a tantalizing prospect: If it were true, then how could these stored memories be accessed? The cartoonist, novelist, and nonce media theorist Du Maurier offered a literary answer in his widely cherished first novel, *Peter Ibbetson*. The protagonist's lover teaches him how to "dream true," or revisit his past experiences while he is sleeping; through their clairvoyant connection, all their consumer experiences of music, food, art, and travel can be played back on demand. In this way, dreamed and re-dreamed experiences enact a paradox of ephemera, that although it is meant to be fleeting, it is instead collected and kept. The conceit of disembodied playback also changes the nature of human memory, converting it into information. Peter Ibbetson's ability to play back his life returns him to his idyllic Parisian childhood, compensating him for the shocks of Haussmannization, and offering a technophilic solution to the ruptures of modern life, since "dreaming true" is imagined as a reparative media technology. By proposing "playback" for all one's memories as a way to insulate oneself from the shock of modern change, Du Maurier participates in a conversation about shock, psychic insulation, and prosthetic media extensions, with theorists such as Freud, Benjamin, and Marshall McLuhan. I trace Du Maurier's fantasy of making all experience ephemeral and thus catalog-able to his career as a cartoonist for *Punch*. Because his cartoon aesthetic described the new breadth and immediacy of public feeling brought about by mass print media in the 1890s, it anticipates the affects that attend our own versions of playback.

How does one fashion an authentic self out of mass-produced ideas, styles, and materials? This book closes by assessing a tremendously influential, extended answer to this question, Oscar Wilde's novel *The Picture of Dorian Gray* (1891). I interpret Dorian Gray as caught in the mass media consumer's dilemma. Since Wilde disguised this dimension of his work by larding the novel with "old" media such as paintings, decorated books, and the theater, my interpretation may seem counterintuitive, yet it builds on recent work that has linked the novel to new nineteenth-century media such as photography and cinema.[66] I trace the paradox of authentic self-making through the concepts of reverie and personality. Wilde represented Dorian's reverie as an embodied, material activity of self-fashioning through mass print culture. Dorian also circulates as a personality, a signature term in Wilde's writings, and a revitalized concept in mass culture and psychology at the century's end. Especially through its connotation of theatrical sex appeal in Sibyl Vane, "personality" increasingly indicated the way people performed their mass-mediated identities for others. Personality was also clearly tied to the novel's own textual history of gay censorship. Prevented from representing gay desire as clearly in the book edition as he had in the *Lippincott's* version, Wilde published a novel full of queerly coded signs that nevertheless assembled a new community within its mass readership. The book concludes here because Wilde's novel reflects a century of questions about mass print consumption: How did light literature become the equipment of reverie? How and why did millions of people begin to read compulsively, distractedly, to stimulate themselves, or to relax? How could one draw on mass-produced tropes to find an authentic sense of self? And how could one use mass culture to connect with others?

The conclusion summarizes the key nineteenth-century formations the book describes, linking them broadly to those of our own moment. In this way, it sketches genealogies yet to be written. Naming and tracing these linked formations will give greater nuance and richness to our ongoing critical narrative of modernity.

CHAPTER I

Temperate Media: Ephemera and Performance in the Making of Mass Culture

> One [sailor] followed me half a mile to return a temperance Tract,
> which among others I had left on board his vessel;
> thus showing his enmity to the cause.
>
> —ANONYMOUS COLPORTEUR "Shipping Committee,"
> *Ninth Annual Report of the New York Tract Society*, 1836

Has anyone ever actually read a temperance tract? Of all the copious material suddenly printed at the turn of the nineteenth century, temperance ephemera seems the most ubiquitous, but the least desirable. The number of tracts distributed is impressive. Beginning in 1795 and running through 1817, Hannah More's Cheap Repository Tracts of moral fables warning against drinking in gin-shops, gambling, and rioting sold millions, competing with chapbooks and broadside ballads.[1] The Religious Tract Society gave away millions of copies of "Tom Toper's Tale over His Jug of Ale," "The Fortune-Teller's Conjuring Cap," and others, rivaling major publishers by the 1840s.[2] Between 1831 and 1834, the British and Foreign Temperance Society printed and distributed over 2 million temperance tracts in Britain; between its inception in 1825 and 1851, the American Tract Society disseminated 5 million.[3] Temperance tracts focused broader efforts at moral reform on getting readers to moderately use alcohol or abstain altogether from it. In their efforts to reform society one person at a time by placing such messages in everyone's hands, the tract societies implemented the financial and distribution networks of modern mass print media.[4] In "sowing the seed" of their message, they first imagined the "broadcasting" central to mass communication.[5] Yet the tracts are a counterintuitive origin of the mass print medium. Given away or priced cheaply, they were not produced in response to market demand. Indeed, their didacticism certainly grated on potential readers, such as the sailor who did his part to reverse their tide by restoring the colporteur's giveaway. Temperance tracts are thus paradoxical documents of the new mass culture of print: They make print ubiquitous, but many seem to have gone unread.[6]

Temperance tracts are more productively considered as media objects than literary ones. Their circulation, along with other ephemeral material and events such as pledge cards, medals, and performances, created affects that unified and mobilized temperance's base toward its political goals—and alienated almost everyone else. As this chapter shows, the movement's aesthetics of sobriety, positioned against the figurative intoxication of ordinary, market-driven literary consumption, were imagined to facilitate a kind of rational recreation.[7] But these aesthetics were most effective when tracts and printed objects interacted with performance to produce a special kind of affect in mass audiences—the feeling of the presence of freedom that was otherwise elusive within political culture. Temperance ephemera may not have been widely and deeply studied or absorbed, but it helped shape modern mass culture.

As a later instance of the explosion of printing beginning at the end of the eighteenth century, which detonated conservative fears of revolution, temperance and especially teetotal tracts were viewed warily by those who still believed that the people should not read. In his classic account Richard Altick observed, "The widespread belief that printed exhortations to 'sedition' and 'atheism' found their way into every calloused hand in the kingdom was nothing short of a nightmare."[8] In response, regressive taxes on printed material, as well as windows, helped stifle the circulation of ideas.[9] Temperance, which advocated restricting the use of alcohol, and teetotalism, which favored total abstention from it, struck many in a traditional drinking culture as outlandish.[10] The ideal of sobriety also had a politically radical edge: Chartist booklets such as William Lovett and John Collins' *Chartism* (1840) made it central to the case for workers' rights, demonstrating the affinity between two radical movements for the improvement of the people. Confronting their opponents' charge that the drunken masses could not be entrusted with the right to vote, they hinted "that the majority of drunken and vicious characters are . . . already in possession of the franchise."[11] To them, established British institutions and classes were already deranged by alcohol. The temperance movement's association with nonconformist religions such as Methodism, marked by adaptable, populist practices and dangerous "enthusiasm," also declared its progressivism.[12] Temperance and teetotalism's share in mass print sparked anxiety and outrage among the conservative middle class. Yet the essential reason and Christian morality of their advocacy of sobriety also proved difficult to assail. Moreover, temperance could also function far less radically: The Cheap Repository Tracts had included temperance narratives and messages as part of the effort to overwhelm the broadside and ballad market, and strengthen the moral fiber of the populace in order to quell rather than enflame their radical political desires. As we shall see, the tracts also reflected an aspirational drive: Saving money and achieving respectability by ceasing to drink could elevate a man's class status, without fundamentally changing social and economic relations. Although temperance was viewed skeptically by many, its politics and media policy were more complex than either its advocates or opponents acknowledged.

As political documents, temperance tracts found receptive audiences among fellow reformers such as workers, suffragists, abolitionists, and anticolonialists. Temperance tried to subvert unthinking norms of sociable drinking, the medical prescription of spirits, the religious distribution of communion wine, and the use of alcohol for basic nutrition. Defying powerful pub owners, brewers, and distilleries who profited from excessive drinking, the movement opened alternative recreational activities to male semiskilled, unskilled, and casual workers who might otherwise spend their wages at the pub. It made visible the violence, starvation, and neglect suffered by many of their wives and children. In the United States, Black temperance groups performed the then-progressive political task of proving the sobriety, reason, and morality of their members to racist and proslavery whites. Temperance ephemera attests to the affective and memorial rituals and practices of self-consciously marginalized groups. The pledge not to drink, performed at a meeting or rally, was supported afterward by the card or medal that helped oath-takers, in dangerous moments of temptation, to hew to their commitments, which were regarded as extreme by mainstream, middle-class readers. Likewise, the material presence of temperance ephemera in public spaces, and its circulation from hand to hand as gifts, exerted subtle social obligations that helped build alternative, sober communities.[13] The tracts indexed living communities that struggled, witnessed, listened, took oaths, sang, entertained, and feasted together at their meetings, including their famous mass tea parties in Britain and, in the United States, their reappropriated Fourth of July celebrations.[14] Temperance ephemera were signs and traces of a publicly performed and viscerally felt politics. The slowly evanescing presence of the live performance remains or builds as a trace in the printed medal, ribbon, card, or tract.[15]

For many tormented by drink or habitual drunkards, such ephemera functioned as maps to survival spaces—temperance halls and coffeehouses, hotels and restaurants, doctors' offices and ships—where sobriety was the norm. Many of these spaces catered to the genteel. But the movement also sheltered the workers, the indigent, immigrants, and women and children who effected the massive historical transition from agricultural to industrial life. Many either used alcohol to blunt the damage this change wrought within and upon them or were affected by others' use. Thus the movement's media policy focused on matching the ubiquity of alcohol: At the World's Temperance Convention in London in 1846, the governing committee planned to counter opposition by "employing more extensively and more efficiently the press. That is the lever to lift every abuse. Our books and publications should be in every house, in every workshop, and in every library."[16]

An improbable origin of mass culture, the temperance movement nonetheless expressed a dialectic central to it, between printed objects and live, mass experience. This dialectic helps us reimagine what liberal individualist ideology has seen as a transition from popular culture, understood to be participatory, interactive, and unmediated, to mass culture, often depicted as passive consumption of media.[17] As the chapter will show, teetotalism's grassroots "experience" meetings, in which attendees took turns narrating their stories, grew in scale, becoming mass events with professional temperance performers such as John B. Gough, advertised and reviewed in the mainstream press. Print assisted this metamorphosis: Media accounts of Gough emphasize their inability to convey the powerful immediacy of his live performance—and thus helped construct it. Although framed by print, this immediacy conveyed feelings of freedom within the massed audience, as they approached the experience of being present together as a body politic. Rooted in the body, affects have been defined as visceral forces beyond cognition and emotion that can propel and extend people into relation to the world and to others, or equally, suspend those relations.[18]

In Ireland from 1839 through 1841 the Capuchin friar Father Mathew held mass temperance rallies like the ones Gough held in England and the United States. Father Mathew gave away medals that became controversial symbols of his political power to mobilize millions. Such printed tokens— along with the cards and ribbons—exposed the enigma at the heart of ephemera, the disposable, trivial printed material of everyday life that is paradoxically collected or kept as a document of community.[19] Critics disparaged temperance medals as crutches or supplements to individuals' wills, which should have operated without rewards; from this perspective, the medals were superficial mass media items that weakened autonomy and encouraged delusive superstitions. Yet the medals, and the aesthetics of sobriety informing them, also moved potent affects to articulation and action. Temperance ephemera and meetings created communal feelings of unmediated presence that outlasted temperance's political demise, remaining central to mass culture. Because this auratic presence informed Walter Benjamin's assessment of the political efficacy of intoxication, in the chapter's coda I trace this opposing aesthetic from its Baudelairean roots, displaying its surprising affinities with temperance discourse.

Temperance Tracts and Sober Reading

Finds tongues in trees, books in the running brooks,
Sermons in stones, and good in every thing.
WILLIAM SHAKESPEARE, *As You Like It*

Temperance writing introduces to modern culture the aesthetics of sobriety, which features premodern, pastoral, and natural settings, and especially, the life-giving force of water. In the typical temperance song "The Farmer May Boast," singers call for water: "The farmer may boast of his acres so fine,/His barley that smiles o'er the lea;/But I will rejoice in the course so divine,/I love to be sober and free/ . . . Then give me beautiful water/ . . . Bright water for me, bright water for me, bright water, bright water for me."[20] Retreating from an unnatural modernity associated with drunkenness, an artificial state of poisoned mind, temperance aesthetics favor water's brightness and lucidity as emblems of Enlightenment and freedom. In this countercultural position, they align with Romanticism's rejection of urban modernity and belief in human potential. Their pastoral streak can be seen in the lines from *As You Like It* that form the epigraph of this section and which were reprinted in temperance and other reform writings. The notion that stones speak sermons and brooks contain books conveys the point that the wisdom of nature is self-evident. But its language also installed mass print media in natural formations, refiguring the wild environment into a comfortable bourgeois library or chapel. In its mid-nineteenth-century cultural function, the passage articulates an idealized wholesome relationship to nature, available to all by virtue of human affinity with God's creation. Yet this direct connection to spiritualized wisdom is simultaneously undone by the figures of mediation required to convey it: tongues, books, and sermons. The tension plays out in the movement's aesthetic valorization of water as the icon of sobriety and the antidote to alcohol. Against the grim realities of its modern, urban contamination, temperance advocates positioned water as the fountain of life, God's gift, and the essence of nature.[21] People were meant to be drawn to it instinctively, yet—as in the Shakespearean quotation—they needed intermediaries to remind them. The spiritualized reason that rendered water's superiority self-evident nonetheless needed supplementation from tracts, songs, sermons, and other ephemera.

The aesthetics of sobriety central to temperance helped effect the mid-nineteenth-century transformation of broadcasting, from agricultural metaphor to the vanguard's use of media to convey its politics to wider audiences.[22] The movements' systematic saturation of public and private spaces with tracts rewrote the Christian idea of sowing the word as a seed by strewing it indiscriminately on the ground. Since not every seed would grow, grace depended on providence, or, to the secular-minded, chance. Accordingly, the temperance movement widely distributed its tracts, translated them extensively, and measured their success in anecdotes of their seemingly miraculous efficacy. In T. S. Arthur's story "The Temperance Tract," a zealous advocate hands an innkeeper a tract; when the recipient becomes irate, the proselytizer despairs and throws his batch of tracts away. When the wind spreads them around, one of them reaches a man who considers giving up drinking; another finds a different publican, disillusioned with his business, and the two meet and strike a temperance bargain: "If you'll quit selling, I'll quit drinking." The scene of psychological conversion possesses the decontextualized simplicity of a fairy tale: "I found a piece of paper on the road as I walked along just now and it had something printed on it that has set me to thinking."[23] In this media dream, the trashed tract beams up from the road, effecting conversion without seeming to be read. Freed from the competing distractions of a print marketplace cluttered with desirable material, the temperance message also directly connects consumer and producer, who then withdraw from their roles. The hero of a tale of spiritualized Enlightenment reform, the broadcast temperance message forges a bond unachievable by commodified printed material, which makes no real demands on its readers. These were not mere fantasies. The temperance advocate Edward C. Delavan recalled his introduction to the movement "after reading a temperance tract placed under my plate by an unknown hand"; he then makes "a mental resolution" to try abstaining for a month.[24] Delavan's conversion could never have happened through the ordinary reading of individual choice, because the encounter with the radical, unfashionable temperance message must be an act of providence. Delavan's chance discovery inspired him to great feats of broadcasting: He sent a temperance tract to every household in New York State, and one to every Union soldier in the Civil War.[25]

Such anecdotes elide acts of reading and contemplation in favor of sudden resolutions. With a similar implausibility, within the movement's ideology of sobriety, consuming temperance ephemera straightforwardly substitutes for drinking alcohol. The abundant anecdotes attesting to the tracts' efficacy establish their interchangeability: "Only a few days since, we were told how a little temperance tract, coming into the hands of a confirmed sot, finally wrought his redemption from the degradation into which he had sunk, and restored him to his family and to society, sober and industrious."[26] The drunkard simply swaps the bottle for the tract, betraying an odd failure to imagine the challenging transition to a non-drinking life. Temperance writers often naively proposed reading as an easy alternative to tippling: "You can find time to sit and smoke your pipe, to go to the 'Cross Keys' or 'Lord Nelson'; suppose you change this habit for a reading habit."[27] In this bourgeois ideology of "rational recreation" described by Peter Bailey, the relaxation, conviviality, and community life associated with working-class pubs are supposed to be blithely renounced for solitary study aimed at self-improvement. Unwilling to credit the human need for social gathering or acknowledge alcohol's age-old facilitation of it, much temperance discourse reflected the top-down wishes of its middle-class leaders. Since More began writing the Cheap Repository Tracts, their reformist principles had set themselves squarely against working-class collectivity, which they feared might easily devolve into riot or revolution. This paternalistic rhetoric differed from the grassroots style of teetotalism, which also disseminated tracts, but emphasized meetings at which drunkards themselves shared their stories. By contrast, rational recreation emphasized the instant, almost magic ability of its message to change worldviews and behaviors, supporting the broadcasting policy.

Even when hyperrationalist temperance discourse compares reading to more literal modes of consumption, it strangely underdescribes their mental and physical processes. The *Lancashire Temperance Messenger* likened reading to the incorporation of the knowledge others gained by experience:

But the true way is to read as you would take food—to digest it, to make it a part of yourself. Books are now cheap, and by the exercise of

> a little self-denial, any person, even in the humblest circumstances,
> may become the possessor of Histories, Biographies, Travels, Essays,
> Poetry, and increase his knowledge a hundred-fold, and store his mind
> with the best thoughts of wise men. To read of the good that men have
> done may stimulate us to follow their example, and to read of their
> errors may teach us to be watchful over our own ways; and thus we
> shall profit by the experience of others.[28]

In this analogy, one incorporates the matter of print and makes it one's own, literally, a part of one's bodily material through an automatic process. The self here is static: It isn't presumed to meditate on or to change its nature, merely to expand by adding new information. The reader becomes a storage unit for high-quality ideas, as if his or her brain were an expertly curated library shelf. Yet there is no psychic structure in which to store the read material, which remains constantly present to the mind; this reader is psychologically unified. The incorporation of useful knowledge such as the temperance message takes place within a body that is perfectly organized and constantly available for action. And indeed, the bourgeois project of working-class edification extended from temperance exhortations to the Society for the Diffusion of Useful Knowledge's cheap publications on dry topics, and similar paternalistic projects.[29] The only concession to physical or psychological desires in the passage is the reference to "self-denial" or delayed gratification, the pillar of bourgeois accumulation. In this way, the strand of rational recreation within temperance discourse proposed a theory of mind as uniform and depthless, the antithesis of the more well-known Romantic interest in unconsciousness, intoxication, and dreams.[30]

Yet temperance was not unaware of more realistic theories that acknowledged the mind's embodiment. It felt the pressure of the literary marketplace and initially resisted it, identifying its absorptive appeal to readers as itself a pernicious kind of intoxication. These depictions formed an opposing aesthetic to that of sobriety. The drunken reader of worldly literature "hastens on with the story, from page to page and from chapter to chapter, forgetful of other engagements and regardless of the passing hours, his mind all the while steeped in a most delicious intoxication." This absorption in print could end only in insanity, as readers invested all their intellect and emotion in unreal scenes, neglecting their own lives. In another description, originally from the *American Messenger* and widely quoted throughout the religious and mainstream press in the second half of the century, the problem of stimulating reading is displaced onto the matter itself: "Bad books are like ardent spirits: they furnish neither 'aliment' nor 'medicine': they are *'poison.'* Both *intoxicate*—one the mind, the other the body; the thirst for each increases by being fed, and is never satisfied; both ruin—one the intellect, the other the health, and together, the soul."[31] Passages such as these influenced the wider, century-long criticism of salacious printed material, especially sensation novels. In them, temperance described the psychology of leisure reading in far greater detail than in its exhortations to replace drinking at the pub with the reading of self-improvement. Railing against the "delicious intoxication" of losing oneself in a narrative, it conceded the delights of fiction. Nord describes the tract societies' ambivalence: They knew they had to make their own reading material enticing to casual readers and so had to deploy characters and dialogue; yet they wished to remain aloof from the moral mire of fiction. In his bid to be allowed to include general news items in his temperance magazines without incurring the newspaper tax, the publisher John Cassell acknowledged that his family-oriented temperance periodicals were "the same thing, over and over again"; to entertain and reach a mass audience, they required variety and novelty.[32] Temperance thus demonstrated an understanding of the absorptive reading taking place in the literary marketplace and eventually adopted a policy to inculcate it by adopting the secular features it abhorred.[33] Songs about the benefits of water gradually made room for lurid depictions of delirium tremens and drunken violence. As I demonstrate in the coda to this chapter, this turn from the aesthetics of sobriety to an aesthetics of intoxication would position temperance fiction as a significant generic source for the sensation fiction of the 1860s and as an interlocutor with other countercultural voices.

The intoxication model of reading itself quietly informed the ideology of reading that stoked bourgeois deep subjectivity and rejected the didacticism of the tract. This ideology opposed temperance, but accepted some of its descriptive terms and conceptualizations. "[I] must confess that I would as soon read a temperance tract as one of those moral tales, where the wisdom floats like the scum of a broth-pot at top, and which the reader is expected to stand by with his ladle and skim off," wrote "An Irish Oyster-Eater" in *Blackwood's*.[34] The truth that temperance activists saw shining forth from the surface of their tracts was, in this criticism, evidence of their overcooked, edifying style. From this point of view, reading was the unpleasant labor of consuming morals without any aesthetic flavoring. Middle-class readers wanted the pleasure of interpretation and the sense of psychic interiority that accompanied it. As Leah Price has shown, novels supplied these demands in part by contrasting their desirability as commodities to the disfavor in which tracts, as giveaways, found themselves.[35] Moreover, the primacy of individual judgment—part of the formation Elaine Hadley describes as "liberal cognition"—stood in opposition to the perceived inflexibility and oversimplification of the temperance and especially the more extreme teetotal message.[36] Harrison observes that "there was a vulgarity and a rigidity about organized teetotalism which repelled many of the finer Liberal minds."[37] Liberals recoiled from teetotalism's apparent production of new mass subjects, whom the ever-present tracts had indoctrinated into radical behavior. The movement's impoverished understanding of how its tracts might effect conversions likely confirmed this vision of psychological simplicity. By contrast, interpretive readers—so the ideology went—could allow themselves to be temporarily absorbed, enchanted, and even intoxicated by more complex material, while retaining their autonomous judgment. As long as their intoxication was private, an interior mental state, it remained discreetly unthreatening and even developmental. The emphasis on mental "play" or lapses into spontaneous, unproductive thinking, marked this aspect of liberal cognition.

Identifying and reframing this logic exposes its endurance within literary criticism and its shaping of academics' own investments in hermeneutic complexity, as remnants of bourgeois privilege. This self-awareness should help us credit collective and working-class activities and modes of knowledge, informed and organized by print, which nonetheless eschewed sustained or deep reading. If the aesthetics of sobriety and rational recreation were driven by a one-dimensional view of individual psychology, it was in order to unite intellect and behavior, politicize personal behavior, and join individuals to reform society. By drinking water, singing, pledging, and uplifting one another, temperance activists performed this conviction and made it present. Temperance's media policy of broadcasting tracts helped invent the mass medium of print, but the mass culture it helped inaugurate was not one of solitary, rational reading, as it imagined. As we shall see, print instead supported other, collective activities and a new kind of affectivity and intersubjectivity associated with live mass events.

The Pledge and Its Souvenirs

The temperance pledge became a flashpoint, drawing the ridicule of those beyond the movement and sparking contention within organizations. Formalized by signing a card or receiving a medal, the pledge declared members' commitment to stop drinking. As with the tracts, the pledge exposed tensions within liberalism. The illustrator and temperance convert George

Cruikshank, whose graphic series *The Bottle* (1847) dramatized the unsavory domestic effects of excessive drinking, refused to take the pledge simply because his status as a gentleman and man of faith seemed to him to preclude it.[38] A character in the novel *Before and Behind the Curtain: A Queer Story about Drinking* (1868), disparaging temperance societies as suited only for commoners, claims that "pledges argue conscious weakness. Taking the pledge is like a man tethering himself lest he should wander where he ought not; or muzzling himself, so that when in a biting mood he may do no one any harm."[39] As a ritualized representation of a willed act, the pledge constrained the liberal individual from the free play of decision-making. In so doing, it threatened to touch the deeper self-divisions that drove excessive drinking. Implying that a man—especially a gentleman—might not be the master of all his decisions, the pledge generated hostility. Critics rehearsed statistics about pledge-breakers; according to one 1848 estimate, 80 percent of those who had pledged in 1840 had returned to drinking.[40] In a screed against temperance and teetotalism, *Blackwood's* charged, "There is a tendency in the pledge to make confirmed drunkards of fifty out of a hundred; for greater is the temptation when there is a bond against it—the forbidden fruit is the sweetest."[41] This preoccupation with backsliding betrayed a characteristic bourgeois failure to sympathize with the struggle to abstain and with working-class life more generally. Temperance organizations themselves battled over exceptions for table wine, medicinal stimulants, communion wine, and the giving or selling of alcohol to others. In Britain, the "short" pledge committing only to personal abstinence from alcohol was associated with the south; the more radical "long" pledge, with the teetotalism predominant in the north and Scotland.[42] "Ultras" within the New York City Temperance Society instituted a new pledge banning communion wine; the group maintained old and new pledges to gradually transfer members to the more radical stance.[43] Rather than petty quarrels, such decisions reflected groups' struggles to integrate their evolving views into existing social structures of hospitality, medical care, religious practice, and commerce.

As the material evidence of the pledge, the pledge card highlighted these broad and specific challenges, while also indexing the shift from oral to printed culture. The pledge card was an elaborate certificate, most closely resembling a modern diploma: It bore Gothic lettering, flowing script, and detailed imagery attesting to the signatory's commitment. Midcentury pledge cards were copper-engraved, whereas later ones might be lithographed in four to six colors, as well as gold; many featured allegorical illustrations of the blessings of abstinence.[44]

Figure 1. Temperance pledge card.
Edinburgh Total Abstinence Society, 1837.

Later in the century, advertisements for pledge cards abound in the pages of temperance periodicals; a column in the *Temperance Record* offers a variety from Tweedie's, ranging from a new, professionally illustrated design for six shillings a dozen to more familiar Band of Hope member cards similar to the one shown in Figure 1 for two shillings per hundred.[45] A tangible reminder to keep one's commitment, the pledge card was, like the tract, a giveaway, but it also resembled a legal document, bearing some version of the statement "I promise to abstain from all intoxicating drinks as beverages" and the bearer's signature. Some had to be signed both by the abstainer and by the administrator, perhaps to impress upon the initiate the gravity of the pledge. Some cards were plain, with lettering only; others bore melodramatic illustrations: tiny scenes of drunkards beating their wives and patients on their sickbeds refusing alcohol alternated with the tableaux of prosperity and happiness that accompanied abstinence. Amy Hughes notes that "illuminated temperance pledge cards . . . allowed consumers literally to put a spectacle in their pockets."[46] The early, text-heavy example that spells out all the exceptions in time gave way to the colorful, simpler late-century version aimed at children. Through image and text, cards and medals communicated the temperance message, especially to those transitioning from the oral culture of rural life to the culture of print associated with urban, industrial existence, for whom miniature printed objects held great allure. Along with woodcuts, penny prints, advertising bills, and trade cards, temperance ephemera helped form the popular visual experience.[47]

To those piqued by temperance, pledge ephemera seemed both too powerful and not powerful enough. It was belittled as ridiculous and charged with spreading benightedness rather than enlightenment. Temperance medals, the bronze or copper chits bearing temperance iconography and mottoes, inspired as much mockery as did the tracts. If virtue is its own reward, wrote Thomas Hood in his satirical story "Mrs. Burrage: A Temperance Romance," "Then what need, say I, of a Temperance Medal," suggesting further that medals, ribbons, and parades were hypocritical, ostentatious shows of morality.[48] Irish temperance was said to be mired in superstition, including the beliefs that the activist Father Mathew could raise the dead, and that the temperance medals he dispensed were "badges of safety" in a coming war and "tokens of salvation" for entry into the next life.[49] Band of Hope ribbons, tracts, and medals, generally aimed at children, were pointless: Since they had not yet experienced intoxication; indoctrinating them into temperance with baubles might perversely increase their interest in alcohol.[50] And as always, the phenomenon of backsliding seemed to prove that the cards and medals were indeed inefficacious. Yet to those taking the pledge, especially in the very early days of the movement, such tokens materialized psychological support for a life-changing project. As Shiman notes, the change was often more dramatic than a baptism, since the pledge-taker would have to avoid many old acquaintances and haunts, and form entirely new habits, to stick to his plan.[51] Harrison observes that drink was so closely tied to religion and culture that renouncing it seemed tantamount to breaking off all social relations.[52] The activist Joseph Barker recounted his pledge, when he felt full of "fear and trembling. I imagined, in fact, that I was risking my life. I thought it very doubtful whether I should survive the experiment or not."[53] Whether premeditated or impulsively taken, the pledge was a moment of affective intensity. Its souvenirs attempted to preserve that passion and courage in the future. Insofar as their legends were read, it was within this simultaneously personal and collective frame of reference.

A more focused and sustained attack on temperance culture and its essence, the pledge, came from Friedrich Engels and Karl Marx. In *The Communist Manifesto* (1848), they classified "temperance fanatics" along with philanthropists, humanitarians, charity organizers, and animal rights activists as those who "want all the advantages of modern social conditions without the struggles and dangers necessarily resulting from them. . . . They wish for a bourgeoisie with a proletariat."[54] For them, the individual's surmounting of miserable circumstances was irremediably tainted because it maintained and even bolstered capital accumulation. As Engels explained in *The Condition of the English Working Classes* (1844), temperance wrongly emphasized individual self-reform, leaving intact the underlying social conditions—poverty, exploitation, lack of cultural resources—that led to habitual drunkenness among workers and the poor. As the enactment of individual moral suasion rather than other temperance strategies such as trade regulation or prohibition, the pledge was an act of false consciousness. Undeniably, the ideology of bourgeois accumulation saturates temperance literature with the constant injunction to spend one's wages not on drink but on more durable goods such as watches, coats, and boots. The sketch "Swallowing a Yard of Land" offers a familiar temperance joke in this vein: "Dick" declines Jack's invitation of a pint, as he "can't afford to drink a square yard of good land, worth £60l 10s an acre." He explains, "Every time you spend threepence in beer, you spend what would buy a square yard of land" and performs the mathematical calculation.[55] Observing the movement's constant advocacy of accumulation, Marx, writing to Engels, referred to temperance as a "bourgeois infection."[56] The visual and material design of the ephemera bolsters this message: The pledge cards resembled bank notes, and the medals clearly evoke coins—ones never meant to be spent.

Though it possessed descriptive accuracy, Marx and Engels's critique of temperance did not tell the whole story. Committed to their grand narrative, they did not appreciate the pledge's value as a survival strategy for everyday life in a punishing, alien industrial urban modernity. Nor did they credit the nuanced political interventions teetotalism made, for example, its creation of public spaces in which working-class and women's voices and experiences could be newly heard, its attention to children's welfare, its role in anticolonial struggle, and in the United States, its productive alliances with abolitionism. Nor did the critique witness the alliances the artisanal class of teetotal leaders forged in attempting to rescue working-class and indigent drunkards by supporting their pledge commitments with material assistance.[57] Temperance indeed was a tactical rather than a strategic response to the rapid, intensive upheavals of the Industrial Revolution. And although it clearly lent itself to class-aspirational motives, it also made key political interventions with lasting legacies.

A brief look at the temperance pledge in Ireland brings into focus its complex power to build communities through mass meetings, oral ritual, and ephemeral culture, in ways that bourgeois commentators found profoundly disturbing. Father Mathew, the famous Irish temperance advocate, held mass rallies in which he seems to have converted most of the Irish population to teetotalism: 100,000 in Limerick; 70,000 in Dublin; 85,000 in Birr.[58] The *Dublin Weekly Herald* estimated that 5.3 million had taken the pledge from him by May 1841.[59] The individual would kneel and recite the pledge, and Father Mathew would make the sign of the cross on his or her forehead. The aspirant would then receive a copper medal featuring Con-

Figure 2. Father Mathew's temperance medal. Image from *Fraser's Magazine*, 1841.

stantine's cross and the motto "in hoc signo vinces" (in this sign you will conquer).

Mathew's political power did not go unnoticed, and although he tried to distance temperance from Irish nationalism, other anticolonialist groups, led by Daniel O'Connell and Thomas Davis, made the connection, for example in the slogan "Ireland Sober, Ireland Free." In October 1841, the *Cork Examiner* stated, "A nation of sober men, with clear heads . . . shall and *must* have the full completion of their liberty."[60] A letter from a St. Patrick's College, Maynooth, student to Father Mathew described his pledge in nationalistic terms: "Yielding cheerfully myself to the many generous examples I had seen in the town and in the college, I did what an Irishman should do under the circumstances. I must be like them, I said; I will do as they have done, and folding my arms in deep deliberation, I knelt among the crowd."[61] The transmitted affect of the live mass audience created the environment for his decision. Kneeling, he performed his feeling of freedom.

Unsurprisingly, Mathew drew fire from English critics, who targeted the pledge and the medals. In *Fraser's Magazine*, a paranoid reviewer interpreted the medal as riven with secret signs of Romish sedition, its imagery of cross and lamb somehow more closely referencing Moloch and Belial than Christ.[62] Harriet Martineau's memorial essay characterized Mathew's success as temporary and fleeting, asserting that "vows and mechanical association" could never bring about true reform. She also repeated the rumor that the proceeds from the sale of medals had never been accounted for.[63] In fact, Mathew lost money on the medals, which cost him 3 ½ pence each and which he mostly gave away until debt forced him to begin selling them for a shilling each in 1840. Even this plan failed, and he was eventually arrested for £7,000 debt to the Birmingham medal manufacturers. The critics also griped that Mathew refused to dispel superstitions about the medals, for example, that they could repel police bullets.[64] Their criticisms echoed familiar antiradical charges against mass media that resound down the ages: that media orchestrators dupe their consumers, spreading ignorance.

Father Mathew's temperance pledge and medals suggested a hitherto unseen social and political formation, a massive live event that was also, paradoxically, mediated, for the medals trouble the category of ephemera to which they belong. Ephemera denotes the quotidian, prosaic documents of ordinary life—bus tickets, business cards, bookmarks—but temperance medals were fully intended to outlast the day of their issue. Not only did they memorialize the pledge-taker's commitment to temperance, they also indexed the person's participation in the mass live event, and interaction with Mathew, its spiritual celebrity. For many poor people, they were a special keepsake of their involvement in a cultural and protonational phenomenon. The superstitions that clung to the medal and the pledge—that they tokened salvation, warded off illness, or brought good fortune—were narratives that embellished the event and gave it a variety of local meanings. Yet the medals and the pledge provoked critics less because they functioned like primitive talismans and more because of their startling modernity as pieces of mass media and emblems of mass culture. Mass culture tends to be refreshed from economic and political peripheries.[65] Mathew's rallies may have had the aura of ancient gatherings, but they were really a new phenomenon—an early instance of live mass performance with audience participation. Moreover, the popularity of Irish temperance was unprecedented. Mathew's millions could not be dismissed as a violent, faceless mob, because they were gathered for the enlightened purpose of an ultimately rational and moral reform. The regeneration of Ireland from its legendary drunkenness to sober enlightenment seemed like a modern miracle that even paranoid and hostile critics had to acknowledge. That this sudden modernization might also involve shaking off the oppression of centuries threw English commentators into confusion, and they scrambled to reassemble the primitive Ireland they thought they knew. As Teresa Brennan has argued, contrary to such individualist, imperialist opinion, large gatherings are actually composed of rational individuals: "Collectivities may have more—rather than less—intelligence, deductive speed, and inventiveness than the individuals within them."[66] This perspective helps us reassess Father Mathew's large rallies. Moreover, English antagonism to the radical press should be included in the familiar critical narrative of domestic repression of revolutionary ideas.

A firsthand account of one of Mathew's rallies showcases their mingling of premodern and modern elements, evidencing a profound power to mobilize meaning through the affects inspired by mass presence:

> But how can I describe the effect of these bursts of a thousand voices, or the variety of emotions depicted on the faces below! . . . Men upon whose countenances I saw the marks of shame and sorrow; women, in a kind of maudlin dreamy state, who threw up their arms, and clapped their hands over their heads, as if bewailing the last "drops of comfort" they had taken; and here and there groups of the poorest peasants from the far west, from the recesses of that rocky shore, whose frowning cliffs protect us from the liquid mountains of the restless Atlantic. . . . Probably not one of them in fifty understood a word of English, and yet there was a language evidently speaking within them, as their lips never ceased to move; and immediately after the ceremony most of them rushed to Father Mathew to touch his person, or be touched by him, doubtless considering *that touch* the perfection of virtue against future temptation.[67]

The passage seems to conjure an ignorant multitude, who could not possibly have understood Mathew's remarks or the pledge, given in English, yet it depicts the workings of meanings deeper than conventional communication. Where critics would have seen the evacuation of reason in the feminized "dreamy state" induced by the frisson of the mass event, we can imagine an apparently undisciplined form of mental and embodied group experience. That its profundity inhered in a moment of tactility—touching Father Mathew—suggests its rootedness in affect rather than egoistic reason. The moment of collective affect attests to a new phenomenon—new to its participants and new in modern history—of shared emotional, embodied intensity.

It is worth pausing for a moment to more precisely describe what I mean by collective affect. How can affect be collective without being homogenous? If we begin, as Brian Massumi does, by acknowledging affect as "trans-individual, directly relational and immediately eventful," then we can reframe its appearance as an aspect of individual psychology as just one mode of its expression.[68] Now we are able to set aside the common assumption of mass psychology, which "only understands the collective as a molar aggregate of individualities that have melted into an undifferentiated magma" (206). But if affect is instead transindividual, then it binds individuals to each other without collapsing their differences. Moreover, affect "is the ongoing force of the social taking evolving form" (205). And in industrial society, the encounters and exchanges that bring people into proximity are often mass mediated. Affect forms the social through "mechanisms of mediation" (205). Thus Father Mathew's rally does not homogenize tens of thousands of individuals, magically flattening all their experiences and perspectives. Rather, we can see its affective intensities registering in different ways across all those individuals, while it drives their formation into a new social body. Mathew, the medals, and the setting all serve as media or tactile environments in which their affect appears and transfigures them. This is the theoretical description of the contagious excitement of the live mass event, which remains fundamental to globalized mass culture.

The novelty of this phenomenon inheres in a dialectic between its live, unmediated quality and its crucial mediation in print, in the pages of *Bentley's Miscellany*. It is here that the author Peter M'Teague disavows his own ability to convey the scene's intensity, a renunciation that produces precisely that effect. As readers, we can credit his reportage with some degree of accuracy while acknowledging that the mass event becomes intelligible only afterward, in a print medium that must call attention to its own failings. In this way, the mass print medium and the mass live event began to co-create mass culture—not as the pabulum of primitives, but as a complex interaction of collective, intersubjective feeling. This collective affect is an effect of modern mass print media.

John B. Gough: Mass Culture and the Feeling of Freedom

In the United States and Britain between the 1820s and the 1840s a similar kind of mass affect arose and thrived to configure intoxication, experience, and mediation. In the Washingtonian movement begun in Baltimore and in teetotal meetings throughout the north of England, local participants stood up and told stories of their personal struggles with drink and the improvements abstinence had made in their lives. Nineteenth-century histories of the larger temperance movement rightly emphasized the importance of these "experience meetings" and their grassroots origins, enshrining them in legend.[69] In many places, they replaced the top-down style of temperance leadership of the kind that Charles Dickens satirized in *The Pickwick Papers* (1837), in the "Brick Lane Branch of the United

Grand Junction Ebenezer Temperance Association," in which self-important windbags read ridiculous reports of conversion aloud, everyone sings "Who Hasn't Heard of a Jolly Young Waterman," and a fight breaks out over accusations of drunkenness.[70] By contrast, converts at teetotal meetings told their own stories, and listeners witnessed and supported them. But only recently have critics such as Thomas Augst and Glenn Hendler made teetotalism's performance of personal narratives central to historical media studies, for example by claiming, as Hendler does, that "the reformed and transformed drunkard stands near the beginning of a history of American mass culture."[71] Since temperance and teetotalism were transatlantic cultural formations, as Amanda Claybaugh has shown, the scope of Hendler's claim extends beyond the United States.[72] Experience meetings dissolved the boundary between audiences, speakers, and classes, embracing even the direst cases. Working men who had stopped drinking—however recently—recounted, in unrehearsed autobiographical narrative, and made visible in their appearance, the transformations that total abstinence had wrought. Augst describes the essence of the experience meeting as the "romance of experience"; but this fascination with true personal events was decisively shaped by print. Hendler places the white masculine body's metamorphosis from figurative "slave to the bottle" to self-mastery at the heart of the phenomenon. I develop his claim by theorizing how speakers communicated the feeling of freedom to their mass audiences in performance and in print, and how this collective experience of intimacy and immediacy reorganized the relationship between mass culture and the public sphere.

The graduation of appealing speakers from their local teetotal meetings to the lecture circuit, traveling to other towns to tell their stories, brings into focus a tension between authenticity and communicative appeal that structured the uneven transition from oral to print culture. Joseph Livesey, the architect of British teetotalism, recalled the "primitive spirits" who gathered at Preston to begin the movement in 1832 and the early days in which "unlettered" speakers such as Thomas Swindlehurst put their hearts and souls into their work.[73] Teetotalism famously acquired its name in a moment of stuttering in September 1833, when a plasterer named Dicky Turner arose at a meeting to argue against moderation, claiming, "Nothing but t—t—total abstinence will do!"[74] Subsequent writers enshrined this moment in legend, flaunting the homespun quirkiness of the word uttered in a moment of disfluency.[75] The flawed public speaking of illiterate and uneducated working men guaranteed the genuineness of their experience with habitual drunkenness, poverty, and degradation. Thomas Carlyle attested to their power: "I could almost weep to hear these poor rude workmen . . . ! They speak evidently from the heart: *this* is something practical and true they are talking of,—while nothing but *organ* psalmody and vague jinnerjanner is going on all round them from those *hired* to speak."[76] Carlyle highlighted the difference between the local, untutored eloquence of random men bearing witness and the formalized, practiced, and superficial message of temperance as a political movement and mode of quasicommercialized entertainment. The former hints at the possible origins of mass culture in lost folkways, imbuing their avatars with a premodern air. To Swindlehurst's and Turner's broken narratives, one might contrast the brilliance of Harry Anderton, who spoke at a Bolton meeting in 1836 for an hour with "an energy and fluency really very uncommon; his utterance was distinct, yet he might be said to talk in demisemiquavers, for he never for an instant stopped."[77] Anderton's vocal polish, as well as the poetry and precision of his speeches, "dazzled the imagination."[78] Harrison, relating him to "a modern pop-singer," likens such performances to the professional ones of the music hall and other popular entertainments competing for workers' attention.[79] These differed considerably from the group singing that inspired so many activists and which at least one temperance writer eulogized as the most efficacious method for effecting sobriety: "Celestial song! Spiritual song! May penetrate all, pervade all, teach all."[80] The difference between broken, heartfelt public speaking and virtuosic entertainment indexes the shift from a local culture documenting itself to a mass culture of performance.

Between these two extremes of crudely pathetic personal testimony and seemingly professional entertainment spoke the most famous temperance orator of the nineteenth century, John Bartholomew Gough. Gough emigrated from England to New York in 1829 at age twelve. Struggling to make a living as a book binder and actor, he endured the death of his mother and first wife through an alcoholic haze. His phenomenal career began when he spoke at an experience meeting in Massachusetts. His gifts apparent, he soon moved on to the temperance circuit, and then rose to dominate the more mainstream lyceum movement, which had sprung up in the Northeast and Midwest in imitation of the British mechanics' institutes model of adult education and enrichment. Gough caught on like wildfire: He gave 605 addresses in 1843 and 1844, and estimated that 31,760 people signed the temperance pledge after hearing him speak.[81] By all accounts, his tours de force transfixed and transformed his audiences. He told his own story, tales of others' suffering from the abuse of alcohol, and action-packed but symbolic stories. When Susan B. Anthony heard him speak in 1849 in New York, she exclaimed, "What a lecture, what arguments, how can a man or woman remain neutral or be a moderate drinker."[82] Harriet Beecher Stowe claimed, "I never heard his equal. He will move this country." Reverend E. N. Kirk described how "for an hour, or an hour and a-half, he pours forth one uninterrupted torrent of anecdote, wit, sarcasm, argument, narrative, appeal, comic description, and tragic delineation of passion, without one improper expression or exaggerated statement. His audience is now convulsed with laughter—now bathed in tears."[83] As in M'Teague's narrative of Father Mathew's rally, printed accounts of his speeches repeatedly claim that although the matter of his talks could be transcribed, "his *manner* is quite unreportable. . . . To be fully appreciated, he must be heard."[84] The dynamic interaction between such disavowals of print and the live performance helped move Gough into the eye of mass culture. He bridged Carlyle's divide between the crudely authentic self-expression of workers and the rehearsed performances of seasoned speakers. By the 1860s he broadened his act. A talented mimic, he leveraged his British background by offering U.S. audiences a panoply of "London Voices" in a comedic vein. Analyzing their cultural work connecting the United States to Britain, Tom F. Wright refers to Gough's "liminal transatlantic larynx" as a figurative Atlantic cable.[85] As we shall see, similar language was used at the time to describe Gough as a machine-like communication medium. His ephemeral performances increased in status and allure in equal measure to the print medium's self-professed inability to convey them.

The discourse of Gough as an unreproducible phenomenon positions him as a new kind of medium that can produce genuine collective feeling. Those who described Gough emphasized his instinctive, raw talent, which grounded his sincerity: "This was . . . the most important element, of his power as an orator. Because what he said he always himself felt, he compelled his audience to feel it with him. He was always real."[86] Gough thus achieves a certain transparency: "The feelings of the orator, speaking through the very tones of his voice, are truthful reporters of his own conceptions" (72). Unlike others, his social surface and psychological depth are identical: He is himself, through and through. Seeming to lack an unconscious and to be incapable of dissimulation, Gough is able to spread his ideas and feelings through the crowd. His apparent purity echoes the movement's valorization of water; as previously noted, within the aesthetics of sobriety, water possesses a clarity that transcends the phantasmagoric deception alcohol conjures in the mind. As the popular temperance song

"The Crystal Spring" put it, "In man's primeval state of sinless purity / He happily knew nought of insobriety, / He drank from the crystal stream, inspiring, pure, and free: / If all would drink the same, the world would sober be."[87] At least one writer developed the contrasting element: "Intemperance, with all its pomp and circumstance, and paraphernalia of specious villainy and humbug, is one of [the world's] *dissolving views*; and glorious humanity will be liberated from ignoble thralldom, like an ice-bound ship in the gushing flood of thought, and speech pouring from the temperance press and platform."[88] The water-like flood of temperance media and performance will be mightier than the murky tide of alcohol inundating society like deceptive visual media. Gough embodies temperance's ability to release the static social body into its own fluids—the sweat of labor and the tears of feeling. Natural human fluids, like water, will melt and cleanse the frozen world. Nicknamed "The Apostle of Cold Water," Gough pointedly drank water onstage and often delivered an "Apostrophe to Water" in which he described it as "beautiful and pure, for God brewed it."[89] Unlike the strand of rational recreation running through temperance discourse, which appealed to an abstract, disembodied mode of communication, Gough's appeal conjures water as a physical medium connecting individual and social bodies.

Gough produced feeling in his audiences through the spectacle of his sweat and tears. But in the odd cultural logic of fantasies about media, his seeming defiance of representation in print and transcendence of mediation in general is likened to a variety of media. William Reid compares him to "an illustrated edition of the temperance advocate" but also describes his voice as more powerful than "the entire press of the kingdom, aided even by the power of steam" (*Sketch of Life*, 74, 92). Others develop this notion of surpassing print by likening him to "an animated photographic apparatus, talking and acting pictures."[90] Gough's verisimilitude, animation, image-making ability, and rapid scene-changing all suggest a dream of cinema, with its strangely "overwhelming reality" (76). Paradoxically, Gough's inability to dissemble distinguishes him from the phantasmagoric "dissolving view," yet his ability to entertain makes him resemble such protocinematic technologies. Together Gough and his audience form a dynamic technology expressed in electrical metaphors: "The man was a galvanic battery, and electrified his hearers"; he was "an electrical battery developing an intense interest, his points sparking and flashing as he went along."[91] Gough himself acknowledged his mechanical compulsion to orate: "It is necessary to my very existence that I make these exertions; for I suppose I am like one of your dolls with quicksilver in them—I must always be moving up and down—(laughter and applause)" (84). Also known as mercury, quicksilver is the only metallic element that remains liquid at room temperature, and is thus known for its motility. Through this discourse, Gough's sincerity and infectious guilelessness render him machine-like, an apparatus for conducting feeling. A human medium, Gough communicates affect, drawing "tears from eyes 'unused to weep.'"[92] Noting Gough's function as an actor as well as an orator, Reid emphatically categorized his lectures as performance—a word that anticipates the reliability with which machine technologies meet industrial standards in twentieth-century discourses of efficiency and logistics.[93]

Accordingly, Gough's machine-like aspects—work rate, wages, and relative consistency as a speaker from one evening to the next—formed a prominent theme in the commentary about him. His claims about the number of miles he traveled and addresses given in certain periods were reprinted and recalculated by observers.[94] The marvelous effects of his onstage performance are reflected in the statistical spectacle of his work performance. The same dynamic shaped the fame of his rival, the Washingtonian John Hawkins, who claimed to have traveled 100,000 miles and delivered 2,500 lectures in his first ten years.[95] In Gough's case, the dynamic generates an interest in his machine-like body, which—true to itself—runs on "cold water appliances, inside and out," as well as weak coffee and tea, but never stimulants (56). His perspiration was so fabled, observers claimed to have seen steam rising from his collar. Gough's sweat and the audience's heartfelt tears were part of the same system for producing affect: On tour in Scotland, he received a cambric handkerchief from a fan, who hoped that when he wiped his brow, he might remember "that he had wiped many tears from not a few faces in Edinburgh" (60). Gough's spectacular work was to make individuals feel together. As Rand sets the scene of his appearance, "There is Gough, that slender, wiry man, all nerve, all intense feeling, who has suddenly come from some place in the rear and now confronts his audience. He goes to work at once. It is very direct work in the case of Gough. He gives himself entirely to *you*. He makes you feel that he is personally interested in *you*."[96] Gough, a tiny machine made of quicksilver and nervous wires, generates tremendous affective output by activating each member of his diverse audience, drawing them into an ever-growing network. In this way, he and his audiences anticipate what Richard Menke describes as the first national media event, President Garfield's 1881 assassination, in which telegraphic and other communication constantly conveyed minute changes in the wounded man's condition, linking the nation in a "psychic and even somatic unity."[97] Gough and his audiences, in print and performance, formed a series of similar, transatlantic mass events that were simultaneously mediated and live. As Gough elicited his audience's tears, laughter, suspense, and other emotions, and as the audience's tears continued to call forth his sweaty exertions, a new fantasy of modern communication as the communal expression of intense affect became real.

Gough's communicative efficacy depended on his sincerity: His audience and commentators were convinced that he could not produce such affect in them without feeling it himself. This belief followed from the empirical basis of teetotalism. Whether it appealed or grated, the common man's narrated experience stood as proof that abstinence could redeem the degraded among his hearers. The truth of individual experience, emotionally related, now carried greater weight than erudition, logical argument, and polished lecturing. It fostered a tremendous immediacy, as audiences believed they were experiencing the speaker's misery and reclamation with him.

Thus when the *Police Gazette*, a newspaper aimed at young men, claimed to have found Gough drunk in a brothel in New York City in September 1845, the scandal threatened his reputation and the movement's efficacy, but it also shifted the relationship between Gough's live performance and print media. The story became an early celebrity scandal by virtue of its extended and heated discussion in the national and international press.[98] By his own account, a new acquaintance had insisted on treating Gough to a raspberry soda that was likely spiked with alcohol; Gough, out of his mind after his long abstinence, then purchased and drank brandy, became completely insensible, and after a week, was found in a bordello with a mysterious woman in black, though he insisted it was not a house of ill repute.[99] The scandal continued for weeks as the *Gazette* produced even more material against Gough, and his own advocates and other commentators parried and rebutted it. The press now varied its relationship to Gough as live phenomenon: Earlier it had played the role of the inferior medium that failed to convey his personal power; now, it revealed that power to be false, because dissembled. Gough moved into the phantasmagoric world of false ideas and images that threatened to undermine the moral basis of his live immediacy. If he had really lapsed, his most ardent followers could forgive him, since teetotalism was committed to reclaiming backsliders. In fact, he had already publicized an early relapse in his 1845 autobiography, dramatizing the power of the movement to take him back.[100] The wider audience for the scandal, however, connected it to older suspicions of mass culture's hypocrisy.

Accordingly, commentators used Gough's public rise and stumble to describe mass culture as mass deception. As an anonymous pamphlet purporting a neutral discussion of the affair put it, "Such a man, if sincere, or if he can mask his insincerity, has his uses. He attracts, he pleases his audience with his cause, as well as with himself. . . . His peculiar talents are to the cause of temperance what a band is to a regiment. They go before and a mob follows, stepping to their music, without knowing why."[101] In this model, Gough's audience is a homogenized, mindless mass, as open to deception as to sincerity. Critics commonly charged temperance with deluding its followers—a particularly specious charge, since they had to acknowledge that the goal of lessening drunkenness was worthy, while condemning the coercive methods, such as the pledge, of obtaining it. Gough's exposure energized such critics, keen to take down a temperance leader whose own example now smacked of hypocrisy. These debunkers combated the powerful affect of the temperance community with the intellectual gesture of defrocking revelation. The rational public sphere they imagined devalued mass collective feeling. But they underestimated the force of the newly configured social energies that Gough's performances had gathered.

These energies drew on and reproduced feelings of freedom. As Hendler describes, Washingtonian performances such as Gough's endlessly rehearsed white working-class men's self-enslavement and self-liberation. In this transformation, the orators figuratively racialize and feminize themselves, and then, through the power of sympathy, are transformed "into their properly white 'manly forms'—pale, respectable, docile," and free.[102] Although this transaction clearly maintained the status quo of white, masculine power, it also opened new political possibilities. To African (-Americans) living under the threats and duress of slavery and to women deprived of civil rights, such feeling was undoubtedly motivating and inspiring. Audiences sympathetic to Gough's temperance message filled the ranks of the abolitionist and suffragist movements. Assembled there, not merely bearing witness to Gough's story, but feeling his degradation, uplift, and personal triumph with him and with each other, they brought a potential new public sphere into being, in which they could undergo similar transformations together. The power of performance to make such collective feeling present lay not merely in Gough's talent—it required the audience's affective engagement. Though teetotalism had struck liberals as narrow-minded and intellectually empty, such events suggest instead its subjective plenitude. Moreover, in its emphasis on personal liberation, it anticipated the widening scope of classical liberalism defined by a sacrosanct self-determination, for example as John Stuart Mill would articulate it in *On Liberty* (1859) and *The Subjection of Women* (1869). Gough's rhetoric of freeing himself from the ravages of delirium tremens and the pernicious temptations of alcohol certainly rehearsed a heroic, masculinist, bourgeois narrative. But by enacting it as a mass phenomenon, it also enabled unforeseen connections and coalitions between individuals and political groups. The concept of mutual self-help balanced the bourgeois individualism informing the phenomenon.

The discourse of Gough and his audience as an electric machine bears on the generation and circulation of the affects subtending personal liberation in ways that ramify the relationship between mass media and the public sphere. Affect is open-ended, even vague in its contours, duration, and effects, whereas machines connote precision, repetition, and homogeneity. The idea that Gough-as-a-machine produces affect thus contradicts a long critical tradition that views machines, especially mass media technologies, as encroachments on human spontaneity. For example, Sigfried Giedion's influential interpretation of nineteenth-century life titled *Mechanization Takes Command* demonstrates the mechanization of all aspects of human life, from automatic bread production to patent furniture to showers.[103] In Benjamin's version of this critical narrative, best exemplified in "The Work of Art in the Age of Its Technical Reproducibility," the new, fin-de-siècle capacity of a medium such as photography to reproduce all original works of art diminishes their aura, the mystical quality of their presence in space and time, to which clings the residue of their forgotten ritualistic uses.[104] In Benjamin's writing, the aura also finds its home in the human person, pitted against the machine. Expanding on Luigi Pirandello's observations about the film actor's "exile from himself," Benjamin claims "for the first time—and this is the effect of film—the human being is placed in a position where he must operate with his whole living person, while forgoing its aura. For the aura is bound to his presence in the here and now."[105] Benjamin's schema suggests that Gough's mesmerizing aura would be dispelled if photographed or filmed, and that print was incapable of reproducing his power seems to confirm this idea. Yet Augst, citing similar Washingtonian autobiographical narratives, suggests that "the story itself became a platform for the mass production of aura"; print became dependent on the civic ritual of performance.[106] In other words, the massive expansion of print relied on, and also continued to produce, auratic live performances such as Gough's. The metaphor of Gough's machine production of his spontaneous "performance" reflects this dialectical relationship. Print and performance operate on each other within mass culture. The metaphors that nineteenth-century readers used to understand Gough and his audience as a galvanic battery or electrified communication medium aligned his auratic magic with machine technology. This association departs from the conventional understanding of the Artwork essay and Benjamin's oeuvre, as lamenting the passing of nontechnologized life in the nineteenth century. The public sphere that mass culture creates might well be one of figuratively machine-produced affect that is not inauthentic. Indeed, communal affect could be a new way to consider the auratic energy surrounding works of art.[107] I discuss a more developed version of this gesture in George Du Maurier's novel *Peter Ibbetson*, the subject of chapter 4.

Coda: Poe, Baudelaire, Benjamin: The Aesthetics and Politics of Intoxication

Edgar A. Poe, Esq.
This gentleman who has been in our city for some weeks past, and who has been ministering to the delight of our citizens in several highly interesting lectures, was initiated as a Son of Temperance in [the] Shockoe Hill Division, No. 54, on last Monday night. We mention the fact, conceiving that it will be gratifying to the friends of temperance to know that a gentleman of Mr. Poe's fine talents and rare attainments has been enlisted in the cause. We trust his pen will sometimes be employed in its behalf. A vast amount of good might be accomplished by so pungent and forcible a writer.
The Banner of Temperance, Richmond, Virginia, 31 August 1849

It is more an individual than a historical tragedy that Poe, who died in the throes of delirium tremens a mere five weeks after taking the pledge, never wrote a word of temperance literature. He had already appeared as a character in a serialized temperance novel, *The Doom of the Drinker*, in 1843, as an inebriated wit.[108] It was just one piece of the legend of his drunkenness, which started the arrhythmia of the heart of U.S. literature. Poe's habitual, irredeemable drunkenness fascinates because it suggests that his literary production happened automatically or unconsciously, in spite of his self-sabotage, and without diligent practice or effort. I describe a similar figuration of Romantic inspiration in chapter 2, with respect to smoking. Poe is the U.S.'s debauched Romantic genius. In this way, his drunkenness has hampered later efforts to account for U.S. literature as clearly and consistently envisioned and produced through rational, democratic institutions.[109] Poe's tremendous transatlantic influence made this figuration of literary drunkenness central to the countertradition of European letters that located modernity in the shadows of technological and political progress. For Charles Baudelaire, the architect of this tradition, Poe—and to a lesser extent, Thomas De Quincey—furnished the plans; Baudelaire saw Poe's compulsion as an irresistible desire "to return to the marvelous or terrifying visions, the subtle conceptions, which he had encountered in a previous storm."[110] Irrational yearning for the altered state of mind that discloses the sublimely spectacular, the ghastly, and the horrific: This affective impulse toward self-shattering sensation forms an enduring aesthetic of intoxication. I draw attention to it here because it contours the aesthetics of sobriety, sharing some of its key assumptions about mediation, transcendence, revolution, and the public sphere.

Poe called this irresistible affect *perversity*, and his inveiglement with alcohol performs his own literary and philosophical interest in it, as "a shape, far more terrible than any genius or any demon of a tale. . . . It is but a thought."[111] Among his writings, the likeliest but nonetheless awkward candidate for a contribution to temperance literature, the story "The Black Cat," described perversity as an "unfathomable longing of the soul *to vex itself*—to offer violence to its own nature—to do wrong for wrong's sake only."[112] This vexation is not only the pleasure of transgression, but an enjoyment in the sensations of self-transgression. By identifying it as "one of the indivisible primary faculties, or sentiments, which give direction to the character of Man," Poe satirized temperance's more narrow focus on alcohol as the cause, rather than the effect, of much human misery. Yet "The Black Cat" can also be read, perversely, as a temperance tale in spite of itself. Its narrator, in a drunken fit, maims his beloved cat, and later kills his wife; just when he has succeeding in duping the police about the whereabouts of her body, a second cat that uncannily resembles the first, gives him away. Since black cats were common nineteenth-century alcoholic hallucinations, alcohol vanquishes the protagonist in the end. Though his own experiences certainly informed his writings, Poe's acquaintance with the temperance writer T. S. Arthur and the temperance lecturer John Lofland would have supplied him with grisly tales of enucleation, immurement, and personal violence featured in this and his other stories.[113] As I mentioned in the first section of this chapter, in an effort to attract more adherents, temperance lapsed from its early resolve not to publish the sensational stories told in experience meetings. Its forays into sensationalism have been characterized as the literary genre of "dark temperance" in the United States. In Britain, lurid temperance novels such as Ellen Wood's *Danesbury House* (1860) furnished the training grounds for masterpieces of sensation such as her *East Lynne* (1861).[114] Arthur, covering the new Washingtonian movement in 1842 for the *Baltimore Merchant*, published the personal accounts again as pamphlets and then as *Six Nights with the Washingtonians*.[115] Poe installed such personal stories within his essayistic and philosophical frameworks, helping to create a new genre, horror. Thus in addition to supplying the aesthetics of sobriety underpinning Enlightenment rationality, temperance also stands at the source of the aesthetics of intoxication, which Poe used to expose the perversities of modern life. Baudelaire cited and developed the temperance language of self-enslavement in *Artificial Paradises*, and De Quincey wrote an essay about temperance.[116] Each was fascinated and horrified by the perverse modern turn away from enlightened self-improvement.

I turn briefly to Baudelaire to efficiently demonstrate that the major difference between sobriety and intoxication is not only between abhorrence of perversity and pleasure in it. Baudelaire, whose writings form the crux of the second set of aesthetics, engaged temperance discourse and pushed it toward a socioeconomic critique. Poe drank, he contended, "because he saw the fraudulence of society and understood it to be no more than a gang of thugs" (87). In a long passage about "literary drunkenness" (l'ivrognerie littéraire), he attributes its prevalence to the dismantlement of the artistic patronage system, which destroyed grand aesthetic traditions, and left artists to struggle alone among the brutish bourgeois.[117] Richard D. E. Burton shows how Baudelaire's prose and poetry ties this modern development to the Revolution of 1848 and its legacy. At first, in *Du Vin et du haschisch* (1851), Baudelaire extolled wine as the people's drink that moved them toward revolution, in contrast with intoxication by hashish, a narcissistic, bourgeois self-indulgence. In a poem from *Les Fleurs du mal* (1861) such as "L'Ame du vin" ["The Soul of Wine"], a personified wine sings to "dear and disinherited" man, saluting his labor: "I know it cost/fanatic toil to make me what I am,/and I shall not be thankless or malign."[118] The wine is happy to slake the worker's thirst, in a life-giving circuit that defies alienation. Water achieves a similar effect in temperance discourse, but it is a gift from God, not part of a secularized nature. Wine also signifies poetry itself, since both awaken utopian visions. But the disappointment of 1848 gradually led Baudelaire to assimilate wine to the hashish model. Wine had led man to boldly imagine a higher station, in defiance of God and the bourgeois order; but later, Baudelaire saw this as mere arrogant pretension. He describes this vanity most clearly in *Paradis artificiels* (1860), when he ventriloquizes the hashish-eater's enchanted visions of "superb cities," "museums crowded with beautiful forms and startling colors," and "libraries that hold the works of Science and the dreams of the Muse" as marvels made by workers and martyrs, *"for me, for me, for me!"*[119] He now believed that a similar bourgeois vanity and contentment characterized the revolutionaries who had drunkenly stumbled forward into revolution in 1848. Moreover, if poetry retained its resemblance to wine, then it became a literary commodity that induced such false, phantasmagoric visions.[120] Wine and hashish temporarily disguise, but in Baudelaire's critical insight, reveal, that without patrons, poets rely on the literary marketplace and the bourgeois readers who command it. The predicament is seen in the prefatory poem to *Les Fleurs du mal*, "To the Reader," with the poet's accusation—also a self-accusation—that the hypocritical reader is his own double.[121]

With temperance, Baudelaire's later writing shares an indictment of the literary marketplace as full of hypocrisy and evil. As in temperance's theory of media consumption, the literary commodity dazzles as one rapaciously consumes it in a "delicious intoxication," but it also leaves one unfulfilled, even damaged. Temperance at first tried to evade this problem by producing dry tracts and distributing them for free, thus competing with the market by erecting a parallel world of sober communities and institutions. Water, the central symbol of temperance aesthetics, produced the clean high of collective feelings of freedom. Baudelaire rejected such an approach, seeing it—as other progressive, secular-minded writers such as Dickens did—as leading to bourgeois hypocrisy. Later, temperance hoped to harness intoxicating literary sensationalism to deliver its message of sobriety. Baudelaire, who more finely described the self-aggrandizing psychology of intoxication in *Artificial Paradises*, took a more pessimistic view. For him, sensational delight could not be recuperated under the sign of reason, because consumers could not be argued out of their narcissistic self-indulgence. In its critical phase, Baudelaire's aesthetics of intoxication begin to describe fetishistic media consumption as a kind of self-consumption, because the artificial paradises evoke mass-produced forms of media. He suggests that the hashish taker's life becomes like "a fantastic novel, which will come to life rather than be written" (52). Absorbed in fanciful images, the hashish-eater's imagination kindles "ever brighter before the enchanting display of his own amended, idealized nature" (69). Participating in this consumer economy, one commodifies and then consumes one's self: "You feel yourself vanishing into thin air, and you attribute to your pipe . . . the strange ability to smoke you" (51). Absorption in mass media is revealed to be self-absorption, underwritten by a media marketplace that commodifies everything and everyone. This proposition shares the same basic description with evangelical-minded descriptions of young women led into the simulated worlds of commercial fiction. In chapter 5, I discuss how Oscar Wilde's novel *The Picture of Dorian Gray* engaged and critiqued this figuration. Rather than attempt to intervene within that world, Baudelaire reinvented lyric poetry in order to expose and shatter its self-centered illusions.

At stake in the temperance aesthetics of sobriety and the Baudelairean aesthetic of intoxication is the perversely irrational role of mediation in the reform and organization of the public sphere. At the start of the nineteenth century, alcohol was a material social medium, connecting people and communities. From the temperance perspective, it reflected social defects that could be corrected through the substitution of water, whereas from Baudelaire's early point of view, it was the means to reform through revolution. Baudelaire's late view came to resemble the oppositional critique of teetotalism: Society, as ruled by bourgeois hypocrites, had been drunk. But sobriety was not an option for Baudelaire, because in its rejection of intoxication, he saw no true exit from the commodity world. For him, the mass was not bound together and inspired to action by collective feeling or rational recreation; rather, it was merely an amalgam of individuals, like Poe's crowd in "The Man of the Crowd." Neither mass drunkenness nor total sobriety offered a vantage point from which to translate critique into collective political action. Baudelaire's latest, most ambivalent word on intoxication can be seen in the prose poem "Be Drunk": "You must be drunk always. That is everything: the only question. Not to feel the horrible burden of Time that crushes your shoulders and bends you earthwards, you must be drunk without respite. But drunk on what? On wine, on poetry, on virtue—take your pick. But be drunk."[122] When the old medium of wine and the reinvented medium of printed poetry combine, intoxication becomes the imperative human condition in commodity culture.

From Baudelaire, Benjamin drew many of his ideas, and at the crux of his own oeuvre remained the dilemma posed by intoxication. On the one hand, it retained the potential of facilitating collective action and even revolution by inducing new, altered visions of reality; on the other, these enchanting visions could always lapse into narcissistic lethargy. Baudelaire's notion that "your pipe smokes you" becomes, in Benjamin's essay on Surrealism, "that terrible drug—ourselves—which we take in solitude."[123] Benjamin elaborates Baudelaire's ambivalence. Drunkenness both potentially illuminates the workers' path to action, and remains vulnerable to a comfortable, bourgeois narcosis. It circumscribes the charmed space of the individualist and the means of escaping this self's confinement. Benjamin linked intoxication to nineteenth-century urban phantasmagorias of the kind consumed by the flaneur, who wanders, as he himself does while high on hashish, figuratively reading urban phenomena such as notices in urinals, the physiognomies of men in a tavern, a menu, a sign on a streetcar—in ways that generate poetic flights of fancy.[124] Yet the flaneur, like Baudelaire's hashish-eater, was also on display, commodifying himself and looking for a buyer. Miriam Hansen describes this dual potential of nineteenth-century mediation in Benjamin's thought: "As mythical images, the phantasmagorias of modernity were by definition ambiguous, promising a classless society while perpetuating the very opposite; yet as dream images they could be read and transformed into historical images, into strategies of waking up."[125] Because intoxication normally suggested sleep or the false consciousness of entertainment, the profane illumination of flaneur-like intoxication is disclosed counterintuitively, through the trope of awakened vision. This is a more refined version of the temperance critique: that society itself is already drunk, and its own vision is the sober, enlightened one. In similar fashion, Benjamin linked institutional technologies and techniques of knowledge to stultifying narcosis: "The history that showed things 'as they really were' was the strongest narcotic of the nineteenth century." Within this analogy of narcotic sleep, he proposes "the sobriety of dawn" that appears when works of art interfere with progress to make what is "truly new" felt.[126] The language of intoxication and sobriety found in temperance discourse appears, surprisingly, in Benjamin's critical vocabulary and theory, which also seek reform leading to social justice. Unlike temperance writers, Benjamin, ever the dialectician, sought an alternative form of sobriety within intoxication.

Affect gives us a set of terms to describe the collective feeling of the mass temperance audience that Benjamin also tried to elaborate. He described the collective, physical impulse to revolution in relation to the mass medium of his own time, film. In the Artwork essay, and "On Surrealism," he harnessed the intoxicating spectacle of film for its revolutionary energies. The latter declares that Romantic views of intoxication, such as that of Engels, are insufficiently dialectical, because they accentuate only its revolutionary potential, which amounts "to a praxis oscillating between fitness exercises and celebration in advance" (216).[127] As Baudelaire knew, one could not return to the revolutionary period when wine facilitated collective action. But Benjamin was also searching for more than just a stimulus to the violent overthrow of the established order. Something like shared affect, his concept of innervation is physical, communal, and illuminating—an intoxication that avoids bourgeois insulation, the flaneur's susceptibility to commodification, and simplistic nostalgia for the people. In "Surrealism," Benjamin writes that innervation takes place in "the space, in a word, in which political materialism and physical creatureliness share the inner man, the psyche, the individual, or whatever else we wish to throw to them, with dialectical justice, so that no limb remains untorn" (217). This maimed body reappropriates the physical wounds, injuries, and missing limbs that register industrial-era violence in sensational temperance narratives. Its figurative violence is the dispersal of individualism, so that torn limbs now reflect the physical feeling of intersubjectivity—the reconstituted wholeness of the collective. It is like intensely present affective bonds resonating within a large group of people. When "revolutionary tension" and "the bodily innervations of the collective" interpenetrate each other, reality, in Benjamin's enigmatic phrase, will "transcend itself" (218). The notion of a self-transcending reality seems mystical, unless we reframe it as the unseen, unquantifiable operation of shared affect to change the social body. According to Hansen, the Artwork essay develops the body's ability to constitute "a medium" and helps imagine "new forms of subjectivity"; Benjamin's models for this physical reorientation include "hashish, gambling, running downhill, eroticism."[128] Although they lack intersubjective power, these individualized disorientations approach the collective excitement and delirium of live mass audiences.

Baudelaire and Benjamin certainly formed a countertradition to temperance, with its rational recreation and bourgeois hypocrisy. But both movements shared an ambivalence about mass media consumption's capacity to effect social change, or to maintain the status quo by gratifying individual desire. As a mass movement advocating sobriety as a form of enlightenment, temperance challenged its opponents to accept the possibility of a rational mass. It also proposed a mass given life by shared affect. Both models contradicted the conventional fear of a violent, mindless mass, which had festered since the French Revolution. A similar contradiction invests Benjamin's theory of a mode of intoxication that would also clearly perceive history and reenvision society. Both the aesthetics of sobriety and those of intoxication sought the felt presence of the social—an elusive, ephemeral affect that transports one from reason and self-interest to an intensive, regenerating togetherness.

CHAPTER 2

Tobacco Papers, Holmes's Pipe, Cigarette Cards, and Information Addiction

The Sign of Four opens with Sherlock Holmes injecting cocaine, opening a book, and lighting his briar pipe—actions that, taken together, suggest a habitual mode of absorptive stimulation and mild pathology. Defending his cocaine use to Watson, he explains that he "crave[s] for mental exaltation"—a desire otherwise fulfilled by his professional activities, the brainwork required to solve his cases. It is an early, defining moment in the Holmes oeuvre, in which drugs, tobacco, and print cluster together and reinforce each other as "artificial stimulants."[1] Throughout the stories and novels, Holmes constantly treats his malaise by these means, rousing himself from the tedium of ordinary life to the highs of intellectual transcendence. Oscillating in energy, mood, affect, and cognitive engagement, he inhabits a nascent paradigm of addiction that was beginning to set the rhythm of modern consumption, but tobacco and print, rather than drugs, are his preferred substances. As Arthur Conan Doyle develops his economy of self-medication, print proves more potent than cocaine, which Holmes takes only "when cases were scanty and the papers uninteresting" (351). Tobacco also supersedes the drugs, appearing far more frequently and consistently throughout the oeuvre as an accompaniment to Holmes's reading and ratiocination.[2] Thus, more than his syringe or magnifying glass, Holmes's tobacco pipe becomes the emblem of his characteristic mixture of intellectual creativity and compulsive dependency. Consider how he responds to a break in the case in "The Red-Headed League": by sinking into a chair rather than leaping into action. "What are you going to do, then?" Watson asks. "'To smoke,' he answered. 'It is quite a three pipe problem, and I beg that you won't speak to me for fifty minutes.'" Tobacco simultaneously frees Holmes's mind to soar and encages him in the armchair, where nicotine in the blood will supply the answers he seeks. Holmes is part genius, part nicotine junkie.

As his intellectual prowess came to be parodied in the 1920s, the curving bowl of Holmes's pipe grew from a modest briar into a voluptuous calabash.[3] A curious emblem of habit, it figures Holmes as both a paragon of spontaneous, organic reason, and as reliant on a mix of tobacco and printed information networks. But Holmes is less original than Watson's accounts would have it: He updates the nineteenth-century figure of the masculine, smoking reader, for whom tobacco smoke mediates a contemplative, daydream-like engagement with printed material, especially ephemera. Throughout the century, a wide-ranging, comic discourse made tobacco smoking a metonym and a metaphor for print consumption; writers constantly punned that men smoked and read "volumes," "leaves," and "puffs" of speech preserved in paper. Andrew Chatto published *A Paper:— of Tobacco* in 1839 under the pseudonym Joseph Fume.[4] T. H. Roberts's appropriately short-lived journal, debuting at the price of one penny in 1898, was titled *The Cigarette*.[5] Joseph Hatton's *Cigarette Papers for After-Dinner Smoking* (1892) advertised itself as a repository of "a passing fact or fancy, a wayside reminiscence, an anecdote, an epigram, a story, or a scrap of what is called philosophy. If the resultant be to your liking, I beg you will roll it up with your cigarette, or drop it into your pipe and smoke it."[6] Such mock-genteel invitations exposed the reading of elite and middlebrow genres alike as the consumption of media objects. Poems, advertisements, cards, and other ephemera had long extolled the peculiar pleasure of smoking the "divine weed"; increasingly, their own disposable status echoed its superfluous enjoyment.[7] Like smoking, consuming print was another nineteenth-century habit that had grown to epic proportions and invaded domestic life, one which, once begun, seemed impossible to quit, one that similarly connoted imitation and unoriginality, and one whose purpose grew ever less distinct. Throughout the nineteenth century, tobacco becomes an instrument by which mental interiority becomes mass-mediated. Holmes shifts the ground of smoking and reading from genteel leisure to something edgier that more closely resembles the physical economy of addiction as that concept emerged. Although Holmes's pipe signifies his reason, it also bears the residue of the genteel smoker's reverie and intellectual sedation.

This chapter demonstrates how tobacco smoking becomes both the material means and the cultural symbol of print media consumption. Visual, literary, and ephemeral culture self-consciously represents the smoker's mental life as mediated, his dreams and reveries populated by mass media materials. The act of inhaling smoke signifies the drawing in of mass cultural material through reading, viewing, collecting, and even playing. Habitual, quotidian, neither fully purposive nor determined, both physiological and psychological, smoking is a scene of affect. The overarching analogy between smoking and reading generated several representational motifs. First, the trope of print "addiction" that I noted in the temperance discourses of chapter 1 develops in Holmes's figurative dependencies on print and tobacco, especially in "The Man with the Twisted Lip." I reinterpret mass media addiction as a generalized response to the speed of modernity, as well as to classed desires for mental stimulation and cultural mastery. Second, as the plethora of informational tobacco ephemera narrowed to the tremendously popular cigarette card in the 1890s, "knowledge" transformed into trivial information. Third, the collection of these cards—as I noted in the introduction, the first ephemera produced to be kept rather than discarded—represents a mode of worlding that reemphasizes mass print's ambiguous relation to the social.

Consuming print increasingly took on the appearance and rhythms of addiction. Compulsive consumption of print, and novels in particular, had been a diagnosis of women's reading at the turn of the nineteenth century and again in the 1860s, the decade of sensation fiction; but in the late 1880s and 1890s, it shed its gendered and genre bias to become an ordinary condition of a literate consumer life.[8] The New Journalism, powered by rotary presses and chock full of illustrations and photomechanical images, created an even larger mass audience, which consumed print at an even faster pace. George Newnes's *Tit-Bits*, launched in 1881, reached hundreds of thousands of readers; his next notable success, the *Strand Magazine*, appeared in 1891 and settled into a circulation of half a million each week.[9] Tobacco smoking, long associated with leisurely reading over a pipe, increasingly featured the cigarette, now mass-produced and increasingly accompanied by series of cards meant to be viewed and skimmed in minutes. Holmes's reliance on precisely calculated doses of tobacco to think through his cases refracted his readers' experiences as consumers of

mind, and put his pipe down upon the mantelpiece.

me

ld-

his
ot
cid

ble
he.
are

iad

in

eft

to

e's

be
he
'o-
ay

en

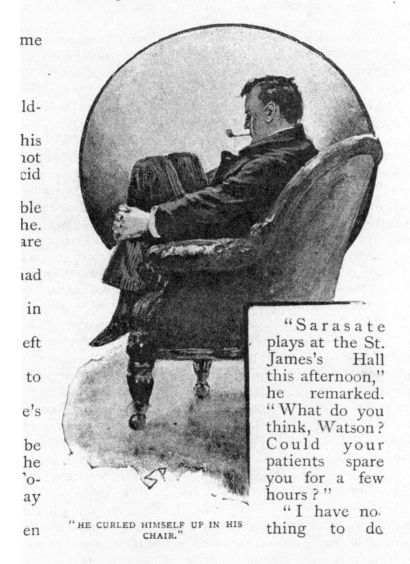

"HE CURLED HIMSELF UP IN HIS CHAIR."

"Sarasate plays at the St. James's Hall this afternoon," he remarked. "What do you think, Watson? Could your patients spare you for a few hours?"

"I have nothing to do

Figure 3. Sidney Paget, "He Curled Himself Up in His Chair." *Strand Magazine*, August 1891.

ephemeral media. Sidney Paget's illustration of Holmes's smoking and thinking evokes such activities, by collapsing, into a single moment, the vacillation between stimulation and sedation characteristic of satiation and withdrawal.

Holmes's pipe stands in for the reams of print that he has collected and memorized, and which we imagine him to be mentally cross-referencing as he inhales and exhales. Conan Doyle writes, "He curled himself up in his chair, with his thin knees drawn up to his hawk-like nose, and there he sat with his eyes closed and his black clay pipe thrusting out like the bill of some strange bird" (184). The pipe makes Holmes into an odd creature indeed, his paradoxical posture suggesting ease and unease, leisure and work, intoxicated absorption and hyperactive stimulation. Indeed, Holmes resembles readers of detective fiction: sitting on the edge of their comfortable seats. Theirs was the reading of leisure, but it was nervously stimulated and accelerated; as Peter Bailey has shown, in this period, leisure itself "was haunted by the imperatives of a rigid work discipline."[10] Holmes's tobacco signifies this new demand that print, resembling both rest and labor, should both soothe and excite. His compulsive dependency on it reflects his readers' industrious consumption of the stories, which made the new *Strand Magazine* such a runaway success. Readers were so hooked on the Holmes stories that when Conan Doyle tried to end them, with "The Final Problem" in December 1893, their outcries persuaded him to resume the supply. Holmes's reading "addiction" indexes just one way the literate masses were consuming print in the 1890s.

Cigarette cards render the object of such addictions more precise: rather than the act of reading or the object of print, it is the acquisition of information. As the mediated mind became culturally recognizable, its knowledge increasingly assumed the character of information and was contoured by the politics of knowledge. The saturation of everyday life by printed material throughout the century generated appetites for information—as some critics sniffed, at the expense of true knowledge and with the effect of creating Philistines.[11] Cigarette cards satisfied these appetites. Tiny items, they harbored an outsized ambition: to inventory everything in the world. They divided this totality into sets of items within natural history (such as tropical flowers, animals and their furs, and birds' nests), cultural history (kings and queens of England, Hindu gods, famous railway trains), and recent popular culture (cinema stars, champion prizefighters, football club badges). This index was dispersed among billions of people, who collected, traded, studied, played with, and discarded its elements in the decades around the turn of the twentieth century. The vestiges of this inventory reside today in libraries, museums, and private collections, where they can be studied as a mass cultural experiment in the ordering of information.[12] That smoking, an infamously unproductive, irrational activity, generated such a vast archive of information, is a conundrum worth contemplating. Holmes and his readers resemble information addicts, but this model must be applied with caution so that it does not obscure the varied affects, mental stimulation, world-making, collecting, play, and cultural mastery that motivated consumers and collectors. As I show, the concept of addiction to information, rather than a straightforward diagnosis, reveals a world of ordinary human longings and needs.

Tobacco, Print, and Addiction

Oh Nymph of Transatlantic fame,
Where'er thine haunt, whate'er thy name,
Whether reposing on the side
Of Oronoquo's spacious tide,
Or list'ning with delight not small
To Niagara's distant Fall,
'tis thine to cherish and to feed
The pungent nose-refreshing weed,
Which whether pulverized it gain
A speedy passage to the brain,
Or whether touch'd with fire, it rise
In circling eddies to the skies,
Does thought more quicken and refine,
Than all the breath of all the Nine—
                WILLIAM COWPER, "Epistle to the Rev. William Bull" (1782)

Smoking and desultory reading had a long, intertwined history in Britain. From the seventeenth century, tobacco had formed a robust topic for publishers of ephemera, such as the anonymously authored *Metamorphosis of Tobacco* (1602). James I's *Counterblaste to Tobacco* (1604) had inspired a smattering of comic and medical defenses, narratives, and poems, such as Richard Braithwait's *The Smoaking Age* (1617).[13] In this period, tobacco and illustrated printed books were expensive, and the presumed genteel masculine readership of tobacco media clung to early nineteenth-century discussions of tobacco. Charles Lamb's letters to Samuel Taylor Coleridge conjure an idealized model of elite, sociable smoking combined with the art of talk and homosocial intimacy: It was an "associated train of pipes, tobacco, egg-hot, welsh-rabbit, metaphysics, and poetry.—Are we *never* to meet again?"[14] Leigh Hunt's essay "Coffee-Houses and Smoking" (1826), with its fantasy of a secret smoking and reading room behind Gliddon's Cigar Divan, demonstrates the transition from such literary talk to solitary media consumption, with tobacco providing the continuity. Over coffee and a cigar, he prepares to stuff himself with "a newspaper, a two-penny sheet, a number to be continued, a magazine, and a review; for I am fond of having too many books at once."[15] In the public-private zone of the cigar divan, the consumption of tobacco and print effect a new pseudosociability that is far less intimate than Lamb's and Coleridge's smoke-fueled discussions: "The conversations were maintained in very quiet and gentlemanly tones: now and then was heard the sound of a leaf turning over; sometimes a hem consequential or otherwise; my own puffs were always distinguishable to myself."[16] Richard Sennett has described such environments as the setting of the privatized public sphere; a member of such a club, "shielded by his right to be left alone, could now also be absolutely lost in his own thoughts, his own daydreams."[17] These were increasingly mediated by print. As tobacco smoking moved unevenly from a customary social activity to a solitary, habitual behavior, light literature nostalgically invoked its genteel intimacy in titles such as *Tobacco Talk and Smokers' Gossip* (1884) and *The Smoker's Guide, Philosopher, and Friend* (1877).[18] The simulated sociability and forced cheer of such titles indicate that smoking while reading was becoming the habit of lonely minds. Holmes preserves the old model, in his use of a cherry-wood pipe when he feels disputatious; but he more frequently engages the new one, smoking his clay pipe while meditating, alone. Affects associated with conviviality turn to ones of solitary, self-contained contemplation.

Watson's observations of Holmes's smoking and reading built on this cultural context, casting the combined and often interchangeable activities as complex, solitary, automatic behavior. In *The Sign of Four*, Holmes declares, "I am going to smoke and to think over this queer business to which my fair client has introduced us," but he immediately reaches for "a bulky volume . . . a gazetteer which is now being published. It may be looked upon as the very latest authority" (127). When Watson arrives at Baker Street with a new client in "The Adventure of the Engineer's Thumb," he finds Holmes "as I expected, lounging about his sitting-room in his dressing-gown, reading the agony column of *The Times*, and smoking his before-breakfast pipe" (276). Watson appears to be catching Holmes indulging in a private pleasure, but there's more to his consumption of advertisements for missing relatives, personal messages, and requests for advice. Holmes is working on the column, rearranging it as so much so-cial data, and thus proving, paradoxically, both his mental superiority to the mass medium of print and his reliance on it.

Similarly, readers had to exert a pleasurable effort to follow the generic cues of detective fiction, weighing narrative clues and speculating on the mystery's solution. In this way, the Holmes stories complemented the puz-zles and brainteasers for which the *Strand* was also known.[19] Moreover, as a pleasant mental challenge, the stories could become the habitual mate-rial of a dependency; reading them was a mode of behavior rather than an utterly willed series of acts, as with Holmes's agony column. Though Holmes's genius always seemed to create a great gulf of difference between him and his ostensibly ordinary readers, in their compulsive reading they resembled each other. If short detective fiction distilled the thrills of mid-century sensation novels into concentrated doses, then Holmes's immense knowledge of sensational literature, which seemed to include "every detail of every horror perpetrated in the century," reflected his own readers' prodigious appetites (22). Tobacco smoking indexed such cravings, not for a specific genre of fiction, but for news, puzzles, illustrations, and advertisements—that is, for the interactive play with information that print supplied.

Smokers literally smoked poetry, riddles, and puzzles as these were printed on tobacco rolling papers, a practice that became a fad around 1840.[20] In 1870, the Liverpool tobacco manufacturer Cope's launched *Cope's Tobacco Plant*, a trade review also aimed at the smoker—"for those hours of ease in which he enjoys his favorite luxury." Cope's equated to-bacco with the new periodical as minor luxury items: "We do not think it improbable that the Tobacconist will find his Customers asking for their monthly 'Tobacco Plant' as regularly as they present their cigar cases, their tobacco pouches, or their snuff-boxes, at his counter."[21] This rhetoric of pleasurable self-medication expanded the activity of reading to include the broad consumption of innovative media formats: The journal offered po-ems, illustrated essays, cartoons, foldout posters, and cards designed by the watercolorist John Wallace, known as "George Pipeshanks," in homage to the famed caricaturist and illustrator George Cruikshank.[22] A. V. Seaton has attested to Cope's tremendous success as an advertiser; this derived from its ability to repackage the leisurely, literary air of earlier books and periodical matter about smoking in smaller, cheaper, attractive formats.[23] One of its blends was named "Our Mutual Friend" after Charles Dickens's 1865 novel. In 1889, the firm began reprising the best pieces from the *Plant* in fourteen illustrated smoke-room booklets, offering them at two pence each: "to the intelligent many who have soothed their lives by the judicious use of Cope's Mixture in their pipes, this enlivening mixture for their minds."[24] This elaborate literary tobacco media flourished in the last third of the century, overlapping with cigarette cards' rise to dominance in the 1890s. Its cultural effect was to compress the leisurely bourgeois tradition of smoking and reading into a briefer, more superficial experience of smoking and consuming ephemera—two compulsive habits that increasingly went well together. In addition to metamorphosing from a social activity to a simulated conversation carried out in print, smoking also shifted from an emblem of expansive literary leisure to brief, self-administered doses of print.

The smoke-room booklet was a unique piece of Victorian ephemera. It repackaged selected writings by famous literary smokers such as Charles Lamb (no. 4); Thomas Carlyle (no. 5), and John Ruskin (no. 13). It took up topics in the history and material culture of smoking, such as "Amber," used to make pipestems (no. 7), "Pipes and Meerschaum" (nos. 11 and 12), and the European "discoverer" of tobacco, Sir Walter Raleigh (no. 14). It also offered poems, anecdotes, parodies, and other tidbits in "The Smoker's Textbook" (no. 1) and "The Smoker's Garland" (nos. 2, 6, and 11). For three shillings, readers could obtain about sixty pages of fine or amusing writing, and the exquisitely charming line-drawing illustrations of Wallace, rendered in gorgeous gold, red, and black on the covers. Seaton claims that Cope's was "more innovative than any nineteenth-century advertiser"— high praise for the era in which the modern practice emerged; likewise, Richard Altick praised the *Plant* and the booklets for their good value.[25]

Alongside this high quality cultural material, however, ran an aesthetic of sedation that permeated tobacco discourse more widely. The visual trope of the dozing, sleeping, or dreaming smoker, which appeared throughout the booklets, did not match a sharp appreciation of the finer points of Carlyle or Ruskin. Linda Austin, analyzing the poet James Thomson's writings for Cope's, which the company interspersed with his essays on Ben Jonson, Edmund Burke, and George Meredith in booklet no. 3, interpreted them as a new, vacant mode of writing that lent itself to leisurely, amused detachment.[26] Because all intellectual pathways in the essays and snippets lead back to "the altar of Diva Nicotina," the booklets cultivate a self-consciousness of their own consumption as so much undifferentiated smoking.[27] Any straightforward reading of them as edifying must struggle with their competing tendency to foreground their own evaporation in the act of consumption. As an accessory of smoking, and an analog to the pipe or cigar, the smoke-room booklet performs the strange feat of converting serious reading into frivolous media consumption.

Smoking furnished an apt analog for consuming print because both seemed to take place in the gray zone between intentional act and habitual behavior—the realm of everyday affects. As Matthew Hilton observes, Holmes's own incessant smoking could have furnished the data for his famous monograph "Upon the Distinction between the Ashes of Various Tobaccoes," which catalogues "a hundred and forty forms of cigar-, cigarette-, and pipe-tobacco, with colored plates illustrating the difference in the ash" (91).[28] Holmes knows the value of ashes—as well as the odor of tobacco smoke—as traces of behavior because he himself smokes promiscuously, inhaling from the briar, the cherry-wood, cigars, and cigarettes. In "The Boscombe Valley Mystery," he identifies the butt of an Indian cigar rolled in Rotterdam as the murderer's signature trace; and the strong odor of one helps explain the intruder's means of entry in "The Adventure of the Speckled Band" (214; 261). Holmes thus catalogues a symptom of mass consumer behavior that he himself exhibits. His investigations construe smoking as habitual, unselfconscious activity, but his own smoking fluctuates between such automatic dependency and personal style. In "The Adventure of the Yellow Face," Holmes interprets a client's briar, fitted with a faux amber stem and mended with silver bands, declaring, "Nothing has more individuality, save perhaps watches and bootlaces" (352). As we shall see in chapter 3, like one's relationship to ink, whether exhibited in handwriting and analyzed by graphologists or produced through inkblot tests, one's taste in tobacco and style of smoking was thought to be unique and beyond affectation. Compulsively expressive, it was always eminently legible to the detective. Reading the body off the pipe, ash, and cigarette butt, Holmes reconstituted personality through identity: Although all indexed a physiological dependency on nicotine, the ash of Trichinopoly, bird's-eye, and hand-rolled cigarettes each would have signified a different mode of masculinity and class. Individuality inheres in the stylistic permutation with which one conforms to the mass activity of smoking. Smoking thus suggested a form for mundane, indeterminate affects that almost all men could inhabit.

Popular and medical writers were beginning to describe smoking as a pathology, although their voices were in a minority; perhaps none sounded the alarm in so grimly comic a fashion as Guy Thorne, who penned the novel *The Cigarette Smoker: Being the Terrible Case of Uether Kennedey* (1902). Uether Kennedey is a hale young English painter who, under the influence of a decadent French colleague, takes up cigarette smoking and finishes the novel as a brain pickled in an anatomy jar. His doctor declares, "I am used to all the various forms of insanity, but I have never yet seen such cases of mania as those induced by the cigarette."[29] Partway through the novel, Uether agrees to sequester himself in a remote south coast cottage to break his habit, and his live-in medical attendant suspects him of secretly smoking again. The discovery, when it comes, is worthy of Conan Doyle: "The room was papered with a pattern of large crimson flowers, each with a centre of a dark brown colour. From the middle of one of the flowers a thin spiral of cigarette smoke poured into the room. They stood watching with amazement. . . . Even as they looked at it the ash at the end began to kindle, and glowed to a bright red point. . . . *Kennedey was smoking through the wall!*"[30] Depicting the habit as a degenerate disease and a secret crime, Thorne tried to turn readers against smoking, but as with similar temperance fiction, he may have simply advertised its allure. Nonetheless, his novel signaled a more modern, scientific understanding of tobacco smoking. We see it as well in Conan Doyle's "The Five Orange Pips," when Watson and Holmes joke about Watson's inventory of Holmes's areas of expertise, skills, and flaws when they first met in "A Study in Scarlet." At the end of a list that includes "botany variable," "anatomy unsystematic," and "violin-player, boxer, swordsman, lawyer" comes the designation "self-poisoner by cocaine and tobacco" (225). This piece of mirth reframes Watson's original diagnosis as a fusty, naive impression of an earlier epoch. Holmes's compulsive smoking, drug-taking, and information absorption reference the old concept of "self-poisoning" to signal its obsolescence. In the 1890s, a new, forensic notion of personhood was helping to remake smoking into a habitual, dependent, stylized mode of self-medication somewhere between unconscious behavior and self-conscious style—a disease of everyday modern life.[31] Long before consensus about its effects on health, smoking exteriorized a less than rational, but not quite unconscious, state of mind and body. This state, characteristically below the threshold of consciousness and sovereign reason, is the domain of affect.

In this affective space, the media consumer was represented psychically incorporating mass cultural materials. Visual and literary representations of masculine, smoking readers had suggested the self-consciousness of the addictive model, in particular, the consumer's absorption in print. An image from *Cope's Smoke-Room Booklets* exemplifies how such absorption in print was thought to shape bourgeois interiority. The book seems to have swallowed up and replaced its voracious reader, who carelessly holds the

"THE PIPE IS WHAT WE CARE FOR."

Figure 4. "The Pipe Is What We Care For." *Cope's Smoke-Room Booklets*, no. 8, 1893.

antique folio while sitting in his armchair. Of visual representations of
people reading, Garret Stewart writes that "the sequestered mental life of
reading is often . . . shown subservient, squandered, drained, evacuated"—
in this instance, overwhelmed by the book and literally effaced.[32] Yet in

the comic spirit of tobacco discourse, the wafting smoke parodies the elite act of contemplative reading or viewing taking place beneath it, like a visual graffito. Print and image refashion subjectivity, but this takes place in a moment—the very one in which viewers spy the figure's ongoing absorption. This glimpse recalls observers of the image to themselves, turning them from a similar absorption to a more fleeting, self-conscious awareness of their own varying levels of fascination by, and dependency on, print media. The figure's eighteenth-century dress and oversize folio enhance viewers' self-consciousness of their modern difference—the way their own absorption may have dissipated into distraction. The exchange suggests a

Figure 5. "Hymn to Saint Nicotine." *Cope's Tobacco Plant*, Christmas 1871.

new mode of absorption that is "no longer related to an *interiorization* of the subject, to an intensification of a sense of selfhood," but rather enacts an outward-facing, depthless mode of attention.[33] This superficial state of mind suggests a psychic porosity through which mass cultural materials drift: the state of mediation.

As part of this visual discourse, the trope of the curling line of smoke turning into printed text or image represented the incorporation of print.[34] Such iconography depicts exhaled smoke as a repository for the rhymes, songs, and images that the mind compulsively reproduces from printed media. In this widely reprinted image from *Cope's Tobacco Plant*, smoke—like a primitive thought balloon—materializes the seated man's imaginative flight of fancy. But its content is nothing more than the half-clad nymphs of middlebrow pastoral iconography—derivative, recirculated images passing through the smoker as media apparatus, much like Oliver Wendell Holmes's poem "The Lover's Calendar" rewritten as an homage to tobacco. In its lines, tobacco becomes a revelatory optic: "I look upon the fair blue skies / And naught but empty air I see; / But when thy circling cloudlets rise, / It seemeth unto me / Ten thousand angels spread their wings / Within those little azure rings." Tobacco becomes the instrument by which the individual smoker's imagination replicates printed mass media. In this common trope, tobacco suggests how putatively disorganized thought—fancy, fantasy, daydreaming, distraction—could be habitually structured by, and filled with, mass-mediated content.[35] Affect describes the mingled physical and psychic states or moods in which these transmissions between mass and individual take place. The figure's respectable, armchair traveler to exotic mental zones hints that this structuring follows a repetitive industrial rhythm of work and leisure. "The Pipe Is What We Care For" represents print consumption as a temporarily depersonalizing process, as the consumer loses himself in his books and pipes. "Hymn to Saint Nicotine" more ambitiously represents the consumer mentally reproducing media content—an automatic, even unconscious process, like inhalation and exhalation.

Literary satires humorously critiqued tobacco smoking as an instrument of the mass-mediated imagination, which "Hymn to Saint Nicotine" so unaffectedly represents. For example, in Bret Harte's short story "Facts concerning a Meerschaum" (1860) the narrator, acknowledging his "besetting sin" of "continually assuming other people's habits," imitates his friend "Puffer" by smoking his meerschaum. Smoking "genuine Latakia (manufactured in Connecticut)," and fantasizing a female figure, he describes his compulsive habit in the nascent nineteenth-century language of addiction:

"You, O Reader, who have . . . indulged in some prohibited vice—you can recall how much easier becomes the descent, after the first downward step."[36] The story mocks the imaginative reproduction of the erotica delivered to consumers' psyches via printed media; moreover, it depicts this consumption as a compulsive dependency on tobacco. These and other examples show that smoking and reading were easily recognized as obsessive, addictive modes of media consumption, and the masculine styles they produced as derivative, rather than natural.

Perhaps the best known of these satires is *The Picture of Dorian Gray* (1891)—a novel I discuss at length in chapter 5. Oscar Wilde writes Dorian's dilemma as one of media consumption: How does one construct an authentic or natural self out of mass cultural materials? Dorian's media consumption, though seemingly of "old," elite late-nineteenth-century modes such as oil painting, decorated books, and theater, symbolizes the pleasures and perils of new, mass print media consumers of the period. Taking a more darkly comic, nuanced view than Harte's broader satire, Wilde nonetheless shows how Dorian consumes mass-produced tropes and styles, and then reconstitutes and reproduces them in his dandiacal style. Moreover, Wilde also invokes the language of intoxication, and then addiction, to describe Dorian's obsessive consumption. His signature emphasis on the figure of the dandy's cigarette smoking conveys Dorian's absorption of Lord Henry's spoken wisdom, as he "talks books away."[37]

As a budding media addict, the smoking reader doubled his role as consumer and reproducer, a figuration that foregrounded unoriginality and conflated labor with leisure. In a tradition hearkening back to Isaac Hawkins Brown's parodies of Alexander Pope, Jonathan Swift, and others in *Pipe of Tobacco* (1736), the figure of the young man as smoker solidified as one of modern literary unoriginality, too: Robert Buchanan described the devotees of the Pre-Raphaelites—themselves, in his estimate, imitators of Alfred, Lord Tennyson—as "young gentlemen with animal faculties morbidly developed by too much tobacco."[38] When Enoch Soames, Max Beerbohm's satiric emblem of Decadence, disappears, "His cigarette floated sodden in his wine-glass. There was no other trace of him."[39] Tobacco exposed modern masculine literary self-fashioning as a drolly failed imitation, necessarily dependent on consuming literature in order to produce it. In this way, the exhausted, used-up, tobacco-saturated male body became a ground of confusion between labor and leisure. The poem about tobacco that was most frequently reprinted throughout the nineteenth century, William Cowper's "To the Rev. William Bull" (1782) illustrates the way industrial-era poetry recruited tobacco smoking to figure poetic composition as consumption and, conversely, literary consumption as a kind of labor. A poem about writer's block, it praises tobacco as divine inspiration, supplying the speaker's need for "a succedeaneum, then, / To accelerate a creeping pen!"[40] Its beneficent wish that Bull might never stop smoking and reading—"And so may smoke-inhaling Bull / Be always filling, never full"—hints, despite its benignity, at the potentially wearying, endless work of modern print media consumption. Gorging on print, consumers—like addicts—could never achieve satiety because such fullness would transcend mediation itself. Conversely, aesthetic producers increasingly felt originality to be harder than ever to grasp unaided.

This cultural logic can be glimpsed, in an understated way, in a well-known painting of the most famous Victorian novelist. In Robert H. Buss's unfinished watercolor *Dickens's Dream* (1875), we see Boz in his study, snoozing as his characters make their way through his mind. Dickens's right hand is holding a cigar, and although Buss doesn't connect the exhaled smoke to the spectral figures wafting overhead, a later painter, E. Gray, did so in an image published in the *Dickensian*, "Charles Dickens in Reverie." The trope is quite like "Hymn to Saint Nicotine," as well as to Luke Fildes's frontispiece for *The Mystery of Edwin Drood* (1871), in which the Princess Puffer and a Chinese man exhale opium smoke that seems to form other characters and scenes from the novel. Neither image of Dickens impugns him as a hack. Yet his cigar is clearly facilitating his imaginative absorption, the psychic state in which he produces his fiction; and in this fiction, characters seem to arrive in Dickens's mind rather than to be created there. Andrew Miller has also observed the way these images abstract Dickens's labor by having him seem to occupy the same ontological plane as his characters, like a Spiritualist medium.[41] Although Miller is uninterested in tobacco smoke, in these and similar images it produces a specific, punning kind of "inspiration." Through it, viewers and readers join the part of mass culture for which Dickens was responsible, but they also see Dickens the author as himself a kind of media consumer.[42] Images circulate through minds, blurring consumption and production; they are reproduced, but the scene of their formation remains elusive.

Holmes's undisputed originality as a cultural figure emerges from this complex logic of print consumption and reproduction: Rather than embodying an idealized model of autonomous creative genius, he inaugurates a new one that is dependent on media and artificial substances as analogous props. Frank Wiles's cover illustration for the first installment of *The Valley of Fear* (1914) demonstrates how Holmes's pipe literally mediates between him and the printed cipher he analyzes, like a lens, filter, or screen. Holmes forms part of a media apparatus, with the pipe visually linking his intent face to the paper. He resembles Egyptian boys, in the speculations of the *Quarterly Review*, whose eyes were fixed on ink that bore projections from mirrors in magicians' sleeves, as we will see in chapter 3. As Alison Byerly has shown, Holmes relies on fast new transportation and information networks: the post, newspapers, telegraphy, telephony; we might even include the Baker Street Irregulars, who resembled Wilkie Collins's Gooseberry in their swift urban circulation.[43] Holmes needs these technologies, broadly construed, to collect and document the traces of others' original misdeeds; his own originality inheres in narrative bricolage. Smoking signifies this new, dependent, belated relationship to print. The idiosyncratic profession of "unofficial consulting detective" links tobacco's older, late-Romantic associations with genteel intellectualism to the newer, harried brainwork of white-collar professionals. In a developing service economy, such intellectual work often relied on new artificial stimulants: cigarettes and, in rarefied bourgeois circles, cocaine and morphine.[44] Indeed, Holmes's energy, which waxes and wanes according to the rhythms of his artificial stimulation and case work, is as rigidly compelled as any dependency. Likewise, his affect surges to mania and quietens to melancholy.

And yet the combined habits of smoking, reading, and thinking also connoted idleness, Bohemianism, and creative artistry, as when Holmes squirrels away his tobacco in the toe of a Persian slipper or appears reading the agony column late in the morning (386). His signature cluster of unoriginal, nonactivities seems to defy industrial work schedules, and his intellectual work resembles idleness, especially since sitting and smoking in solitude was the iconic performance of bourgeois, masculine leisure throughout the century.[45] Yet his strongest appetite is for work. Quipping like his fellow smoker and aesthete Lord Henry Wotton, but expressing a conventional Victorian sentiment, he jokes, "I never remember feeling tired by work, though idleness exhausts me completely" (127). The fantasy of thrilling intellectual labor that Holmes embodies enlists tobacco smoking to disguise the physical and material economies that support it. Thinking, for Holmes, seems as easy as breathing. It is afterward that he collapses. Holmes's scrambled work and leisure—his brainwork looks like idleness, so it must be later seen to have depleted him—reflects the new industrial regime of intellectual labor that depends on information media and artificial stimulation. Holmes's voluminous reading, smoking, and drug-taking gloss this new mode of professional productivity as eccentric Bohemianism. Addiction develops unnoticed by disguising, as pleasure and style, the labor and other costs involved in its maintenance; it only becomes visible when excessive consumption loses the guise of enjoyment and novelty, and begins to resemble work.

Affect may seem a counterintuitive optic for viewing Holmes, who has traditionally been viewed as a reasoning machine. But that is precisely why his psychological and bodily economy, with its rhythms, dependencies, and mood swings, requires finer description. Affect helps name these zones and forms of self-reproduction from mass-mediated materials. Smoking, which connects body, unconscious mind, and self-conscious pose, suggests the space and time of everyday affect. It also signals the self's porosity: its unconscious reliance on mass culture that remains incompletely determined by it. These exchanges suggest the self's work on itself.

"The Man with the Twisted Lip": Smoking and Detective Fiction

I'm the king of the *Cadaverals*,
I'm *Spectral* President;
And, all from east to occident,
There's not a man whose dermal walls
Contain so narrow intervals,
So lank a resident.

JOHN LUCAS TUPPER, "Smoke" (1849)

Holmes's and other detectives' smokiness runs the narrative machinery of the genre. Although he disdains the comparison, Holmes resembles his predecessor, Edgar Allan Poe's Dupin—another voracious smoker, reader, and contemplator of the abstruse, who similarly defies commercial work schedules by roving through his city at night. "The Purloined Letter" invokes the trope of smoky, desultory thought: It begins with Dupin and the narrator sitting in silence in the dark, apparently "intently and exclusively occupied with the curling eddies of smoke that oppressed the atmosphere of the chamber," but truly thinking hard.[46] Likewise, Gabriel Betteredge, house steward turned detective's assistant of Wilkie Collins's *The Moonstone* (1868) linked smoking, problem solving, and books by habitually smoking a pipe while randomly consulting *Robinson Crusoe*. As a sign of the leisure required for mental activity, whether fantasizing, problem solving, speculating, reading, or viewing media, tobacco smoking offered an action to dramatize the detective's thinking while hiding his thoughts, thus generating suspense. In *The Moonstone*, the gentleman detective Franklin Blake smokes to attenuate his own suspense, when he awaits the emergence of Rosanna Spearman's hidden box from the quick-sand: "This was one of the occasions on which the invaluable habit of smoking becomes especially precious and consolatory. I lit a cigar, and sat down on the slope of the beach." Yet this cigar does not work as advertised: The tide turns, terrifying feelings erupt, and before he finishes the cigar, Blake flings it away and hurries from the scene.[47] Blake's hysterical smoking aligns him with the page-turning reader, who endures the chills of sensation fiction, the genre from which *The Moonstone*—and detective fiction in general—unevenly emerged. I discuss this readerly intoxication and addiction in greater detail in the next chapter. To smoking's connotations of leisurely, genteel intellectualism, Poe and Collins added the narrative function of regulating the flow of information. Smoking signified the situation of the consumer of detective fiction: Sitting, reading, and thinking had never been so exciting.

It is Holmes, however, who perfects tobacco's narrative instrumentality to detective fiction; and none of his adventures demonstrates tobacco's self-reflexive comment on the genre more clearly than "The Man with the Twisted Lip." In this story, Holmes investigates the disappearance of Neville St. Clair, last seen in an opium den; he hypothesizes that a beggar with a scar named Hugh Boone has murdered him, until he realizes that St. Clair and Boone are one and the same person. Instead of going to work each day, St. Clair has been disguising himself as a beggar, and making more money sitting on a street corner offering witty quips to passersby than he did as a journalist or an actor.[48] As in "The Red Headed League," tobacco solves the case for Holmes. In St. Clair's suburban villa, Holmes clads himself in an Orientalized blue dressing gown, arranges pillows on the floor, and smokes and thinks through the night. As Watson narrates, "In the dim light of the lamp I saw him sitting there, an old briar pipe between his lips, his eyes fixed vacantly upon the corner of the ceiling, the blue smoke curling up from him, silent, motionless, with the light shining upon his strong set of aquiline features" (240). The aestheticized spirals of blue smoke and empty gaze connote passive absorption, but it is mingled with the intellectual force of his racialized British profile, the contour of alertness and focused attention. Here, smoke depicts Holmes as both an intellectual factory and as a votary, burning incense for an oracle: It both indexes a productive mental activity and hints that the answer to the riddle will be given—as it typically is, in the denouement of the detective narrative. Readers cannot hope to solve the mystery themselves, though they must be given the illusion of being able to do so. Inspector Bradstreet voices a common curiosity when he tells Holmes, "I wish I knew how you reach your results." Holmes replies by frankly admitting, "I reached this one . . . by sitting upon five pillows and consuming an ounce of shag" (244). The punch line cheekily comments on the story's own generic formula: Since Holmes's thinking cannot be narrated without spoiling the revelation, smoking substitutes for his thought process. Smoking, an affective form, humorously supplies the new pose of reason.

"The Man with the Twisted Lip" pointedly alters its source material to promote this ideology of tobacco smoking as enjoyable consumption. In a *Tit-Bits* feature titled "A Day as a Professional Beggar," a journalist decides to impersonate a beggar for a day to generate fresh copy; he too displays boxes of matches bought for a penny each, to avoid being arrested for begging. The story concludes by soberly asserting that begging involves effort: "Standing is by no means such easy work as it looks. Yet the people who do this every day for a living are called lazy."[49] Conan Doyle, crucially converting the journalist-beggar's standing to sitting, the characteristic posture of the leisured smoker, accordingly inverts this moral to emphasize begging's illegitimacy, as shameless nonwork that St. Clair must keep from his family and that the police must stop. Whereas the *Tit-Bits* writer subversively suggests that tobacco was an alibi for the paradoxical labor of begging, Conan Doyle rewrites it as a disguise for indolence. More scandalously, he makes Holmes's smoky brainwork resemble Boone's begging. Boone "takes his daily seat, cross-legged, with his tiny stock of matches on his lap"; these are "wax vestas," which he pretends to sell; Holmes likewise "perched himself cross-legged, with an ounce of shag tobacco and a box of matches laid out in front of him" (235; 240). Just as Boone's matches cover his nonwork, so too the matches in Holmes's lap are the narrative's alibi for his mystified means of production. Just as tobacco smoke delivers the mystery's solution to Holmes, so too does it permit "a small rain of charity to descen[d]" into Boone's cap on the pavement (235). Holmes's cheeky retort to Bradstreet, that he solved the mystery by smoking, winks at readers: Tobacco proves that thinking really is pleasure rather than labor—the abiding working-class fantasy of intellectual work that Holmes embodies. Holmes's solving the case by smoking mimes readers' experience with the story, which was likely consumed while sitting, and as with tobacco, once finished, used up. Pleasure and effort combine in a smoky spectacle that self-consciously rewards readers for their compulsive consumption.

Tobacco was crucially suited to play this role of aggrandizing consumption, disguising its physical toll, and flattering readers that they resembled genteel intellectuals, because it formed a contrast to a more clearly damaging smokable substance that was embroiled in a history of forced labor: opium. "The Man with the Twisted Lip" accordingly deploys tobacco to suburbanize and anglicize the urban and foreign custom of opium smoking, which had been a feature of English journalism and fiction for a generation. Conan Doyle opens the story with the figure of Isa Whitney, who, "having read De Quincey's description of his dreams and sensations . . . had drenched his tobacco with laudanum in an attempt to produce the same effects" (229). Since Whitney shares this affinity for drugs, tobacco, and print media with Holmes, he must also be differentiated quickly as a garden-variety sot: The habit has made him, in conventional nineteenth-century terms, "a slave to the drug" and "an object of mingled horror and pity," who Watson must restore to wife and hearth (229). The description of the Bar of Gold elaborates the slavery metaphor, by conflating such addicted, idle dreaming with the most painful, dominating compulsion of all, chattel slavery. The den, with its "wooden berths, like the forecastle of an emigrant ship," is populated with human cargo that, in its anatomizing and fetishizing prose, hints at the middle passage: "bowed shoulders, bent knees, heads thrown back and chins pointing upwards" (231). This whiff of more literal enslavement, however, is subsumed again by the metaphorical bondage to opium, which commands the "dark, lack-lustre eye[s]" of its devotees and reduces their discourse to a single "strange, low, monotonous voice" (231). Holmes, in lurking there in disguise, flirts with opium and slavery, but distinguishes himself from them through his more mainstream smoking choice.

Lurid descriptions of opium dens elided the realities of Chinese and other immigrants' work and leisure; the fabled dens that had entertained readers since the period of Charles Dickens's *The Mystery of Edwin Drood* (1871) were likely nothing more than boarding houses where Chinese seamen rented rooms.[50] The purpose of the description, in that novel, the Holmes story, and the welter of periodical features, was to briefly titillate slumming readers; unlike Whitney, Watson—and readers— "have not come to stay" (231). When he encounters Holmes, Watson packs Whitney into a cab, and opium, with its connotations of migration and enslavement, is also driven out of the narrative. Holmes reconstitutes their dangerous allure, as armchair visionary travel, when he erects his own makeshift opium den in suburban Kent, with his pillows, dressing gown, and tobacco. Holmes's tobacco-smoking sanitizes the history of racialized labor associated with opium dens, placing it in safer, plainly English confines, and making it a spectacle of consumption.[51] This is just what Victorian gentlemen had done by dressing in Oriental drag—

fezzes, frogged jackets, printed robes—and smoking narghilés, hookahs, and other exotic pipes.[52] Both deployed the ideology of tobacco-as-inspiration as a mass aesthetic, an ersatz, English version of opium minus the compulsion and desuetude of both the metaphorical "slavery" to the drug and the historical slavery that produced and distributed tobacco throughout the world.[53]

In contrast, the white, masculine, knowledge-worker's acrid inspirations of tobacco Romanticized and effaced labor. The sinuous line of exhaled smoke that suggested imaginative potential, evident in visual and literary tobacco discourse, promoted the ideology of tobacco smoking as effortless aesthetic and cognitive inspiration: smoke simply rises, forming castles in the air. In this ubiquitous theme, tobacco was a muse, and thus a force variously natural, divine, and mythological, as well as a godly gift. Visual puns on "Pan pipes" abounded in this pastoral iconography. Forming countless voluptuous nymphs, sprites, and other feminine figures of fecundity and energy, smoke obscured the real labor of tobacco production and trade. Even realistic representations of such work, like "A Day in a Tobacco Factory," from *The English Illustrated Magazine* or F. Marion Crawford's best-selling novel *A Cigarette-Maker's Romance* (1890), sentimentalized and eroticized women's labor rolling cigarettes, probably under the influence of Georges Bizet's *Carmen* (1875).[54] This sentimentality was mingled with nostalgia, after the Bonsack machine began to displace hand-rolling techniques, manufacturing cigarettes at the rate of 300 per minute, in 1883.[55] Within the U.S., the visual iconography of tobacco crop harvesting resonated as a spectacle of national commercial might, often powered by the effort of fetishized black bodies; but British imagery dwelled in the pastoral and supernatural, emphasizing the smoke rather than the leaf or the bale. Such play on "inspiration" was a refusal to acknowledge both the physical labor of tobacco production, and the aesthetic and intellectual effort involved in knowledge and cultural production. Smoking seemed to promise that writing, making art, or solving complex problems could be as natural and effortless as breathing; this is the cultural fantasy subtending "The Man with the Twisted Lip" and the Holmes persona. The disavowal of the material exchanges that grounded smoking echoed in a disregard of its addictive aspects—that is, of the body's own efforts to supply and maintain its dependency. Likewise, they were blind to the intellectual laborer's own dependency on mass print as the source of putatively original ideas. That this ideological nexus was ripe for satire, by Harte, Beerbohm, Wilde, and others, suggested a self-consciousness of a complex set of dependencies: of consumers on producers, of intellectual labor on physical condition, and of literary originality on its print medium.[56] Tobacco's association with print, especially paper, revealed this constellation, setting the scene of addiction to printed information.

Holmes turns to his pipe for answers, but he also smokes more modern, mass-produced cigarettes; in them, the literalizing, self-referential drive of tobacco discourse heightens the reminder of his and his readers' dependencies on the disposable material of paper. Cigarettes make Holmes fully self-referential, or, coexistent with his printed medium—a resonance echoed in his narrative status as media icon, since he is the subject of Watson's stories.[57] A man of smoke and paper, he coalesces, as a character, the habitual punning of tobacco discourse. Years earlier, a poem by John Tupper in *The Germ* had given voice to smoke, which described itself in terms that resemble Holmes: "lank and slim," "an authority / on all things ghastly," and a reader of "tractates musty, / Dry, cadaverous, and dusty."[58] Smoke refigures the human body as so much old, dead, paper—a medium that has been digested and preserved. Insofar as Holmes is a repository of knowledge, he incorporates and reembodies the print media that conveys it; these range across the life of paper from ephemeral gossip columns to ancient black-letter volumes.

The disorienting effect of such wide-ranging media consumption registers on Holmes as an imagined exhaustion and nausea from print culture. Conan Doyle, perhaps feeling his own pen creep with fatigue, and wishing to write something new, attempted to kill Holmes off at the beginning of the end of "The Final Problem." There, Watson is struck that Holmes "was looking even paler and thinner than usual. 'Yes, I have been using myself up rather too freely,' he remarked, in answer to my look rather than to my words; 'I have been a little pressed of late. . . . Might I trouble you for a match?' He drew in the smoke of his cigarette as if the soothing influence was grateful to him" (469). When Holmes's pipe reaches its apotheosis, it becomes a cigarette. His affinity with the paper makes him resemble it: pale, thin, pressed, used up. At the same time, these words all describe Holmes's existence as the object of readers' own print dependencies—and the fatiguing labor of maintaining those dependencies, too. Conan Doyle wanted to quit Holmes, but consumers of the *Strand* were too habituated to give him up. Sure enough, when Conan Doyle resurrected him in 1903, in "The Adventure of the Empty House," he "lit a cigarette in his old nonchalant manner" (486). Holmes's smoking mirrored readers' consumption of his adventures: a pleasurably effortful dependency that, below its scrim of nonchalance, signaled a significant if subtle change in a culture's relationship to print.

Cigarette Cards: Trivia, Mastery, Play

Holmes, of course, never ceases to bounce back to life. One of his manifestations was as the first of a series of Turf cigarette cards in 1925, where he is depicted, with scrupulous accuracy, smoking a bent briar pipe. "Conan Doyle Characters" is a fairly standard set: image on the front, informational text on the back, along with advertising for the brand. Its other items include major characters such as Watson, Moriarty, Lestrade, and minor ones like Tonga, Miss Mary Morstan, and Dr. Grimesby Roylott. Aficionados of the Holmes stories may be disappointed by Turf's copy on number one: "The nature of a detective's work makes it essential that he should avoid publicity. Perhaps that is why no 'real life' detective has the notoriety of Sherlock Holmes, the hero of so many of Sir Arthur Conan Doyle's tales." This copy doesn't tell you anything you don't already know—unless you don't know the term "detective," the name of the author of the Sherlock Holmes stories, or that Holmes is a fictional character. And yet each of these would have been a perfectly reasonable missing piece of cultural information within many working-class, quasi-literate, or immigrant communities circa 1925.[59] "Sherlock Holmes" may have become a popular byword for genius, but the very fact, let alone the details, of his literary existence was not universally known. The card thus offers access to cultural information that may be new to its readers or hearers. More finely imagining the contexts of the cards' circulation deepens and complicates the informal model of addiction to narrative information that Holmes's smoking and the *Strand* consumers' reading exemplified. As mass-mediated interiority became a modern norm, cultural information gained currency; smokers and readers eagerly sucked it in, filling themselves and establishing social status.

The cigarette card turns from the sedative effect of the text-heavy smoke-room booklets to quick mental stimulation. Cigarettes themselves signified a new kind of mass modernity. They streamlined the Victorian jumble of smoking implements: pipes of clay and wood, meerschaums, and cigars; cheroots and narghilés.[60] A pipe suggested the comfort of a domestic habit, something soothing to be enjoyed between a home-cooked meal and sleep. Cigarettes signified publicity, mobility, speed, stimulation, and convenience. Manufacturers such as Allen and Ginter in the United States and John Player & Sons in the U.K. quickly realized that the cardboard stiffeners designed to protect the delicate rolls from being crushed in their packets could also advertise the brand. The high volume of individual consumption required variety and novelty in every pack, and advances in color lithography and flat-press printing obliged, generating vivid pictures and miniature text for each tiny card.[61] Typically, the image depicted the subject of the series, the brand name, and some descriptive text; cards often came in sets of twenty-five or fifty, though there was no standard. The longest series, Ogden's "Actresses, Prominent People, and Subjects of General History" ran from 1899 to 1910, comprising more than 20,000 cards—"a complete social history of the period."[62] Before long, the acquisition of such trivia about celebrities, flags of the world, swimming champions, and lighthouses became known as "cigarette card knowledge."[63] The cards seemed designed to supply the sort of information one needed to keep pace with modernity: not practical knowledge relevant to direct experience, but trivial facts. Detective fiction, which I explore at greater length in the following chapter, generated an appetite for narrative information to solve a mystery; cigarette cards stimulated and supplied a desire for trivial information to be collected and displayed.

True to their historical moment, cigarette cards organized information like world fairs did. By featuring famous leaders, battles, and coins, they emphasized nations; by showcasing folk costumes and dances, they foregrounded cultures; and by enumerating steamships, airplanes, and inventions, they highlighted manufacturing achievements. The ambitious scope implied by the titles of the sets—"Arms of All Nations," "Wild Animals of the World"—made their inventories seem complete or somehow official, and their accuracy was fabled. Cigarette cards were even used as references in court cases, to settle disputes about Scottish clans' tartans and types of fish.[64] Today, their objectivity and comprehensiveness seem fatally compromised. Sensational series, such as Kimball's "Savage and Semi-Barbarous Chiefs and Rulers," cast people of color as thrilling objects of Western knowledge, valorizing modern imperial conquest.[65] Numerous card sets deployed female figures in visual aesthetics that ranged from the genteel exhibition of yacht club colors to the quasi-pornographic performance of gymnastic exercises and bicycle tricks. The cards' bluffness, in this respect, could be amusing: One set of international flag signals featured sexy women demonstrating messages in semaphore such as "I am on fire" and "Let go the buoy."[66] The card series' seeming ambition to document all of nature and culture was shaped by their consumers' impulses toward entertainment, producing a world inventory from a masculine, juvenile, working-class perspective. As attitudes and markets changed, their catalogues of "a thousand . . . homely things we love to remember" increasingly exhibited the racism and sexism underlying that worldview circa 1900.[67]

Cigarette cards produced the modern phenomenon of the boy collector. "God, we had thousands and thousands of them. . . . We used to go on all over swapping. . . . And I had train cards, birds, cricketers, football," recollected one.[68] Roy Genders described accosting men outside the pubs and theaters of Sheffield to ask if they could spare him their cards.[69] "Before 1914 it would have been hard indeed to have found a boy in the working class without at least a few dog-eared cards about his person, dreaming of making up, by swap and gambling games, that compete set of fifty," claimed Robert Roberts.[70] The boy collector was such a well-known figure that the tobacco company W. Duke and Sons featured him in its "Postage Stamp" series. Manufacturers were accused of using them to entice boys to smoke, but the brightly colored cards with their tidbits of precise information were themselves desirable. Genders amassed his collection without ever becoming a smoker. In urban areas where people absorbed information from hoardings, posters, advertisements, newsagents' windows, and postcards, cigarette cards offered "a panorama of the world at large."[71] To minds absorbing information from such legible environments, the cards presented opportunities for interaction and learning. For the price of a packet of cigarettes—or less, if they could be found on the street or cadged from a stranger—one could begin to convert phantasmagoria into domains of knowledge. Walter Benjamin observed that children's collections renewed the old world, like "the painting of objects, the cutting out of figures, the application of decals—the whole range of childlike modes of acquisition, from touching things to giving them names."[72] Boys rather than girls became the cards' most enthusiastic consumers because they were incipient smokers who enjoyed greater urban mobility; in turn, the cards conferred on them a vague authority as organizers who could manage a quasi-technical system. The next generation of boys would furnish ham radio with its aficionados. Boys were not the only people to collect cigarette cards, but they were the most visible, especially when, in the mid-twentieth century, they became old men who bequeathed their collections and wrote their memoirs, as Genders and Wharton-Tigar did.

Collectors' informal self-education took place within the context of corporate advertising, although it also exceeded it. Once the craze for keeping them set in, cigarette cards became the first ephemera to be produced purposely for collection by consumers, to ensure brand loyalty in a competitive market. Canny tobacco companies would often withhold a single card within a set as a rarity, to stimulate sales.[73] Sets could also be turned in to manufacturers in exchange for albums and other giveaways. For smokers themselves, the cards' variety, action, and engagement with a vibrant world may have compensated for a monotony—that of consuming a seemingly infinite number of identical cigarettes. Perhaps the completion of a card set offered a satisfying endpoint to balance the ongoing effort of managing a nicotine addiction. In any case, by removing the object from the market, the act of collecting alters and expands its meaning. Benjamin struggled to decide whether or not collecting was truly radical. His collectors, like Romantic travelers, flaneurs, and gamblers—possessed passions that seemed "dangerous though domesticated."[74] A casual hobby, collecting cigarette cards required little or no expense, and not much time, so it made collectors of people who might not otherwise have asserted principles of order and taste to organize an aesthetic whole. In this way the cards, incidental to the main activity of smoking, crystallized something central to it: intellectual creativity, reduced within industrial modernity to the interstices of addiction or the minutes-long span of the work break.[75] In these small spaces, one's thoughts and affects could wander far— around the world, through history, and within all the realms of nature. Individual cards facilitated this self-extension, but the act of collecting them went even further, toward a figurative world mastery. Acquiring and arranging facts about the world, whether through memorization or simply possessing these small, colorful pieces of cardboard, held the powerful allure of transcending one's immediate circumstances.

The world-making of cigarette card collecting resembles the activities of Dorian Gray, who wishes for "a world in which things would have fresh shapes and colours," and has the means to create them in the infamous eleventh chapter of Oscar Wilde's 1891 novel, the subject of chapter 5.[76] It may seem counterintuitive to compare Dorian's esoteric, expensive enthusiasms for papal vestments, gemstones, and exotic musical instruments to working-class experiences of cigarette cards. Yet both engage ephemeral print culture: As I demonstrate in that chapter, Dorian's collections are as much about the acquisition of information through excessive reading as they are about his lavish expenditure, and the chapter reads as a condensation of his own reading. Wilde borrowed from *Women's World* and mimicked a growing genre of feature story in which arcane historical materials were mined for sensational oddities. Dense as it is, that infamous chapter attempts to convey the obsessive consumption of printed information as a mode of entertainment. We might even see Holmes as a mediating figure between working-class cigarette-card collectors and Dorian Gray's curations. Holmes collects cigarette ashes and writes a monograph on them, dwelling in the pleasure of organizing worlds of knowledge, like the card collectors. Yet, as I have shown, he also has aesthetic tendencies, and his

Figure 6. "Edgar Allen [*sic*] Poe." In
Histories of Poor Boys Who Have Become Rich,
and Other Famous People. Duke, c. 1889.

smoky reveries resemble Dorian's short-lived, contemplative studies of his various interests. In each case, collecting ephemera performs a form of world-making and self-making through the entertaining consumption of trivial information.

That commonality notwithstanding, cigarette cards participate in a literary idiom of enchanted transport, and this sense of intellectual and affective mobility was frequently attached to social mobility. In an origin story of cigarette cards, the author and editor Edward Bok recounted his boyhood surprise when, picking a card with a lithograph of an actress off the floor of a restaurant, he found the verso blank, and—in classic entrepreneurial fashion—resolved to make a business out of writing 100-word biographies to fill them.[77] One of the early forms, miniature books, was Duke's "Histories of Poor Boys Who Have Become Rich, And Other Famous People," issued around 1889. It offered biographies of luminaries such as Buffalo Bill, Thomas Huxley, Edgar Allan Poe, and Cornelius Vanderbilt, some of them running to twenty micro-printed pages between two thin cardboard covers. This tiny card includes the surprise of a book inside. As one begins to read, learning the story of Poe's rise to fame—if not fortune, happiness, or long life—the book as media affordance becomes apparent: It extends the duration of one's consumption, the detail of one's knowledge, and an opportunity to absent oneself from one's surroundings. At the same time, the cultural trope of achievement materializes in the theme of Poe's similar good luck, in being singled out for greatness. Early cigarette cards, following the model of the still earlier tobacco papers, contained more text; later ones reduced it, speeding up their own consumption. "Edgar Allen [*sic*] Poe" is technically a book, and it suggests the cards' general characteristic of alluding to other worlds or orders of reality organized by longer print forms and their literary and historical narratives. This imaginative space of dreaming frequently overlapped with the aspirational aesthetic of dreaming big. The temperance movement's earlier exhortations to workers to improve themselves by studious reading, which I discussed in chapter 1, have been transformed by generations of mass print into an appealing mainstream idiom, in which edification takes place in small doses of unrelated information. In this metamorphosis, the imagined knowledge acquired through focused concentration becomes the veneer or show of irrelevant factoids.

Literary cigarette cards especially contributed to the project of worldmaking: Their references to books were to specific alternative worlds of knowledge and imaginative spaces, whereas cards depicting prizefighters and ocean liners remained within the domain of reality. Carreras Ltd.'s "Figures of Fiction" and John Player & Sons' "Characters from Dickens" featured images and descriptions of Hamlet, Robinson Crusoe, The Vicar of Wakefield, and The Artful Dodger, using popular novels and plays to sell tobacco. If smokers couldn't read all of *Oliver Twist* or attend a Shakespearean tragedy, they could snatch a fragment of that complex experience. The cards were part of a new image culture of mass photography and cinema, but their promotion of reading and allusion to books glanced back to the past, seen as a trove of cultural tradition, and thus gave consumers a chance to obtain cultural capital.

Dickens offers an interesting case of the literary cigarette card, since his popular canonization took place during the cards' heyday, culminating in the centenary celebration of his birth in 1912. The term "Dickens" in this period conjured a world populated by eccentric and sometimes fiendish characters but ultimately governed by conviviality and good cheer. Titles such as Percy Fitzgerald's *Bozland* (1895) and Snowden Ward's *The Real Dickens Land* (1904) enhanced this sense of alternative space. Likewise, the card sets mixed characters from various novels together in one, such as "Dickens Character Series" or "Cope's Dickens Gallery." In this virtual, intertextual space, Paul Dombey could presumably mingle with John Jasper or Lucy Manette.

"Cope's Dickens Gallery," issued in 1900, links characters to their signature quotes; for example, number 15, "The Artful Dodger," bears the quotation, "Hello, my covey! What's the row? I suppose you don't know what a beak is, my flash com-pan-ion." Number 8, "Bumble the Beadle" from *Oliver Twist*, says, "Mr. Limbkins, I beg your pardon, Sir! Oliver Twist has asked for more!"; and Number 17, "Thomas Gradgrind," says, "In this life we want nothing but Facts, sir, nothing but Facts."

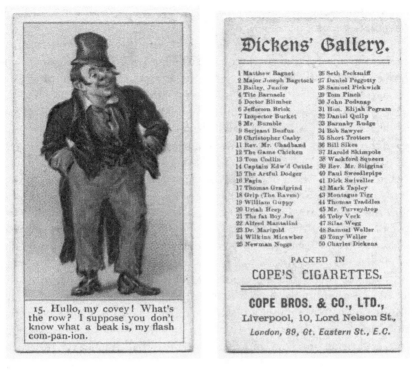

Figure 7. "The Artful Dodger." *Cope's Dickens Gallery.* Cope, 1900.

George Orwell saw such cards as a sign of Dickens's failure as a great writer: "[Dickens] is able to reach simple people, which Tolstoy is not. Tolstoy's characters can cross a frontier, Dickens's can be portrayed on a cigarette-card."[78] While it has merit, Orwell's point has been usefully opposed by an alternative, which accentuates Dickens's original affinities with the transition from popular to mass culture that nostalgically rendered working-class life.[79] The novels were embedded in contexts of popular entertainment that they themselves came to replace. For Juliet John, Dickens's flat characters are less negative than "transferable to other media"—a sign of the calculated canniness that led him to cultivate his performances, invent protocinematic prose, and ensure his longevity in mass culture.[80] In this context, the cards are less derivative reductions of the novels than they are Dickens in another medium. Appearing at the very moment when Dickens was becoming a canonical author—a moment prepared by the cheap editions of the novels issued after his death—the cards helped extend his longevity as a mass media referent. Since the Dickens world was already a knowledge set, the cards could circulate minute information about its features as cultural capital.

"Cigarette-card knowledge" is part of the unwritten transatlantic nineteenth-century history of trivia, itself a kind of knowledge game. Popularized by quiz shows in the United States from the 1940s through the 1960s, trivia began in nineteenth-century parlor games. For example, the game "Characters—or, Who Am I?" relied on the common knowledge of the details of Dickens's novels and Shakespeare's plays: People were sent out of the room, characters chosen, and when the absentees returned, they had to solve the riddles of their identity as the other players fed them hints.[81] Such games required a command of facts that seems astonishing today. Take "Interesting Sevens," which required players to name the seven wise men, the seven stars, the seven sleepers, the seven chief virtues, and the Seven Wonders of the World.[82] Other games, such as "Useless Information," were homages to the very concept of trivia: The leader would demand answers to questions such as "What per cent of sulfur does a man's body contain?—I want the exact per cent!" Players guessed, with the closest guess winning a prize.[83] Such games arose in part because the burgeoning of print throughout the nineteenth century conveyed more information to readers than ever before. In these games, and in cigarette cards' collection of trivial information, I see a small turn in the history of media consumption, toward the acquisition and memorization of facts. Although it was certainly underwritten by class aspirations, and involved a certain amount of performative gentility that the social historian Melanie Dawson has called "laboring to play," it nonetheless marks the deployment of information as entertainment.[84] Dickens, who, as Paul Schlicke notes, viewed popular forms of entertainment with nostalgia, making his novels seem a generation or two behind their own moment, thus looked backward rather than forward in his characterization of the fact-enthusiast Thomas Gradgrind in *Hard Times*.[85] Creative play increasingly dissolved the boundary between facts and fancies. Cigarette cards lived in a social context that increasingly absorbed the flow of information by collecting it in pieces and reconstructing it in games.

This concept of play and mastery helps frame my discussion of information consumption as a kind of addiction. In the context of the fevered reading of a detective story or puzzle, the desire to obtain the information that will resolve the narrative certainly resembles an addiction, as I demonstrate in greater detail in chapter 3 with respect to Wilkie Collins's *The Moonstone*. The chronic stimulation and disappointment of desire by which mass culture governs self-fashioning can also be described as addictive, as in *The Picture of Dorian Gray*, discussed in chapter 5. And earlier in this chapter, I showed how Holmes's physical economy of heightened nervousness followed by collapse constitutes a developing paradigm of addiction. Yet, as I have been demonstrating, as a simple diagnosis, the term "addiction" can obscure the cards' unpredictable circulation and their affective and intellectual roles in adults' and children's play. Moreover, these social uses should be imagined within the legacy of what Alan Rauch has called the "knowledge industry" that flourished in midcentury publishing. All the encyclopedias, miscellanies, and penny magazines through which organizations such as the Society for the Diffusion of Useful Knowledge attempted to effect the "mental improvement" of the working class had created a welter of information that had long been parodied.[86] Writing in 1858, Margaret Oliphant frankly acknowledged that these texts "dropped one by one into oblivion, and nobody missed them; and lo, rushing into the empty space, the mushroom growth of a sudden impulse, rapid and multitudinous to meet the occasion, came springing up a host of penny magazines—spontaneous and natural publications, which professed no artificial mission."[87] By the 1890s, the concept of "useless information" had become an occasion for mirth and play. Thus Altick's portentous pronouncement—that "the reading habit among the masses was contributing nothing to their cultural improvement. Reading had become a popular addiction. . . . The British masses had won their cheap periodicals"—requires some tempering.[88] It was addictive, and it felt like cultural improvement to them. Subtracting judgment and opprobrium from the observation, Raymond Williams declared, "I doubt if any educated person has not used books—any books—[as easy drugging]."[89] The tremendous popularity of cigarette cards as informational play suggests instead that consumers responded to them with intellectual creativity—and above all, without taking themselves too seriously. They may have been metaphorically addicted, but their engagements were still varied and robust.

Why did cigarette cards disappear? They vanished from Britain in 1940, due to wartime paper and labor shortages, and were never widely resumed.[90] In the United States, their reign ended when manufacturers discontinued regional brands, devoting advertising dollars to national print campaigns in the 1950s. By this point, when all segments of society seemed to smoke, the cards' association with trivia and especially juvenile masculinity—reflected in their emphasis on sports, actresses, and adventure—likely seemed quaint. Moreover, the modernization of marketing and publicity in the 1920s and 1930s, the increasing influence of psychoanalysis on advertising, and the ubiquitous appearance of cigarettes in films conjured them as erotic accessories and icons of freedom for adults.[91] In this period, women began to smoke more, moving from the objects depicted on the cards, to the subject of advertising appeals. In these new cultural contexts of cigarette smoking, the cards began to seem naïve, if not utterly innocent.

After their retirement from popular culture, the cards began to hold out the promise of a materialist history—the thrill of touching the past. They became objects for adult collectors, whose enthrallment by historical ephemera echoed the boy collectors' original desires for the cards. In her engaging little book *Collecting Cigarette Cards* (1966), Dorothy Bagnall recounts a bicycle excursion to Horsham, Sussex, just before D-Day, where, in an antiques store, she finds a valuable set of cards. Fashioning them into a bundle and tying it on the back of her bike, she commenced her return journey to London on a road roughened by the passage of military vehicles to the coast:

> Negotiating a particularly bumpy hill, the utility, wartime string gave way, and the collection formed a paper trail on the highway. Fortunately the weather was fine and with some effort I salvaged the lot. Happy with this ending, the sun shining and the birds twittering in the hedgerows, I relaxed on the grassy bank by the roadside and set about restoring some sort of order to my scattered cards. There was a war on, however, and soon the peace of the countryside was a-clatter with the hob-nail boots of marching men. The remarks of the passing soldiery were, as usual, raucous and witty: their advice fantastical and impracticable. They must have wondered what kind of "nut" this was, sitting at the roadside sorting cigarette cards as the world marched into battle.[92]

Bagnall was the daughter of Colonel Charles Lane Bagnall, who had coined the term "cartophily" to denote the practice of collecting—and indeed, loving—the cards. Updating their association with boys, his daughter's book modernized the pursuit for the serious collector. Yet her affinity for cigarette cards similarly evoked a delight in the paradox of ephemera: "There is some communicative quality about paper itself. A spirit informs its substance, or seems to. . . . In handling an old card I feel often I am in touch with the many hands through which it has passed—a thin little piece of paper, delicate, destructible, and yet it has survived."[93] Bagnall's exquisite observation describes an effort to remake a world threatened by war and to reconstitute the social through its tiniest, most trivial materials.

CHAPTER 3

Ink, Mass Culture, and the Unconscious

My inkstand is made of a flat piece of Untersberg marble which is
hollowed out to receive the glass inkpot; and the inkpot has a cover
with a knob made of the same stone. Behind this inkstand there is a
ring of bronze statuettes and small terra cotta figures. I sat down at
the desk to write, and then moved the hand that was holding the
pen-holder forward in a remarkably clumsy way, sweeping on to the
floor the inkpot cover which was lying on the desk at the time.

—SIGMUND FREUD, *The Psychopathology of Everyday Life*

As one might imagine, Freud's clumsiness was no accident. His sister had
visited his office and mentioned her plan to replace this inkstand with one
that better matched the desk; his desire for her to return bearing this gift
led him unconsciously to annihilate the inkstand while sparing the statuettes. For this reason, he argues, seemingly accidental motions, rather than
being simply spastic anomalies, are guided by a hidden intention. To sketch
the anatomy of this quotidian mishap, Freud lingers on the materials and
construction of the inkstand, giving us a sense of its thinghood. As the exception to the figurines, which retain specific psychological and cultural
significance, it is a utilitarian object—all the better to invest with psychological intricacy. With this anecdote, Freud rewrote a nineteenth-century
running comic narrative of shattered inkstands and spilled ink. They all
turned on ink's ironic status, as the ephemeral material and recalcitrant
technology that betrays or exposes the individual's abstract ideas and expressive intent. Normally, ink was the unnoticed vehicle of rational communication. In Freud's story, and in the turn toward psychoanalysis, it
shifted from ground to figure, coming to represent the unconscious. This
chapter shows how, along the way to this transformation, the dark, messy

chaos of spilled and pooled ink materialized a diverse array of minor affects and states of mind, from frustration and rage to flashes of genius, automatism, zaniness, clairvoyant information transmission, intoxicated absorption, and enchantment.

The central evidence for my claim is a forgotten popular parlor trick and common nineteenth-century cultural reference, ink-gazing. In this mystical practice, participants peered into pools of ink to see fleeting images of remote people and events, or the future. Ink-gazing, a subset of "scrying," or striving to see images in highly polished surfaces, crystals, and pooled liquids, was a participatory visual entertainment with the air of divination. When George Eliot opened *Adam Bede* (1859) with a reference to ink-gazing, she borrowed the allure of this magic vision to glamorize printed fiction: "With a single drop of ink for a mirror, the Egyptian sorcerer undertakes to reveal to any chance comer far-reaching visions of the past. This is what I undertake to do for you, reader. With this drop of ink at the end of my pen, I will show you the roomy workshop of Mr. Jonathan Burge."[1] Ink-gazing, a pastime of wealthy tourists to Cairo in the 1830s and '40s, had been so long debated and referenced in print that it had become common knowledge. Was staring into the ink pool in an enchanted Orientalized reverie, to see a remote relative or a celebrity, genuine clairvoyance or charlatanism? Ink-gazing attracted debunkers who regarded it as optical deception, yet it also offered a deeply personal experience that rebuffed such cynicism. In her account of her attempt to conjure visions in ink, Harriet Martineau reported seeing such strange things that "I thought it more prudent to shake off the influence while I could, than to pursue the experiment."[2] Her self-consciousness reveals ink-gazing to be a nascent psychological performance. Within a mind-set of cultural imperialism, she also frames it as a racially black experience, available for consumption by sensitive white Europeans like herself. But the most influential and transformative representation of ink-gazing was that of Wilkie Collins in his novel *The Moonstone* (1868). Collins moved the practice from the early Victorian discourse of deception to a mid-Victorian version of unconscious memory. Combining information retrieval with visual enchantment and psychological projection, Collins's novel constructed a paradoxical model of controlled reverie that could produce the truth without full self-awareness.

The enchantment of ink-gazing formed the opposite of the everyday task of writing as rational communication. Gazing at ink's slick, reflective surfaces was a "screen practice" of visual entertainment and fascinated reverie; it was the inverse of painstakingly forming ink into correct alphabetic and numeric patterns. Driven mainly by the market and related educational efforts, tens of millions of new writers trained themselves to manipulate ink with machine precision, mimicking mass print culture with its neat, standardized lines of type. Yet ordinary writing was inevitably marred by spilled and blotted ink that recalled the disorder of its sensuous, material aspects. Whenever one saw ink, one was not seeing the information or meaning it conveyed in clear handwriting or print, but the chaos of raw material in which it originated and to which it might return. As its mere, illegible self, ink deconstructed its ordering into written and printed communication. Spills and blots thus indexed ink's technological aspirations and failures. In the early twentieth century, the practice of gazing at pooled ink would transform into that of staring at blotted ink, to produce psychological content for professional evaluation. In the Rorschach and similar inkblot tests, the material of this unconscious was the calculatedly random inkblot, deliberately designed to evade easy reference. As the chapter will demonstrate, only in a mass culture that saturated the individual's consciousness with ephemeral words and images written, drawn, and printed in ink, could the shapeless inkblot come to signify the individual's hidden mind.

The story of ink may seem like a tangent to media consumption, but it is integral to it. Ink was a material component of mass print, but it was also a material of mass writing: Over the course of the century, legions of new writers had to learn how to use pens and ink to communicate. They produced countless pages of private, commercial, and other writing; and in doing so, they consumed ink. In the process, they spilled quite a lot of it. Rebellious clerks, unruly students, furious children, and careless servants—all new or potential writers—came to be represented hurling inkstands and spattering and blotting ink. The word "blot" generally lost its eighteenth-century meaning of editorial correction, retaining its sense of accidental disfigurement.[3] In a competitive new sphere of writing, spilled ink suggested an eager rush to public expression, debate, and feeling—a surplus of varied affect. This chapter turns the midcentury metaphorical reference "much ink has been spilled" inside out, to examine its literal inspiration. Excessive, rash, or meaningless commentary reflected the entrance of new social actors into the public sphere, as well as the accelerated pace of communication motivating it. The inkblot's formlessness recalls the mass—that entity that both constitutes and threatens the public sphere as a scene of rational communication. The inkblot thus has two intertwined genealogies: a psychological one that leads to the individual unconscious and another one that is more akin to the political unconscious. To understand their overlap, I briefly interpret two exemplary figures, the genius whose illegible handwriting conveys his or her obscure brilliance; and the clumsy clerk, who—like ink itself—constantly fails to meet modern demands for copy as clear, error-free, and systematic as print.

My attention to ink in the hands—and on the hands—of new writers readjusts Friedrich Kittler's account of nineteenth-century media history. In *Discourse Networks 1800/1900* (1990) and *Gramophone, Film, Typewriter* (1999), Kittler argues that the unconscious is structured like a machine and divided between the Lacanian real, signified by the gramophone; the symbolic, associated with the typewriter; and the imaginary, driven by the cinema. These late-century technologies transform the earlier network of 1800, grounded in the orality of children's reading education, typically conducted phonetically and orally by mothers, and flowering in Romantic poetry. Keen to find the origins of postmodern subjectivity in the later nineteenth century, Kittler selectively emphasizes machine-based media technologies as models for human automatism.

Focusing on ink, which Kittler mentions only in passing, redirects critical attention to the primary mass medium of the nineteenth century, print, and its relation to the mass practice of handwriting. Rather than link psychoanalytic structures to ink's affordances, I assemble the historical record of the disorganized affects and psychological performances associated with ink. Truer to its mid-nineteenth-century contexts, the result is an unconscious that looks quite different from Kittler's and Lacan's schematic, post-Freudian formulations. Although it shares the same feature of automatism, it is significantly less fraught, operating more like a storehouse for information than a roiling stew of psychosexual conflict. This paradoxically rational unconscious simply continues on from consciousness, forming an unusually flat, unvaried psychic terrain. Although this chapter shows how the rational unconscious turns, at the century's end, into the Freudian and psychoanalytic model we know so well, it never completely disappeared from Western cultures. In the conclusion, I suggest how it still abides in twenty-first-century technophilic discourses.

The chapter begins with ink as an everyday problem, a faulty modern technology and focus of cultural ambivalence; I show how the figures of the illegible genius and the clumsy clerk signify its idealization and its disappointing reality. This cultural-historical framework prepares readers to understand ink-gazing as a screen practice, an Orientalist touristic pastime, and a psychological performance in Martineau's memoir and Collins's novel. As long-form detective fiction, the novel developed ink-gazing's visual enchantment into a delirious drive for narrative information—that is, the enactment of the metaphorical addiction I introduced in the previous chapter with respect to Sherlock Holmes. The last, short section demonstrates the late-nineteenth- and early twentieth-century transformation of ink-gazing into inkblot-gazing in art, games, and psychological testing.

Much Ink Has Been Spilled: Pens, Ink, Clerks

I am jet black, as you may see,
The son of pitch and gloomy night:
Yet all that know me will agree
I'm dead except I live in light.

JONATHAN SWIFT, "On Ink"

The grey goose was an Enlightenment creature. "Whatever there is . . . that relates to morals and government, to literature or science, to the pleasures of the imagination, and to business of any and every kind, proceed all from the goose quill," wrote Ezra Sampson in 1818.[4] One hundred and fifty years later, Marshall McLuhan agreed, suggesting that the quill diminished cultures grounded in conversation: "It abolished mystery; it gave architecture and towns; it brought roads and armies, and bureaucracy. It was the basic metaphor with which the cycle of civilization began, the step from the dark into the light of the mind."[5] Since Roman times, geese, turkeys, swans, ravens, pheasants, and crows had furnished Europeans with writing implements; but the grey goose feather surpassed all the others. From the eighteenth century, the British imported them from Canada, Germany, and Ireland. Small farmers in the Lincolnshire fens also bred geese, selling their wing feathers for quills, their short feathers for bedding, and their carcasses for Christmas dinners. Isaac Taylor described "large flocks, of eight or ten thousands . . . driven to London. A piece of red rag, on a stick, scares them on. They travel about eight miles a day."[6] Writing with a quill proceeded at a similarly bucolic pace: Because quill pens wore down quickly, they had to be frequently re-cut, their nibs mended constantly with penknives. The geese had slowly ushered in modernity. But their reign was about to end.

In the mid-nineteenth century, the steel pen usurped the goose. A hollow tube with a detachable nib required less maintenance than a quill, allowing ink to flow smoothly and continuously. The technological marvels of the steel pen factories that sprang up in Birmingham made the new gadget an emblem of modern speed and efficiency throughout the century.[7] Contemplative writers rebelled. Eneas Sweetland Dallas claimed they were fine "for school ushers and counting house clerks," but that "authors and domestic correspondents prefer nibbing their pens while collecting their ideas."[8] Another writer claimed the steel pen, with its greater speed, facilitated rash and regrettable self-expression: "[A] steel pen ready made to one's hand is a dangerous temptation to a man in a fit of passion."[9] The steel pen's speed was that of commercial modernity, whereas the quill pen partook of nature, the realm of the poets. "Who ever heard of a great poet who wrote with a steel pen?" asked a literato in 1869.[10] As late as 1881, in *The Portrait of a Lady*, Henry James referenced steel pens to illustrate the gulf between Gilbert Osmond's overweening aestheticism and Henrietta Stackpole's plainspoken pushiness: "Do you know what she reminds me of? Of a new steel pen—the most odious thing in nature."[11] By the 1860s, the feeling of feathers curling gently around the knuckles, or dancing along to the rhythm of one's prose, had vanished from all but the most affected writers' hands. Odes to goose quills became odes to metal pens, and the seventeenth-century wisdom of James Howell, that "The Goose, the Bee, and the Calf (Meaning Wax, Parchment, and the Pen) rule the world" passed from quaintness to obsolescence.[12]

Ink complicated the distinction between quill and steel, past and present, sloth and speed, thoughts collected and flashes of genius or rage. Although the steel pen modernized handwriting, it did not solve the ubiquitous and wearisome problem of managing ink. Dallas, speculating on the inventions to emerge from the Great London Exhibition of 1862, conceded that steel pens improved upon quills, but he raged against ink:

> What a nuisance is ink! It is a barbarism altogether. . . . Where is the
> house in which there has never been any spilling of ink, in study,
> drawing-room, boudoir, or kitchen? Look at counting-house desks and
> school-room tables! Look at the dusty, brown, thick fluid in the vestry
> inkstand and the small shop! Look at the troubles of the traveler who
> would keep a journal in a far country![13]

The challenges of spilled, smudged, blotted, evaporated, thickened, moldy, crusty, dried, frozen, and faded ink can be inferred from the high number of new and improved inkstands advertised and reviewed throughout the century. "There are few articles upon which so much ingenuity has been employed as inkstands, but hitherto no person has succeeded in producing one wholly free from exception," began a piece about a rubber diaphragm–regulated inkstand.[14] Others describe inkstands fitted with caoutchouc

Figure 8. "The Inexhaustible Magic Inkstand." *Publisher's Circular*, 1874.

or India-rubber to prevent leaking; piston-operated inkstands that force ink to rise into the barrel; and similar "gravitating" inkstands that preserve ink from air and dust.[15] Sampson and Low claimed that their "Magic Inexhaustible Inkstand" made writing "a luxury, rather than a vexatious labor."[16] Despite such inventions, tidy writing ink remained a desideratum throughout the century. Ink's messiness was a drag on the swift, clean, ideal efficiency of the steel pen and the accelerated modern writing it enabled.

The idealized swift current of writing ink facilitates the absorptive psychological experience Mihaly Csikszentmihalyi has described as flow. An "optimal experience," flow is "a sense of exhilaration, a deep sense of enjoyment" that occurs "when a person's body or mind is stretched to its limits in a voluntary effort to accomplish something difficult and worthwhile."[17] In moments of engaged creative production or athleticism, self-consciousness, distractions, and awareness of the passage of time all fade away, and one achieves something resembling presence. Csikszentmihalyi's model is ostensibly transhistorical and it resembles Samuel Taylor Coleridge's theory of the imagination as the "inward eye" uniting reason and idealization, which suggested a similar sublimely absorbed state of mind. To illustrate it, Coleridge imagined an ideal inkstand that would connect thinking to writing without distraction: "The pen should be allowed, without requiring any effort or interruptive act of attention from the writer, to dip sufficiently low, and yet be prevented, without injuring its nib, from dipping too low, or taking up too much ink."[18] Perfectly calibrated pens and ink permit thoughts to flow from the mind onto the page. Yet modern ink both enabled and hampered unfolding thoughts. Dallas pleaded, "Can we not have . . . a kind of pencil which shall make black and indelible marks without being heavy, without needing cutting, and without using up too fast? Till some magical method is flashed upon the world, whereby ideas can be recorded as the sunlight records form and shadow, we must demand more convenient implements."[19] In Dallas's imagination, ink would flow as apparently effortlessly as the new medium of photography harnessed the sun. Industrial demands for productivity, speed, and efficiency sparked the dream that the writer's mind and hand could keep pace. The happy, generative state of flow reflected the individual writer's absolute synchronicity with modernity. In its ideal form, ink manifested the writer's reason; in its actuality, it often seemed to impede it. Swift's poem, which forms the epigraph of this section, captures this frustration: Ink comes to life only in the light of the writer's animating mind, but always threatens to lapse back into moribund inertia. Ink bore the weight of cultural expectations for swift, clean communication and for the absorptive reverie of a mind communing with itself. Like many communication technologies, it embodied a disappointed dream of attaining presence.

The exasperating reality of ink's messiness and interruptions to thought found cultural expression in the common trope of inkstands accidentally overturned or hurled in anger. Few other household items exceeded the spectacular mess of ink, or the painful injuries it and its containers inflict, especially in the hands of wrathful children. Flying ink and inkwells ruin the order of the schoolroom, where middle-class children, as new writers and readers, are meant to be learning their appropriate uses. When the schoolmaster Ichabod Crane is invited to a frolic at the van Tassel house in "The Legend of Sleepy Hollow" (1820), he hurries his pupils to finish their lessons, wreaking havoc: "Books were flung aside . . . inkstands were overturned, benches thrown down, and the whole school was turned loose an hour before the usual time, bursting forth like a legion of young imps."[20] In Dickens's *Bleak House* (1853), Esther finds the "jaded and unhealthy-looking" Caddy Jellyby with ink on her face, as she miserably attends to her mother's pointless charitable correspondence regarding Boorioboola-

Gha.[21] And in *Alice's Adventures in Wonderland* (1865), Lewis Carroll, ever ready to mock educational order, has the Queen of Hearts lob an inkstand at Bill the Lizard, who pathetically commences writing on his slate with his finger, "using the ink, that was trickling down his face, as long as it lasted."[22] In these and similar narratives, ink and its accessories elicit and reflect a hotheaded physical expressivity that will not wait for writing. Ink stains fingers and faces instead of flowing from minds. Such representations register the uneven transition to literacy and increased writing activity of minor social actors: children, servants, women, soldiers, clerks, and others. The mayhem of thrown ink and inkwell narratives reflect the friction of their entry into a world of writing and print dominated by propertied men. Formerly incidental to the public sphere, new social actors forced it to include them as participants in its communicative networks. They were the mass effaced in Freud's anecdote of his violently erupting unconscious wish to destroy his inkstand. I describe them here to show how ordinary people directly engaged the mass media of modernity, getting their hands dirty in their materials.

A complementary analytic move deconstructs the figure of the illegible genius, and inserts him or her into the genealogy of the inkblot's figuration of hidden psychic depths. His or her inky illegibility stands as a mysterious exception to print culture's constant, voluminous communication to the masses. "It was long a vulgar opinion, which is, even in these matter-of-fact days, not quite obsolete, that writing illegibly was a token of genius," wrote one reformer of penmanship in the 1880s.[23] The genius wrote illegibly because he or she was translating divinely ordered nature for readers, and the traces retained some of its inscrutability. Frederic Myers's *Lectures on Great Men* (1841) claimed for philosophers and scientists "the skill to read the generally illegible handwriting of Deity which is inscribed upon His works—to interpret appearances, to discern and to reveal the hidden springs of things, their Laws and Life."[24] Nature conceals divine intentions or world spirit, which are opaque to ordinary observers; a visionary few could produce their own extraordinary works as a translation or decipherment. The illegibility of God and nature remained in the translators' scrawling traces and could be glimpsed in the strange natural materials that constituted the great variety of ink recipes. A standard 1830 ink recipe incorporated oak galls, or wasp eggs that grew on oak trunks, as well as gum arabic, cloves, indigo, and sugar.[25] As both writing and printing ink unevenly transitioned from artisanal to mass production, eventually incorporating aniline dyes, their recipes remained variegated, secret, and a little odd, such as the one that called for "stones of peaches and apricots, the bones of sheep, and ivory, all well-burnt."[26] In the genius's illegibility, ink seemed to return to the wilderness of incomprehensible signs from which it came—a place where apricots might mingle with ivory. Traced backward, meaning moved from print to illegible handwriting to genius to nature to God. In this way, the material of printed modernity sheltered sacred remnants.

The genius's flashes of insight came too fast even for the steel pen. Although many affected literary types clung to the quill, slowly arranging their thoughts while mending its nib, the genius's lightning-quick thoughts rendered his writing unreadable. The foremost English graphologist, Henry Frith, explained that fiction writers such as Charles Dickens wrote illegibly because "in writing of romances, the speed at which the imagination travels induces a corresponding speed in the hand."[27] Men of letters were not the only ones. Napoleon Bonaparte became well known for his hieroglyphic handwriting and for his self-defense that the ideas of the man of affairs "must flow faster than his hand can trace them . . . he must . . . let the scribes make it out afterwards."[28] Ludwig van Beethoven explained his own indecipherable writing, associated with his growing deafness and thus with the myth of his triumphant musical genius, by the quip that "life is too short to paint letters or notes," punning on *noten* and *nöthen*.[29] Dickens, Bonaparte, and Beethoven established reputations as intellectual forces of nature in part through the mystique of illegibility. When ink was hurled and splashed by children or the working class, it was meaningless; when scrawled by geniuses, it was too meaningful for common understanding. For new writers struggling to master the art of clear handwriting, the example of the illegible genius might have formed a wishful aspiration.

The genius and the ink-thrower occasionally converged. In a letter to Thomas Moore, Lord Byron wrote, "Before I left Hastings I got in a passion with an ink bottle, which I flung out of the window one night with a vengeance;—and what then? Why, next morning I was horrified by seeing that it had struck, and split upon, the petticoat of Euterpe's graven image in the garden, and grimed her as if it were on purpose."[30] Byron's hurled ink besmirches the allegory of musical art, sparking the amusing possibility that he wished to insult the muse. The story also conjures the eroticized force of his poetic genius and compositional zeal. At the same time, it undermines his aesthetic power, suggesting that his poetry may be nothing more than offensive ink splashes. The randomness of its landing hints that the genius's feeling may not translate to mass understanding. Elsewhere, Byron had used the irony of the ink drop to dramatize communicative power: "But words are things, and a small drop of ink, / Falling like dew, upon a thought, produces / That which makes thousands, perhaps millions, think."[31] But the thrown ink anecdote balances this depiction of such as enlightened public sphere of mass print with one of chaos, randomness, and meaninglessness. Although a household item often consumed in private, ink always recalled the wider sphere of mass print culture, the tensions surrounding its production and consumption, and the possibility that its variety and extent might reflect the chaos of nature.

Like the illegible genius, the zany clerk focused cultural ambivalence about mass print's machine precision and speed, which set impossible standards for writing by hand. As copyists, the massive new workforce of commercial and government clerks was supposed to write quickly and legibly: "Handwriting was indeed the one accomplishment a junior clerk needed: day after day he was set to work copying—copying letters into the letter book, minutes into the minute book."[32] Throughout the century, an array of manuals, guidebooks, periodicals, and even a device called a tantalograph attempted to train young men to be clerks and nonwriters to be writers, by calculating the correct distance of the hand from the inkwell and offering precise advice on the minor strokes of letters.[33] In this way, mass print supplanted the elite private training of the eighteenth-century writing master. Although the ideal clerk was a writing automaton, clerks also quickly became celebrated for their excesses. Charles Lamb and Edgar Allan Poe each observed their fashionable, petit-bourgeois modernity.[34] E. T. A. Hoffmann's "The Golden Pot" (1814), translated into English by Thomas Carlyle, featured a hapless student, Anselmus, who blots an original document while hallucinating fantastic visions.[35] When a poodle runs off with his hairpiece and he gives chase, Anselmus stumbles against the table where the Privy Councillor has been breakfasting and working, "and cups, plates, ink-glass, sand-box rush jingling to the floor, and a flood of chocolate and ink overflows the Relation he has just been writing" (204). Anselmus's comic comportment, which includes several devastating ink spills, falls into the aesthetic category of zaniness described by Sianne Ngai. The zany redefines personhood "as an unremitting succession of activities" rather than static psychological depth.[36] Readers reveled in the clerk's hapless transgressions, as his inability to manage ink echoed their own. A human inkwell, the clerk characteristically lapsed from rote labor into individuality. Dickens emphasized this exceptional lapse in *Bleak House*, when his copyist Nemo's usually speedy, machine-like handwriting initiates the plot by catching Lady Dedlock's eye.[37] Endlessly, swiftly copying, the clerk represents mass print culture itself—perhaps most of all when he makes it go awry.

Herman Melville's "Bartleby the Scrivener: A Tale of Wall-Street" (1853) offered its titular clerk as a similarly overzealous but ultimately dysfunctional copyist, who refuses to do all other tasks with his signature demurral, "I would prefer not to."[38] His office-mate, "Turkey," recklessly blots his papers, sometimes spilling his sandbox, splitting his pens and throwing them on the floor, but Bartleby, "as if long famishing for something to copy, . . . seemed to gorge himself on . . . documents," and copies all of them perfectly (24).[39] Bartleby's intensive devotion to copying displays the affective overcommitment of Ngai's zany as "the unhappily striving wannabe, poseur, or arriviste" (Ngai, *Our Aesthetic Categories*, 193). Bartleby proves that even when he seems to succeed at being a machine, the clerk fails, reframing humanness as physical excess and expressivity, not unlike the inkblot. Thomas Augst interprets Bartleby as a symbol of the clerk's specific dilemma of alienated labor: Becoming an excellent penman also limited the interest in one's work, especially in a new mass print culture, in which reading and writing index depth of character.[40] But Bartleby may be even further mired in the capitalist machine than Augst envisions. What if he prefers not to read his copy back because, like Dickens's Krook, and other real-life clerks, he can't read?[41] Many clerks simply imitated writing without understanding it. Anthony Trollope describes a clerk who, confronted by his manager with a letter book, is told that he will not be fired if he can read his own writing. "This the lad, could not do, and so was dismissed. In fact, the book had been scrawled over with a pen, and no words had been written."[42] Rather than challenging his alienation, Bartleby may be hiding illiteracy; his increasingly spectral appearance might suggest not the tortured poet, but the harried, underqualified worker. As such, he draws attention to fast, legible handwriting as a new personal skill requisite for gaining a foothold in a modernizing economy, yet falling short of the fuller literacy that would maintain or advance him within it.

The illegible genius and the clumsy, possibly illiterate clerk are human equivalents of the inkblot with which they were associated; they illustrated the new, widespread pressure to learn to write clearly. In Britain and the United States, the illegibility of too-visible ink was associated with the ink-hurling masses, the divinely inspired genius, and the zany clerk. All three contoured a conservative fear that new and popular writers would pull the elite sphere of letters down into the mire of the mass.[43] This analysis departs from Kittler's description of the "discourse network" of 1800.

Kittler's psychoanalytically inflected media history was based on a German context, in which state-sponsored training in handwriting and maternal, domestic education in phonetic reading, produced clear, neatly connected handwriting as Romantic subjectivity. In Britain and the United States, however, training in handwriting was a market-driven, ad hoc affair that took hold over decades; significantly, it emerged through mass print culture. In the pressure to produce neat handwriting, and the likelihood of generating blots instead, the illegible genius departs from Kittler's easy association of Romantic poetry with clean, readable handwriting. Likewise, the range of literacies associated with the clerk overturn a long literary critical tradition that assumes there is only one, complete, recursive mode of literacy, and links it to subjective depth. Instead, practicing writers, the partially literate, and those with visual rather than alphabetic understandings of writing suggest an array of engagements with the materials of mass print culture. As ink amply demonstrates, millions of people learning to read and write was a long, messy affair, even after the geese vanished and hands began to habitually grip steel pens.

This section has sketched aspects of ink's role in nineteenth-century life, emphasizing the way its materiality constantly undermined its conscious purposes, as unintended spills and blots disfigured clear handwriting. Every writer attempting to form ink into legible, flowing words confronted the divide between the mechanistic precision and speed associated with the ideal of print, and the spontaneous, organic expression inherent in handwriting that always risked illegibility. They also confronted the divide between their conscious intentions and the accidental forces that hampered their writing, the painstaking, conscious efforts to form letters, and the "flow" of productive reverie. In Kittler's media history, the transition to full literacy as an index of psychological depth happens suddenly in 1800, but in Britain and the United States it was an uneven, ongoing process, notwithstanding Romantic ideology. For example, when Wilkie Collins wanted to conjure the ignorance of "the unknown public" in 1858, he offered a list of editorial replies to readers' questions about ointments, crinolines, and handshakes that also included the tip, "If you want to write neatly, do not bestow too much ink upon occasional strokes."[44] "The Unknown Public" is best known for its bourgeois discovery of a "reading" public who favored ephemeral, illustrated, lowbrow printed matter; its advice about managing ink reminds us that this "mass" was also learning how to write and that writing was a consumer activity. As varying levels of writing proficiency spread through the middle and working classes throughout the century, the illegible genius and the zany clerk traced the cultural contours of ink. The genius's overflowing illegibility, a vestige of his or her translation of nature, set him apart from the industrial precision of print and its analogues, such as the steel pen; the hapless clerk also remained at a distance from it, his human difference always exceeding its modern demands. Their excessive relationship to ink framed questions about their inner mental lives. Did geniuses really have a direct intellectual conduit to nature and God? Were zany clerks tremendously mentally focused on the automatic task of copying, or were they concealing incomplete literacy? If writing was ordinary thinking, then the nonwriting of the inkblot suggested a variety of possible oppositional mentalities and mental states, from genius to automatism. At the same time, such questions and judgments were always embedded in the social and economic contexts of the uneven transition to mass literacy in the first half of the century. If spilled ink began to suggest accidental, irrational, supernatural, and automatic psychological forces, then it also conjured new types of subjects that mass print had called into being.

Ink-Gazing: Egyptian Magic, Visual Media, and The Moonstone

> The little chap unwillingly held out his hand. Upon that, the Indian took a bottle from his bosom, and poured out of it some black stuff, like ink, into the palm of the boy's hand. The Indian—first touching the boy's head, and making signs over it in the air—then said, "Look." The boy became quite stiff, and stood like a statue, looking into the ink in the hollow of his hand.
>
> WILKIE COLLINS, *The Moonstone* (1868)

Ink's association with the visionary genius who can translate the mystical signs of nature into alphabetic language informs the practice of ink-gazing, practiced by British and other tourists to Egypt, debated in print in the 1830s and 1840s, and so commonly referenced in the decades afterward that Charles Dickens and others could drop it into their novels in passing in the 1870s.[45] The question was whether young Egyptian street boys could see remote people and places or the future in pooled ink. The Orientalist Edward William Lane (1801–76) was the first to describe the practice in enough detail to ignite public interest, in a chapter of his *Account of the Manners and Customs of the Modern Egyptians* (1836). Lane recalled a story told by Henry Salt, the Egyptologist, collector, and British consul-general in Cairo, who suspected one of his servants of stealing from him and accordingly sent for the famous magician Maghrab'ee, to intimidate the thief into confessing. The magician proceeded, according to custom, to draw numeric grids on the hand of a boy, incense was burned, prayers were chanted, and ink was pooled in the boy's cupped hand. Eventually, as the boy's sharpened vision focused on the ink, the image of the thief appeared. The suspect was identified and confessed. Impressed, Lane arranged his own ink-gazing session with Maghrab'ee, which featured various experiments, some more successful than others, in which prepubescent boys—supposed to be free of sin—are made to gaze into the inky "magic mirrors." Lane and other English tourists ask them to see public figures, such as Lord Nelson and Shakespeare, and private ones, such as family members; the boys describe these people, with varying degrees of success. Lane prevents private communication between Maghrab'ee and the boys, who are chosen randomly and who do not speak the magician's dialect; and the boys decline Lane's attempts to bribe them into confessing the act a hoax. He is forced to conclude his narrative in ambiguity: "Neither I nor others have been able to discover any clue by which to penetrate the mystery."[46] Lane's inconclusiveness set off a flurry of comment and speculation. Could the boys really see visions in ink? Or if the ritual was a fraud, then how was it perpetrated?

As this section will show, ink-gazing operated through an intriguing configuration of visual print culture, optical entertainment, and psychological performance. In the previous section, we saw how spilled ink began to assume the structural position of the unconscious for individuals trying to form their thoughts, and for economies producing copyists as mass writers. This section turns to visual culture, showing how mass print media provided the key to the trick's operation. Running alongside the tropes and narratives of spilled ink, the participatory visual culture of ink-gazing began to develop ink's materiality into a slick surface or screen onto which the mind cast its images. This shift toward a formalized, aesthetic practice made ink-gazing a screen practice and a visual technology similar to photography and cinema; its gamelike, parlor-trick aspect classified it with optical toys such as the thaumatrope and kaleidoscope. The context of Egyptian visionary skill established ink-gazing as a racialized mode of expertise distinct from ordinary consciousness and cognition. When Wilkie Collins featured ink-gazing in one of the first full-length detective novels, *The Moonstone* (1868), he adapted its visual aspects, psychological performance, and racial meanings. Borrowing the allure of its enchantments, he also embedded it in a critical, suspicious, even paranoid reading practice that tested statements against themselves and restlessly sought new information. These were the contexts in which the ink pool, simultaneously the site of illusionism, magic, visual entertainment, and psychological and racial performance, continued to materialize the unconscious.

English travel narratives about Egypt could neither ignore nor resolve the question of ink-gazing's possible fraudulence. Writers ranged from declaring absolute faith in the boys' ability to see, to disparaging the procedure as the worst kind of trickery designed to beguile credulous English tourists to Cairo.[47] Writings on Egypt were manifold as "Egyptomania" gripped actual and armchair British tourists.[48] A. C. Lindsay, in his *Letters on Egypt, Edom, and the Holy Land* (1838), concluded, "One thing is unquestionable—that the children do see a crowd of objects. . . . How is this to be accounted for? Collusion is out of the question."[49] Yet that was the conclusion of John Gardner Wilkinson, who speculated that the magician asked the boys leading questions.[50] The answer to the riddle indeed involved a conspirator—but it also foregrounded print media. Lane's sister Sophia Poole published it in *The Englishwoman in Egypt* (1845). She quotes his discovery that when the magician Maghrab'ee was successful, an acquaintance named Osmán Efendee had been his interpreter.[51] According to George Nugent-Grenville's interpretation in *Lands, Classical and Sacred* (1846), Osmán was "very probably acquainted, through portraits or otherwise, with the general appearance of most Englishmen of celebrity, and could certainly describe the peculiar dresses of English professions, such as army, navy, or church."[52] Osmán capitalized on his knowledge of English celebrities—those whose public image made them distinguishable through verbal descriptions. Figures who were recognizable from the ordinary consumption of print culture, such as Queen Victoria or Shakespeare, could be maneuvered into the boys' visions through leading questions; famous people who were missing limbs, such as Lord Nelson, or the quadriplegic artist Miss Biffin, were also good candidates. In a comic dialogue in an installment of *Noctes Ambrosianae*, John Wilson wrote, "Don't you see that any print-book must have made this scoundrel familiar with phizzes [faces] such as these?"[53] Moreover, in the sphere of mass-printed illustration, "By pictorial representations, or descriptions otherwise procured, many public characters might admit of accurate description."[54] Neither the trick itself nor its narration in the pages of British periodicals works without the quiet operation of the visual culture of print in the background: Readers must be able to see the people mentioned in their minds' eyes. Staring at ink, gazers recalled and reproduced mental images from illustrations; the ink pool thus dissolved and reproduced print culture. Like clerks, the boys bore the ambiguity of the ink as a new mass medium— this time, not of writing, but of visual entertainment.

The practice imagined pooled ink as its own liquid screen and even a kind of stage, a strange, imaginary medium. The illusion performed the magical dissolution of printed images back into the hidden processes of the visual imagination, but it also invoked the enchantments of live visual performances such as automata, stage magic, and phantasmagoria. Speculating on a "concealed confederate," the *Quarterly Review* likened ink-gazing to Wolfgang von Kempelen's chess-playing Mechanical Turk, ventriloquist acts such as the Invisible Girl, and phantasmagoria.[55] Many such spectacles were featured in the late eighteenth and early nineteenth centuries; the spectacles were part stage illusionism and part technical demonstration, performed at venues such as Spring Gardens and Egyptian Hall. The newly thriving print culture published speculations about their mechanisms. The *Quarterly Review*'s most ambitious description of ink-gazing posited an odd media apparatus indeed:

> The reflected objects of a series of pictures are thrown from the surface of a concave mirror, fixed, probably, to some part of the magician's garment, and concealed by the ample and cumbersome overlapping of his outer dress; the burning of frankincense and coriander seed, and of the slips of paper, in the chafing-dish, repeated from time to time, afforded both light and a cloud of smoke, under the very nose of the boy, on which those images were received—for Mr. Lane tells us, the magician, the chafing-dish, and the boy, were in a line, and must have been close together, since the former held firmly the fingers of the boy's hand, no doubt to keep it and the ink spot in the proper focus; and the interdiction of the boy from 'raising his eyes' was, no doubt, to prevent his seeing the spot from when the stream of reflected light, conveying the images, proceeded. All this could be easily managed without Mr. Lane or Osma'n knowing anything of the matter, or seeing any of the representations described; they were seated behind the mirror. (202)

In this fascinating passage, the ink becomes a screen onto which images are projected. As a surface that receives projected light, ink alludes to early experiments in photography; the images' motion anticipates cinema. The images resemble dissolving views, panoramas, camera obscuras, tableaux vivants, and other visual media entertainments from the period. The images develop, move, and change in sequence, perhaps offering a loose narrative, as in phantasmagoria. The boy's eyes and body, precisely controlled by the magician's grip on his head, are mortised into a media apparatus consisting of the stream of light, smoke, and ink. Recalling the ideal clerk, and the Turk, the boy resembles an automaton, merely conveying what he sees. Detached from pens, ink conveys information directly to sight. The theory's inaccuracy makes it even more telling, as it speculates about how images might be produced for viewers' delighted enchantment. Here, deliberately pooled ink simultaneously reconstitutes printed visual illustration and performs as its own black page, to form images within itself—a kind of ink within ink.

Ink-gazing confronted an Enlightenment discourse keen to indict visual and fictional entertainment as psychological and optical deception, and yet this very impulse to debunk was reincorporated into the entertainment as a screen practice relying on what Neil Harris has called "the operational aesthetic," or the desire to see how illusions, machines, and systems worked.[56] The *Quarterly Review* participated in the operational aesthetic when it conjectured how the trick succeeded. It borrowed the idea of the concave mirror from David Brewster's *Letters on Natural Magic* (1832), a text written to debunk mysticism and enlighten his readers and audiences, since the mirrors' effects on "ignorant minds" is "altogether overpowering."[57] Brewster was especially concerned about visual entertainment as "a national system of deception, intended as an instrument of government" to dazzle and confuse the masses.[58] Brewster, who also invented the kaleidoscope, felt that optical displays should furnish a scientific education for their consumers; they should clarify rather than confound reason. Helen Groth describes his ambivalence about the success of the kaleidoscope; he was haunted by the idea of an "indiscriminate crowd who consumed every new craze with a voracious appetite and paid little attention to the integrity of forms and sources."[59]

Alexander Kinglake, in his travel narrative *Eothen* (1844), and the *Quarterly Review* author, similarly linked ink-gazing to the biblical deceptions of priests imitating God.[60] In Patrick Brantlinger's sketch of this paradox, mass media spectacle was a powerful tool for disseminating culture but in the same ideological formation also a tool of civilizational suicide.[61] Such cultural ambivalence resolved ink-gazing into a "screen practice." As defined by Charles Musser, screen practices configured a relationship between producers, images, and audiences, in which the technical apparatus was exposed, thus demystifying the image and rendering it art rather than deception.[62] This demystification premises most modern popular visual entertainment, though it is essentially intermittent: Audiences must be absorbed into the imagery in order to experience fright or delight, but not thoroughly deceived. As Terry Castle points out, "Clever illusionists were careful never to reveal exactly how their own bizarre, sometimes frightening apparitions were produced."[63] A dynamic alternation between knowingness and absorption structures all such illusionistic culture involving screens. The notion that one was temporarily and trivially deceived ensured ink-gazing's popularity.

The rationalist tradition of debunking mass optical deception extends through Karl Marx's writings to the Frankfurt School; my claims about ink, print media, visual entertainment, and mass culture connect the pieces of the tradition into a new frame. When Marx referenced phantasmagoria to describe the coup of Louis-Napoleon Bonaparte in *The Eighteenth Brumaire* (1852), he also derided "the thunder from the platform, the sheet lightning of the daily press" that "have vanished like a phantasmagoria before the spell of a man whom even his enemies do not make out to be a magician."[64] Marx's castigation of live entertainment and print culture—not to mention faulty government—as sorcery implied a psychic space of deception, lying somewhere between vision and understanding. Like Brewster and Carlyle, who railed against the magician Cagliostro, Marx conflates the visual trickery of stage illusionism with cognitive and psychological deception.[65] Into this space grew two distinct but related critical concepts, the false consciousness identified by Marxism and the repression conjured by psychoanalysis. Focusing on the latter, Castle's classic article shows how, in phantasmagoria, screen images haunted the mind and "a new kind of daemonic possession became possible."[66] When, in *The Arcades Project*, Walter Benjamin adjusted Marx's concept of phantasmagoria to realign these two trajectories and re-theorize the deceptive capacity and illuminating possibilities of nineteenth-century commodity culture, he raised the stakes on the political potential of mass culture.[67] His most important essay, "The Work of Art in the Age of Mechanical Reproduction," performed a similar gesture, attempting to rescue a glimmer of collective consciousness in the new techniques of Soviet cinema.[68] Ink's role in this long history is overlooked, but also overdetermined, because it operates both as the material of mass print, and, as I've been demonstrating in this section, as a screen within visual culture. Ink is a crucial, undertheorized element of media history. However, when I claim that ink was phantasmagoric and that it materialized the unconscious, I am not suggesting that it operated deceptively. Rather, I am reframing the twentieth-century theories as part of a cultural discourse that begins a century earlier. I aim to describe the practices whereby consumers incorporated and reproduced mass media images in a psychological zone that becomes the unconscious. This is done not in the spirit of debunking their individualized expressive authenticity, but to show how the unconscious unevenly emerged in relation to mass media. Ink-gazing was one of these practices.

No nineteenth-century writer did more to align ink with the unconscious, and with racial blackness, than Harriet Martineau, in her account
in *Eastern Life Present and Past* (1848) of her ink-gazing attempt. Two kinds
of visual, mental functioning mark her travels in the Middle East, and con-
textualize her ink-gazing experience. Following Mary Louise Pratt, critics commonly emphasize the power of Western vision to objectify and
rationalize foreign people and places.[69] Martineau certainly exerts Western scopic power, but not without surmounting the challenge of Eastern
enchantment: "[I] verily thought, the whole journey through, and especially at Cairo, that I was losing my observing faculties,—so often had I to
rouse myself, or to be roused by others, to heed what was before my eyes"
(2:118–19). She invokes a familiar dichotomy, of sleepy Eastern reverie and
alert Western observation. But she reverses their valuation: Empirical vision is the lower faculty, whereas mystical gnosis is the higher. "There
is something in the aspect of Oriental life and scenery which meets and
stimulates some of one's earliest and deepest associations, and engages
some of one's higher mental faculties too much to leave the lower free"
(2:119). Martineau imagines a reservoir of psychic plenitude formed at an
"earliest" moment; it helps construct the Western individual's bi-level
subjectivity. Preoccupied at the higher, mystical level, the busy mind ne-
glects the empirical or lower vision of the mundane world. Martineau reas-
sures her readers that she functions equally well in the conscious world of
rational observation and memory: "I arrived at last at knowing and re-
membering almost every peculiar object in Cairo;—of such, I mean, as offer themselves to the eye in the streets." Her touristic, acquisitive desires
motivate this feat: She was vexed by "the longing to have for one's own
forever every exquisite feature of the scene" (2:119). Martineau's mapping
enacts imperial visual power, but it also leaves open the possibility of a
spiritual, enchanted mode of vision that captures and archives unrecord-
able, extraordinary sights. This mode adumbrates the space in the mind
that reason cannot enter and order.

When Martineau attempts ink-gazing, she conjures her own psychic
depth, in contrast to her empirical vision. Although the magician's incense
makes others in the English party drowsy, Martineau has no such debil-
ity: "I, having no sense of smell, and being therefore unaffected by the
perfumes, was wide awake, and closely on the watch" (138). Eyes peeled,
she immediately notices the signs of mesmerism in one of the boy's
"peculiar quivering of the eyelids" and—as a practiced mesmerist and
clairvoyant—asserts herself to take his place (138). Martineau had estab-

lished her expertise on the healing powers of mesmerism in *Letters on Mesmerism*, published in the *Athenaeum* in 1844. In Cairo, as in her writings on mesmerism, she asserts her authority at both levels of mind. "Presently, I began to see such odd things in the pool of ink . . . that I felt uncertain how long I could command my thoughts and words; and, considering the number of strangers present, I thought it more prudent to shake off the influence while I could" (140). Reasserting her mental self-control establishes the ritual as a psychological performance. Martineau cleverly omits the specific content of her visions, since including it would depict her as fanciful and compromise her authority. She thus reframes ink-gazing as a scientific experiment, though it clearly tests the propriety of bourgeois self-concealment. It hardly matters what "odd things" she sees. The fact that she sees anything establishes her as "a very good mesmeric subject," a special, sensitive soul with access to a space both beyond and within. Her narrative positions this space as a new version of the unconscious that is both mystical and rational. In this way, Martineau helps move the history of the unconscious from Franz Mesmer's magnetic passes to Freud's talking cure. The enchanted reverie of ink-gazing, as both an indirect mode of print-media consumption, and a visual entertainment akin to other mass spectacles, formed a missing piece of this genealogy.

For Martineau, the unconscious—like the ink—was distinctively black. She laments that she cannot conduct further research during her travels, because "as far as our knowledge goes (which is but a little way, at present), it appears that the dark-skinned races,—as the Hindoos and the negroes—are eminently susceptible; and it is a loss to science not to ascertain what they can do" (141). As if racial blackness replicates the dark mystery of the ink, people of color are thought to have magic abilities to see forms in the ink. Martineau leverages soft racism to lend credence to mesmerism and clairvoyance as scientific rather than mystical phenomena. In imperial modernity, the visual excess of dark skin matches the visionary excess of second sight. The association of dark ink with racial blackness was long-standing. It can be seen in the poem by Swift that supplies my earlier epigraph, which anthropomorphizes ink: "I am jet black, as you may see, / The son of pitch and gloomy night." In the previous section, I described poets' seeming spiritual access to nature and the vestiges of their decipherment of it in spilled ink and illegible handwriting. Here, we can see Martineau making this spiritual access to nature into a visual technique and racializing it. In this early form of primitivism, racial blackness aligns with intuition, clairvoyance, and second sight—mental states that later psychologists would draw on to formulate the unconscious. The most obvious example of the racialization of lower mental states is found in Freud's classic essay "The Uncanny" (1919). There, Freud claims that civilized, nonneurotic readers leave behind a childhood phase dominated by narcissism and the omnipotence of thought—mental structures akin to superstition in which primitives and neurotics still dwell.[70] Marianna Torgovnick notes Freud's slippage from the analogy between children and primitives into factual claim.[71] It supplies the psychic structure of the psychoanalytic subject, who develops from the implicitly racialized darkness of infancy and the primal demands of the id into the light of reasoned, ostensibly white, civilized adulthood. As a talented white mesmeric subject, Martineau contains racial blackness within herself, as a form of the unconscious—a mysterious depth that yields up images and ideas according to the obscure logic of gnosis. Her solution to the ink-gazing conundrum features this idea: She thinks that the magician is consciously purveying an illusion but unknowingly taps into unexplained forces he cannot understand. The psychoanalytic turn would formalize this lack of self-knowledge, hypothesizing that everyone's mind included an inky black depth where unknown affects, drives, and repressed memories might swim up to a limpid surface.

Wilkie Collins engaged ink-gazing in his novel *The Moonstone*, developing a new literary genre, detective fiction, and a new consumer behavior, addictive information gathering, to transform it. He adapted Brewster's and others' practice of debunking visual deception to the reading process via the hermeneutics of suspicion, a skeptical mode of reading that relies on collecting and comparing information. In his novel, ink-gazing scripts the unconscious into a psychological performance of information hiding and revelation. Moreover, he elaborates Martineau's idea that people of color have greater access to hidden, mystical mental depths into a politically progressive program of racial and imperial representation. The novel's overarching plot develops the discourse of optical deception to form the unconscious: Rachel Verinder sees her sweetheart, Franklin Blake, enter her bedroom and remove a diamond she has just received for her birthday. She spends most of the novel assuming that he has stolen it, but he has no memory of the crime—it turns out that he had been doped with laudanum by a country doctor, Mr. Candy. The drug, combined with Blake's shattered nerves resulting from his efforts to quit smoking, had put him into a trance and given him amnesia. Since Blake cannot remember having taken the diamond, he initiates a search for it, and for the culprit, ultimately discovering himself as the doer of the deed. Crucially, since his motives remain pure—he was removing the diamond to keep it safe—Rachel's eyes, though accurate, have deceived her. If an article in *Blackwood's* debunking spiritualism could have lectured her as it did its own readers, it would have said, "It is one thing to believe what you have seen, and another to believe that you have seen all there was to be seen."[72] Such a lesson, drawing on screen practice and the operational aesthetic, expands to include Blake's discovery of his own unconscious. They both share an addictive drive to know more by seeing, or reading, more.

The novel's structure trains readers in the hermeneutics of suspicion. It is formed by different witnesses' accounts of the interlocking events, compiled by Blake himself after the fact to exonerate himself. Readers hear from the crusty house steward, Gabriel Betteredge; Rachel's interfering aunt, Miss Clack; the dry lawyer, Mr. Bruff; and Blake himself, reading each account against the others and itself, in an effort to solve the mystery. Collins's method exemplifies a characteristic of mass media described by Niklas Luhmann: "Every statement draws the suspicion upon itself of wanting to say too much. . . . Everything that is uttered is deciphered in terms of the one who utters it."[73] From the perspective of systems theory, Luhmann is describing the characteristic mode of modern consumer skepticism neatly nutshelled in the phrase "We Know What That Means."[74] Collins gave this paranoid mode of reading a genial face; he made the hermeneutics of suspicion an enjoyable pastime. Since it consists principally in observing the linguistic and other personal tendencies of characters of which they are themselves unaware, it is the reading technique that most clearly anticipated the psychoanalytic version of the unconscious. As this section shows, Collins's novel moves ink-gazing from the sphere of visual culture into the realm of lettered print and serial fiction, while developing the terms of the debate over its authenticity, its racial aspect, and its relationship to the mind. Teaching readers to compare the different witness accounts and collect relevant information from each one, the novel both models and induces print-media consumption as delirium.

Collins changes the ink-gazer's race so that he, like Martineau, contains blackness—here, extrasensory access to imagery and information—within himself. As Blake travels to the Verinders' Yorkshire house to deliver the diamond, a trio of Brahmin Indians—no longer Muslim Egyptians—force an excessively white English boy to ink-gaze, in an effort to locate the diamond, in the passage that forms the epigraph of this section.

> The Indian took a bottle from his bosom, and poured out of it some
> black stuff, like ink, into the palm of the boy's hand. The Indian—first
> touching the boy's head, and making signs over it in the air—then
> said, "Look." The boy became quite stiff, and stood like a statue,
> looking into the ink in the hollow of his hand.[75]

This description clearly describes the ink-gazing trick, which had been
common knowledge in English culture since the 1840s. The boy answers
their questions until he tires. By converting Egyptians to Indians, was Collins playing on the fabled superiority of carbon-based "India ink"? Perhaps; perhaps not. India ink was increasingly used for drawing rather than
writing, so it would suit ink-gazing as a practice of visual culture. Yet the
term referred to India's supply of raw materials to China, so that India ink
was "more properly [known as] China ink."[76] Moreover, Martineau pro-
claimed the visionary prowess of ink-gazing to belong to people of color
in general. The Brahmins had found the boy abandoned in a London market; by making him a street urchin, Collins renders his whiteness equivo-
cal, like that of a "street Arab." By having the boy initially refuse to gaze
at the ink, Collins played to readers' skepticism and established him as a
disinterested medium, rather than a deceiver, with the result that readers
credit his visions. Indeed, the novel's signature symptomatic reading leads
its consumers to dismiss Betteredge's assertions that ink-gazing is merely
"hocus-pocus, like actors rehearsing a play" and "juggling, accompanied
by a foolish waste of ink" (*Moonstone*, 72, 71). In this way, the novel establishes the truth of an unconscious zone of images conjured in ink, as an
element of black racial vision possessed by the white subject.

Moreover, this racialized vision is rational; it dwells more in the realm
of information than of emotion. Though the clairvoyant boy quickly disappears from the action, a character introduced late in the novel takes his
place. Gooseberry, the small but quick-witted, unusually observant junior
detective who can follow suspects unseen through the metropolis, echoes
and elaborates on the clairvoyant boy's visual prowess. Also associated with
the streets and poverty, Gooseberry too is employed by adults, the lawyer
Matthew Bruff and the detective Sergeant Cuff, as the Indians employed
the nameless London orphan. Like the nameless boy, he produces his
knowledge in replies to his masters' interrogation. Gooseberry's nickname
comes from his signature feature, his prominent eyes: "They projected so
far, and they rolled about so loosely, that you wondered uneasily why they
remained in their sockets" (405). Gooseberry's lucid eyes assume the function of the ink, since they are like a visual media device that can extend

the ordinary range of human vision. In their potential detachability, they literalize Marshall McLuhan's theory that media apparatuses extend the human sensorium.[77] As prosthetics, they anticipate the handheld "detective" camera that would become popular in the early 1880s.[78] Like the hidden camera, Gooseberry can circulate throughout the metropolis, seeing without being seen. His quasi-mechanized vision surpasses that of the clairvoyant boy, who gets fatigued and loses focus, as well as that of the adults, who lose sight of the diamond at the bank. Gooseberry, unlike them all, "has [his] eyes about [him]"—quite literally, and it is this portable, mobile quality that allows him to successfully track the gem (*Moonstone*, 507). Gooseberry modernizes the Brahmins' primitive ink-gazing ritual. The enchantment of clairvoyance gives way to a new kind of enthrallment, with the information flow of modern technology and the young, pliable, boy who literally gives it a face.

As the reader's avatar, Gooseberry is innocent and disinterested in the machinations regarding the diamond; like the reader desiring more information, he consumes the operational aesthetic in the theatrical set piece that resolves the mystery. In The Wheel of Fortune, a public house where adults attempt to shield him from the diamond's theft and Ablewhite's murder, Gooseberry subverts them, delighting in the spectacle of Ablewhite's corpse in blackface. His rolling eyes in comic contrast with the over-delicate revulsion of Blake, who must look away, Gooseberry's narration reprises the role of the clairvoyant boys who narrate their inky visions to breathless audiences. "He's pulling off his wig!" "He's pulled off his beard!" "He's washing off his complexion now!" (*Moonstone*, 520–21). These are spectacular moments, but they are like a magic trick in reverse: Instead of the deceiver Ablewhite conjuring illusions onstage, Gooseberry and readers see him inert, anatomized, progressively stripped of his disguise, and in this way they learn the techniques of his tricks. Collins adapts the impulse behind Brewster's *Letters on Natural Magic* and the *Quarterly Review*'s piece on Lane's book, with their hypotheses about mirrors and leading questions. Moreover, Gooseberry's swelling eyeballs perform the same excessive function as the genius's and the clumsy clerk's ink splashes: They add a touch of pleasure, zaniness, and mayhem to the situation by overflowing their function of registering and conveying information. Prepubescent boys were chosen to gaze at ink because they were thought to be morally pure and less likely to deceive those who played the game. Like the clairvoyant boy, Gooseberry faithfully conveys the information he discovers; they facilitate the flow of information to the other characters and to the reader. Gooseberry's prurience adds some sensation to the transmission. He hints at the degeneration of the ink-gazing boys as described by Dickens, who felt the original seers had been succeeded by "little ragged boys [who] would run after the passers in the street and offer to see—anything that might be required of them—for an anna, or even a cake or sweetmeat."[79] Gooseberry's urban mobility similarly resembles that of telegraph boys, who would later feature as prostitutes in the Cleveland Street scandal, but whose moral welfare was already a public question at midcentury.[80] Collins borrows this seediness to give readers an extra thrill as they consumed the novel's events via Gooseberry's throbbing eyes.

As ink-gazing moves from a small, elite practice of visual culture to a discourse in print that speculates on its relationship to truth, to a signature feature of a new kind of print media consumption, that of reading detective fiction, it acquires sensational, intoxicating, and addictive qualities. Collins cheekily advertises this new sensation in the mock condition Betteredge dubs "detective fever": "If there is such a thing known at the doctor's shop as a *detective-fever*, that disease had now got fast hold of your humble servant" (182). It heats up when clues emerge and cools down when no information is forthcoming. Blake dubs it "an irresistible malady" (372). Moreover, Betteredge likens this condition to intoxication: "The horrid mystery hanging over us in this house gets into my head like liquor, and makes me wild" (205). Collins likens the collection of information to pathological intoxication: Readers' reconstruction of the narrative is like a drunken delirium. Luhmann describes the addictive aspects of mass media, which "engage body and mind more directly—for example, where erotica is concerned, or detective stories which initially mislead the viewers who know they are being misled, and especially foot-tapping music."[81] Intoxication and addiction are less than fully conscious states of mind; they take temporary or fluctuating possession of a person, blunting his or her self-awareness. In Collins's metaphorical physical economy, information operates as a dose, stimulating the appetite for more. Collins was undoubtedly responding to the critical diagnosis of sensation fiction reading, recently made by Henry Mansel and others, as a kind of addiction.[82] Comparing the reader to a "dram-drinker," Mansel wrote that sensation novels "had been called into existence to supply the cravings of a diseased appetite . . . and to stimulate the want which they supply."[83] *The Moonstone* was the novel from which long-form detective fiction emerged from sensation fiction.[84] Collins's audacious references to "detective-fever" throw the charges back in Mansel's and other critics' faces, encouraging readers' absorptive, compulsive pleasure in learning the information that completes the mystery.

The intoxication and addiction that Collins induced in readers involved both narrative and typographic techniques. Alison Winter has described his concern for "the relationship of ink to eye" as he generated "line-by-line excitement" in *The Woman in White* (1860), working with typographers to arrange capitals, italics, and white spaces for maximum effect. "As readers' eyes made passes down each page, the optical sensations created by the running pattern of black and white were coordinated by the novelist."[85] Collins gave similar care to *The Moonstone*. The affordances of *Household Words,* in which the novel appeared in serial form, helped him dole out narrative information in precise doses of print. Mass print consumption of his novels became a paradoxically irrational state of delirious information gathering.

Collins's discourse of intoxicated reading and its wider context of addictive print consumption engage the motif of media addiction I have been describing. In chapter 1, I showed how the temperance movement rhetorically substituted the rational study of books for alcohol, positioning print media as an object of habitual consumption. This not entirely convincing ploy had to compete with the long-standing discourse of women's "addiction" to engrossing novels, exemplified by Mansel's and others' comparisons to dram-drinking. Collins pioneered long-form detective fiction, not to mention sensation fiction, as genres capable of stimulating and satisfying compulsive desires for narrative information. Conan Doyle would perfect the short form of the genre in his Sherlock Holmes stories, as we saw in chapter 2. Here, Holmes's obsessive consumption of, and dependency on, printed information grew from the earlier, more sedative effects of tobacco ephemera; and it anticipated the bite- or puff-sized addiction to trivial information found on cigarette cards. In *The Picture of Dorian Gray*, the subject of chapter 5, Oscar Wilde constructs media addiction as an essentially paranoid affect associated not with new media, with their multifarious appeals to a porous self, but with the old medium of oil painting and the aristocratic privilege it connoted. Unlike other instances in which collecting ephemera and acquiring information lead to self- or cultural mastery—in the case of temperance medals, cigarette cards, and Dorian's relation to the "poisonous" book—for Collins, information gathering is instrumental to the consumption of narrative. Reading a detective novel, a project like ink-gazing, is about seeing remote information, ascribing value to it, and then storing it in an unconscious for later use.

Absorbed in optically and cognitively consuming narrative information, readers of *The Moonstone* and other nineteenth-century detective fiction construct an unconscious that more closely resembles information storage

than repressed desire.[86] Collins's novel models this formation in its
pièce de résistance, Ezra Jennings's experiment to reproduce Blake's cognitive state on the night of the diamond's loss. Re-creating details down
to the withheld tobacco that throws his nerves into a state of withdrawal,
Blake's resulting automatic actions reveal how he took the diamond without intending to steal it. The experiment reinforces the unity of Blake's
mind: Whether conscious or hidden, his intentions remain the same. His
simplicity reflects the "lost parcel" model of the unconscious, associated
with the mesmerist John Elliotson, whose story of an Irish porter Collins
cites: The porter gets drunk, loses a parcel, and must get drunk again
before he can find it. Finding the answer is a problem of memory or information storage and retrieval. Jenny Bourne-Taylor, assessing the novel's
engagement with models of the unconscious, makes E. S. Dallas's theory
of the "hidden soul," from *The Gay Science*, central to her reading. Dallas,
in trying to recuperate the imagination as a rational force integrated into
all realms of thought, also described it in terms of the unconscious, as a
hidden, automatic agency. Bourne-Taylor interprets this terminological
slipperiness as an index of the diamond's "vague force" as projective surface and, ultimately, the novel's tendency to undo itself by making its own
ambiguity ambiguous.[87] But the imagination's covert rationality also suggests a distinctively mid-nineteenth-century version of the unconscious
as a storage area for memories and knowledge that, with effort, can be
retrieved for conscious contemplation. Not yet the Freudian zone of
drives, repression, and affects in turmoil, this unconscious is a strangely
quiet place. Another writer had characterized ink-gazing similarly, as an
internal psychological circuit in which "images are reflected to the eye of
the seer from his own mind and brain."[88] The metaphor of reflection invests the process with the rationality of vision. Ink-gazing, which in the
novel detects the whereabouts of the diamond missing from the Brahmins'
care, performs this searching-the-mental-files as intoxicated absorption.

    The biracial Jennings's authority on this cutting-edge theory of the
mind is part of Collins's racially progressive program in *The Moonstone*; so
too is his replotting of ink-gazing as something other than stupefied deception at the hands of Eastern tricksters. The novel's implicit advocacy
of irrational states of mind includes claims of cultural legitimacy for hitherto absurd, foreign practices such as ink-gazing. As readers shift from an
older model of optical deception to a newer visual pleasure as information
gathering, the stock identities of the conjurers and the duped also trade
places. Not only is Blake, the hero of the tale, positioned as the thief, but
the villains spectacularly morph from the exotic Egyptian magicians and

Brahmin priests of the ink-gazing ritual and its paratexts into a markedly white British preacher. Ablewhite's hypocrisy and deceptions pointedly reverse the narrative of "deceptive priests of failed religions" whom Kinglake, Brewster, and others had vilified. Collins makes his diamond thief a white preacher and allows the Brahmins to murder him and flee the country with impunity as part of a large, loose political project of paying respect to Indian customs, practices, and worship. When ink-gazing ceases to be a technique by which East entrances and deceives West, becoming instead a means of acquiring information, then the diamond itself can also be respected as a culturally different but legitimate object of worship, as the final narrative by Murthwaite dignifies it.

The novel achieves closure by restoring the appropriated diamond, thus offering a desultory counterimperialism: It puts slight progressive pressure on the topics of looting, religious dignity, and racial discrimination, without synthesizing them.[89] As Jaya Mehta argues, were Blake ever to remember stealing the diamond, the narrative would self-destruct, and this necessary forgetting secures English tranquility, confining colonialism to the colonies.[90] Especially one decade after the Uprising of 1857, Collins cannot write a comprehensive critique of British imperialism. However, by removing ink-gazing from the older imperial order and the racial values that underwrote it, he modernizes it as a technique of productive knowledge; and this modernization ameliorates British antagonism to culturally different practices. The novel achieves this feat with no uncomfortable reckoning of Britain's own imperial violence, which remains safely stored out of sight.

Ink-gazing returns in altered form in Collins's last scene, in which a vast Indian crowd worships the restored diamond. Gazing at precious stones and gazing at ink were both modes of "scrying," or attempting to see visions in reflective surfaces; the most famous English scryer was John Dee, about whose obsidian stone Collins wrote in "Magnetic Evenings at Home."[91] What the English regarded as an occult pastime was a Hindu form of devotion, Collins believed. His bid to end the novel with a spectacle of mass worship anticipates the comparative-anthropological approach to occult practices that would further shape the unconscious as a universal mental feature in the 1880s and 1890s. "There, raised high on a throne—seated on his typical antelope, with his four arms stretching towards the four corners of the earth—there, soared above us, dark and awful in the mystic light of heaven, the god of the Moon. And there, in the forehead of the deity, gleamed the yellow Diamond, whose splendour had last shone on me in England, from the bosom of a woman's dress!"

(542). Collins's inclusion of the details of Hindu worship generates respect in readers, especially when the devotion is juxtaposed to its salacious, frivolously consumable image in the English context. Geraldine Jewsbury claimed the epilogue's "solemn and pathetic human interest": "Few will read of the final destiny of the Moonstone without feeling the tears rise in their eyes."[92] Later in the century, writers and folklorists would build on Collins's gesture of respect, approaching ink-gazing, crystal-gazing, and other paranormal phenomena from the point of view of comparative anthropology and religion. In *The Making of Religion* (1898), Andrew Lang sought to rescue so-called savage or primitive beliefs and rituals from critical dismissal—even to distinguish them as vestiges or survivals suppressed in less soulful modern times. In his chapter titled "Crystal Visions, Savage and Civilized," Lang contextualizes Lane's ink-gazing with Maori divination in drops of blood and Native Americans' "hydromancy," or water-gazing; such comparisons ground his protopsychoanalytic declaration: "In modern language, the instinctive knowledge existing implicitly in the patient's subconsciousness is thus brought into the range of his ordinary consciousness."[93] By the turn of the century, ink-gazing—like a host of similar practices around the world—occupied the overlapping zones of different cultural beliefs and unconscious events.

At the same time, psychical research into ink-gazing and crystal-gazing gathered up the threads Collins had introduced—remote viewing, information gathering, and internal suggestion—moving toward a paranormally inflected model of the unconscious. The mysterious and controversial figure "Miss X"—also known as Ada Goodrich Freer—had written two definitive essays on ink- and crystal-gazing, to which Lang was indebted.[94] Goodrich Freer was a telepath, paranormal investigator, and folklorist who had helped write and edit W. T. Stead's journal *Borderlands*.[95] She claimed that seeing visions in ink and crystals was probably the result of "self-suggestion": "I believe the suggestion is made, not by one's normal but by one's subconscious self."[96] By "subconscious," Goodrich Freer meant a person's repository of both visual memories and imagination—a mental filing cabinet that the crystal could index. Her colleague at the Society for Psychical Research F. W. H. Myers had classified the images generated from crystal-gazing as "automatisms," or messages from a lower stratum of a person's mind to his or her consciousness. "Originating in some deeper zone of a man's being, they float up into superficial consciousness as deeds, visions, words, ready-made and full-blown."[97] Myers made it clear that the crystal had no mystical agency in the generation of images. "The effect is said to be not like that of 'conjuring up a scene,' but rather of looking tranquilly into a camera obscura, where light and movement are given correctly, and with no effort of one's own."[98] A distinction emerges between an imagination that invents a scene and an unconscious that renders one a passive spectator. The camera obscura, long a seaside attraction in Britain, furnishes yet another media metaphor for Myers's conceptualization of the bi-level mind. In these ways, British paranormal research characterized activities such as ink-gazing as an internal psychological communication technology.

Although psychological and occult discourses begin to construct an unconscious or "subconscious," the principal task of storing information does not result in psychologically deep characters. Rather, the unconscious-as-information-storage generates flat subjectivities—ones that lack affective range. Blake is the best example of the novel's failure to conjure the embedded emotional conflict that drives the Freudian unconscious. Collins makes Blake's superficiality his most prominent feature, especially as interpreted by the equally flat Betteredge. Blake stares into the shivering sand, but when he dredges up the box containing Rosanna Spearman's letter and the incriminating nightgown with his name on the label, he does not confront his deepest self. Rather, he finds information. As the novel doles out such information to him and to readers, they piece it together until it forms a rational, if implausible solution to the mystery. When he re-develops ink-gazing, the unconscious that Collins produces clings to the surface of character; rather than introducing affective tension or change, it generates compulsive but rational behavior: the collecting and arranging of information and evidence that formally constitute the narrative. Readers of *The Moonstone* do the same with the information the individual narratives dispense. In the next chapter, I discuss how George Du Maurier's novel *Peter Ibbetson* advances this model of the unconscious, depicting a similarly flattened subjectivity in his title character. In the fantastic plot of *Peter Ibbetson*, the main character can archive and play back all his experiences—a conceit that drains them of affective and bodily meaning, rendering them into information. Peter's playback takes place while he is sleeping. During the time when the Freudian subject's dreams are obliquely expressing repressed material, Peter's clairvoyant "true dreams" help him relive his fondest memories. The resulting bodiless experience and static, predictable affective responses make Peter strangely psychologically flat, despite his elaborate psychic architecture. Together, Blake and Peter articulate a distinctively organized, rational Victorian unconscious.

Moreover, Du Maurier will develop ink-gazing's emphasis on visual enchantment through entertainment media metaphors. Recall Martineau's touristic desire to visually consume and retain Cairo: "the longing to have for one's own forever every exquisite feature of the scene" (*Eastern Life*, 2:119). Du Maurier seizes on this wish and invents a fantastic means for realizing it, in Peter's capacity to replay, in luminous visual detail, everything he has even seen. In his depiction of Peter's clairvoyant true dreaming, he also echoes Myers's formulation of crystal-gazing as passively gazing into a "camera obscura" and receiving its images without effort. In both instances, the mind consumes its own memories as if they were spectacular entertainment; the unconscious in each is an internal media technology that recalls illustrated print and photography, and, in its movement, anticipates cinema. They remap psychology as enchanted media consumption.

We have seen how spilled ink, the topic of my first section, formed the opposite of the conscious, rational activity of writing, betraying and spoiling writers' intentions. In the rush to become modern by writing as speedily and flawlessly as possible, spilled and blotted ink slowed new and professional writers' progress, generating frustration; in some instances, the steel pen's fast performance encouraged hotheadedness, allowing inappropriate affects into writing and print. A cultural ambivalence surrounded ink as a media material throughout the century. At the same time, a second strand of cultural significance attached to the ink pool. Here, ink's disordered materiality permitted it to act as a screen, its motile, liquid body offering visions to viewers. From a paradigm of reading and writing, with their criteria of legibility, ink's cultural meanings expanded to include the enchantments of visual entertainment, which relieved ink of the obligation to form recognizable characters in handwriting and type. These two spaces, though different, were not utterly separate: The key to the ink-gazing ritual remained printed illustration. To see visions in ink, one must first have seen printed illustrations of famous faces. Ink-gazing engaged paradigms of other visual media; as a screen-practice, it suspended consumers between a desire to know how the trick operated and a wish to be enchanted and transported by imagery. Collins's novel modernized the practice into one of information retrieval that emphasized white European unconsciousness of imperial appropriation. Collins used ink-gazing to help invent the unconscious as information storage. The end of the novel, with its invocation of Hindu spiritualized scrying, anticipated the treatment of ink-gazing within comparative anthropology and psychical research, which would more fully describe a "subconscious" that mirrored pools of ink, crystals, and other projective surfaces.

In this way, a latent concept of projection emerges and moves from visual media to psychology. Freud would develop this concept into one of psychic and affective depth, a model that stands in contrast to its Victorian formation as information storage. In the last section of this chapter, I describe how aesthetics, children's games, and science used inkblots to fully develop projection. In doing so, they banished the Victorian model of information retrieval, and made psychic depth visible as a response to mass cultural imagery.

The Calculated Blot: Ink and Projection

The inkwell, crystalline like consciousness, with its drop, at bottom,
of shadows relative to letting something be: then, take away the lamp.
    You noted, one does not write, luminously, on a dark field; the
alphabet of stars alone does that, sketched or interrupted; man pursues
black upon white.

STÉPHANE MALLARMÉ, "Restrained Action"

I preface this section with Mallarmé's poem because it succinctly performs the reversal of ink from figure to ground—from the efforts of new writers to gazers at the ink pool to psychologists' ironic calculations of randomness. Stars write their transcendent meaning in light, but humans' "restrained" writing and drawing remains shadowy, opaque, always on the verge of meaning and begging interpretation. When artists, children, and psychologists purposely begin to make blots, they therefore cultivate a new engagement with the stubborn substance of ink. Ink that has been blotted takes on a stability of form that makes it an aesthetic object, albeit a random or desultory one. Blotted ink, like other accidental aesthetic forms, reflects a cultural shift from deliberate artistic choices to reflexive psychological behavior. As the blot is standardized, becoming the deliberate and precise object of printing, it ushers in an era of psychological testing and personality classification. These tests were inevitably tests of mass media literacy, since imaginative acumen had to be proved against the allegedly standardized imagery and ideas of mass culture. And yet gothic imagery, proposing itself as countercultural but truly mass circulated, dominated the most significant inkblot test, the Rorschach, linking it to the strand of German Romanticism best exemplified by the fantastic tales of E. T. A. Hoffmann. As discussed by Harriet Martineau and later, the Society for Psychical Research, ink-gazing was already a psychological performance that involved some sort of "self-suggestion"; but as the inkblot became the instrument of psychological research, it nourished a more elaborate concept of projection. Mallarmé hints that if the inkwell is consciousness, its depths suggest an unconscious of suspended potential. The practice of interpreting inkblots brought those shadows into form.

To see how ink begins to shift the trajectory from the unconscious as information storage, with its attendant flat subjectivity, to the Freudian unconscious of hidden drives in conflict, we begin with an unlikely piece of ephemera: the advertising blotter. In the 1860s, advertisements began to appear on the cheap blotting paper used to dry ink; when used, handwriting traces would overwrite these ads. The original advertising blotters bore only simple line-block printing, but by the turn of the century, they featured glossy, colorful half-tone illustrations, often with a calendar.[99] As the interface between wet writing ink and dried printer's ink, advertising blotters literalized the interaction between expressive and purposive writing, and the phantasmagoric world of mass print media. Ads for apothecaries, photographers, grain and feed shops, steam laundries, jewelers, opticians, tailors, and undertakers intruded into the scene of private writing. As an everyday item, blotters were thought to infuse the unconscious with the random, quasi experiences of mediated modernity—or so the advertisers hoped: "The more mental impressions [the advertiser] can secure from each printing impression, the greater the value of the medium."[100] "Just as Your Name Soaks Into This Little Signature Blotter May the Name of the Fully Protective Peerless Check Writer Soak Into Your Memory. R. K. Slaughter, Boston," wished an early twentieth-century blotting card of about 2 ½ by 4 ½ inches.[101] Printing happened on paper and in the mind.

The advertising blotter thus offers a more realistic analogue for unconscious memory than does Freud's similar "Wunderblock" or "mystic writing pad." To Freud, the celluloid cover of the mystic writing pad was like the perceptual system that received impressions from the stylus of phenomena, and the wax pad beneath was like the unconscious that retained them as permanent memory traces, constantly overwritten.[102] Similarly, the advertising blotter soaked up the aftereffects of experience—the original writing; but the blotter also mingled it with printed media. A shadowy, indistinct place where direct experience blurs with the impersonal addresses of mass culture, the promiscuous, imprecise, disposable blotting paper exemplifies the unconscious within mass culture. Jacques Derrida observes Freud's lapse, in the "Wunderblock" essay, into a Platonic model of writing as a bad supplement for embodied memory, a "writing of the soul" that can somehow simultaneously perceive and store perception.[103] Freud's covert commitment to the sovereign subject of empirical experience and organic memory prevented him from fully recognizing that subject's inextricability from social worlds of representation, or in modernity, those of mass culture.[104] The advertising blotter attests to this entanglement, whereby one's name and identity are repeatedly imbued with random, apparently unrelated consumer messages. Mass print culture updated the old model of the mind as palimpsest to include mediated experience, but as we shall see, artists and game-makers rather than psychologists first took up this task.

The most famous nineteenth-century practitioner of the quasi-modernist practice of inkblot art was also the period's great sentimental and bombastic novelist Victor Hugo.[105] Hugo made several thousand blotted drawings, experimenting in many of them with washes (*taches*) and folded paper (*pliages*). Hugo played with pen, ink, and paper, rotating his outdated quill pen to use the feather end as a brush. He also incorporated random household items such as burned matchsticks, coffee, and toothpaste, anticipating the readymade art of Marcel Duchamp, Hans Arp, and other Dadaists.[106] As Hugo's grandson recalled, "He scattered the ink haphazardly, crushing the goose quill which grated and spattered trails of ink. Then he sort of kneaded the black blot which became a castle, a forest, a deep lake or a stormy sky."[107] Where representational, these blots rehashed gothic clichés; in Luc Sante's opinion, they were "Romantic boilerplate."[108] This gothic imagery linked the German Romanticism of the early part of the century to Freudian and Rorschachian constructions at the end. Hugo's physical engagement with his materials made his blots into unique bodily and affective expressions. He tilted the paper, marbled the ink by pressing two pieces of paper together, rubbed, dabbed, wiped, and smeared ink as his fancy took him. His ink play elegantly parodied printing, especially in his pliages, made by folding paper over a blot to transfer ink to the other side. Visually, the symmetrical, repeating figures of the pliages recalled mass production, especially of wallpaper design or architectural ornament. This automatic quality also made them seem unconscious: The blank white page of paper served as a screen on which the black ink spot figured forth images, letters, and ideas from Hugo's psychic deeps—as mediated by gothic tropes. He even described producing the images in "moments of almost unconscious daydreaming."[109] As ink moves from liquid to solid, wet to dry, formlessness to form, it generates the effect of a psychic source projecting its singularity into mundane material. The purpose-made inkblot becomes itself uncanny, repeating the truly accidental one.

The century's other notable inkblot artist was, like Hugo, a belated Romantic: the German poet, mystic, and physician Justinus Kerner, who wrote and drew *Die Klecksographien* (1857), a series of macabre inkblots and accompanying poems. Kerner also touched up his blots, but he more systematically developed his klecksographien to represent the otherworldly creatures that formed the visual and folkloric vocabulary of German Romanticism. His eyesight failing in old age, Kerner's pen would drip on his papers; without noticing, he would stack them, and blots resembling humans, animals, skeletons, and arabesques would result. Kerner emphasized the randomness of this process: "[The images] did not emerge as a result of my will or power—I'm quite capable of drawing—rather they came about in [a way] that could only be revealed by ink blotting, often necessitated by the negligible assistance of a few strokes of the pen or artificial tracing of faces."[110] Whereas Hugo's imagery dwelled in the melancholic Romanticism of seascapes and ruined architecture, Kerner's featured corpses, skulls, dungeons, and the Black Death. He referred to them as "Hades images," and wrote little poems to caption them. In a passage from "Memento Mori," the poem accompanying Figure 9, Kerner meditates on his compositional method:

> These images from Hades
> All black and terrifying
> (They're spirits, of a very low grade)
> Made their own pictures

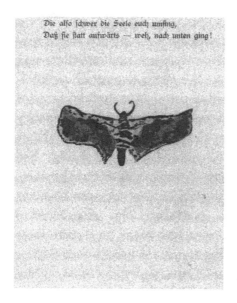

Figure 9. Inkblot ("klecks") accompanying the poem "Memento Mori." In *Klecksographien* by Justinus Kerner (1857; Berlin: Hofenberg, 2014).

Without my assistance, and to my fright
Only—from ink drops.
I always thought that wherever it's black and night,
It's haunted by the eerie race,
Therefore also in the inkwell.
Those of you who write, take care!
Since I, klecksograph, discovered
That the power of a noxious demon
Often hides in the inkwell. (7)

As with Hugo's process, the unconscious develops in the obscured domain of the inkwell's interior. For Kerner, however, the image comes from
hell, a supernatural space that introduced mysticism and divination to the
preservation of spilled ink. The conceit of the demonic or fanciful supernatural creature formed the eldritch side of human nature that gave rise
to the unconscious.

Kerner distributed his image-texts himself, and they achieved a local
popularity: "This 'game' with the thick blots then soon spread among
many, and was for a time in our area and also afar, almost a game of fashion for both the old and young, and even in schools (often to the great grief
of teachers)" (5). Ink-blotting became an actual game: Klecks in Germany;
Blotto in England; Gobolinks and Blottentots in the United States.
Participants used the folding technique of the pliage to make symmetrical
patterns of blotted ink, then wrote accompanying poems under timed
conditions, with prizes awarded for the best compositions. Ruth M. Stuart and Albert Bigelow Paine's charming book *Gobolinks* (1896) collects
some examples, and offers rules for the game; it describes the Gobolink as
"a veritable goblin of the ink-bottle, and the way he eludes the artist's design proves him a self-made eccentric creature of superior imagination."[111]
In the opening poem of John Prosper Carmel's *Blottentots* (1907), one is in-
structed, "To make a funny Blottentot, first take a piece of paper,/Splash
on some ink, a single spot,/Crease, press, but cut no caper."[112]

The images are comically monstrous figures such as "The Graceful Pol-
lywogs," "A South-Sea Idol" (*Gobolinks*), "A Little Grass Midget," "The
Kangar-Rooster-Roo," and "Sorry Grigs" (*Blottentots*). The names of these
otherworldly creatures echo nineteenth-century racist discourses of "Hot-
tentots" and "Golliwogs."[113] To white European audiences, they suggest
the cute domestication of sinister forces. By the century's end, child writers were better controlled by educational systems, so that their spilling of
ink could become an appealing form of play rather than a wasteful irritation

Figure 10. "A Flit-Flit Flitter." In *Blottentots* by John Prosper Carmel (San Francisco: Paul Elder, 1907).

and sign of deficient literacy. Like Hugo's and Kerner's blots, theirs represent a vestige of the Romantic desire to be enchanted by an illegible nature, now organized by practice, testing, and competition. These elements would carry forward into psychological testing; as would the dark, creatural imagery, which coincided so well with the primacy of childhood fancies in psychoanalysis. The Butterfly Man, like the Sand Man, is an ephemeral, dream creature who may outstay his welcome, archived in the unconscious mind, and popping out randomly.

Around the turn of the twentieth century, schoolchildren had played Klecks; this game was the particular delight of young "Klex" Rorschach, who became posthumously famous as the deviser of the psychological test that bears his name.[114] Hermann Rorschach was interested in the psychology of visual and aesthetic perception.[115] He wished not merely to interpret the content of the forms seen in the inkblots, but to consider engagements with detail, motion, and color. Though he was influenced by psychoanalysis, his test ran along different lines, seeking to reveal people's "experience types" rather than their personality types.[116] Rorschach likely brought his artistic talent to bear on the construction of his ten standardized images, accenting them as Hugo and Kerner had done. The forms had to be simple, but not so simple that "they will not be suggestive, with the result that many subjects will reject them as 'simply an inkblot' without consideration of other possible interpretations."[117] Conversely, they could

Figure 11. Card 5 of the Rorschach test. Originally published in Hermann Rorschach, *Psychodiagnostics*, translated by Paul Lemkau, edited by W. Morgenthaler (1922; Berne: Verlag Hans Huber, 1942).

not be too recognizable, or they would yield only straightforward description. Seeking exactly the right image, Rorschach mimicked ink accidents in what Peter Galison has described as "an exquisite art of artlessness."[118] Moreover, these finely calculated accidents now operated as keys to psychic depths. The Rorschach test standardized, systematized, and made productive the nineteenth-century new writer's accidentally or deliberately spilled and blotted ink.

Cultural and aesthetic norms calibrated Rorschach's quest for images that would be neither too formless nor too formed. Ernest Schachtel observes that the inkblots, "by striking at the empty shell of cliché recognition . . . speak to something deeper in the person."[119] Schachtel cites the images' fantastic, grotesque quality as unique, but as we have seen, they are part of a gothic counter-aesthetic, which self-consciously opposes the mass culture to which it truly belongs.

German supernatural stories had wielded tremendous influence on the British short story from the 1820s, helping to transfer popular oral tales to the new marketplace for print and remaining popular throughout the century.[120] Gothic aesthetics continue—to this day—to connote Romantic, creative, and imaginative alternatives to the more realistic genres of mass culture. One of the Rorschach test's requirements was that testers deceive subjects into thinking their imaginations were being evaluated, since this would free them to speak, when in reality they were producing unfiltered unconscious data. In this way, the aesthetic of the Romantic imagination transformed into that of the unconscious. Through the end of the twentieth century, individuals would generate unique psychological data by responding to images inspired by popular culture circa 1800.

The disavowal of mass culture as cliché is part of the ideology of projection. Freud had first limited projection to psychopathology and then broadened it to a defense mechanism, defining normal subjects' relationship to the external world: One attributed one's own characteristics to the outside world because they were too anxiety-inducing to acknowledge to oneself.[121] Projection thus culminated the social logic of the hermeneutics of suspicion, which characteristically unearthed and decoded the unconscious; everything about a subject became interpretable to an expert, and opaque to himself or herself. This idea in turn overdetermined the key concept of the "private world," articulated in Lawrence K. Frank's definition: "The essential feature of a projective technique is that it evokes from the subject what is in various ways expressive of his private world and personality process."[122] The private world represented one's uninhabitable psychic deeps, but these were also a utopian land free from the oppressive norms of reality, as David Rapaport wrote: "When a procedure is so designed as to enable the subject to demonstrate his psychological structure *unstilted by conventional modes*, it is projective."[123] Conflated with bourgeois privacy, the unconscious becomes a rebellious, countercultural space. The idea is part of a durable nineteenth-century genealogy in which the individual tests himself or herself against everyday life imagined as machine production. Walter Benjamin carried it forward when he wrote that the actor performing for the camera "must operate with his whole living person, while forgoing its aura."[124] Yet Benjamin's aura and Frank's private world are brought into being by the very mechanized apparatuses of mass culture against which they are ostensibly arrayed. The opposition aligns with the internal contradictions of ink as an apparently normative technology of reason, and, as I have been exploring, as a natural wilderness of incomprehensible signs, chaos of disparate materiality, pool of hidden information, and reservoir of divine insight. The psychologized inkblot attempts to colonize this unorganized cultural material and the array of affects attached to it, and make them productive. In the process, however, it had to pretend that the fantastic, the eccentric, the accidental, and the otherworldly lacked a mass cultural aesthetic.

The final irony of standardizing randomness informed the printing history of the Rorschach test. Rorschach had fought his first publisher, Ernst Bircher, to obtain the precise size, proportion, number, and composition of the card images that he wanted.[125] The printing process introduced unintentional shading into them; Rorschach realized that this chiaroscuro effect "could bring out finer nuances than were possible on the original inkblots, and he immediately adjusted to that."[126] Indeed, Rorschach introduced an entirely new category of "affective adaptability" that could be revealed by attention to shadow. The terminology points precisely to the intertwined relation of affect and the materiality of mass print culture that I have been tracing in this chapter and book. The anecdote opposes the two faces of ink—that which is precisely and rationally controlled for effective communication, and that accidental one which blots, spills, exceeds its bounds, and appears darker or lighter than intended. The drive to standardization balances the openness to the accident, which now becomes the creative force behind the test itself. The accident always undoes itself, since, within the ideology of projection, the hermeneutics of suspicion, and the recuperative forces of industrial modernity, it can be made meaningful.[127] As Schachtel later noted, almost anything test subjects might say could be included as evidence of a diagnosis, since they were always projecting their unconscious material.[128] Rorschach's mentor Eugen Bleuler conjured the tests' capacity to deliver up the whole person from the most trivial of his answers: "The intent to infer the entire personality from the individual's handwriting, the physiognomy, the shape of the hand, or even the style and the use of the shoes are not aspirations without a basis."[129] Such traces are accidents—like ink spills—that require a standardized system of interpretation; hence the drive to organize and uniformly apply projective techniques. Well into the twenty-first century, Hogrefe AG Switzerland (formerly Verlag Hans Huber) uses the same, nearly century-old printing presses, and follows secret instructions to replicate the original temperature and humidity of that first printing in an effort to reproduce the cards precisely—a further irony in the play of accidents that informed their origins.[130] We can only assume they take the same care to replicate the printing ink of 1921.

In this way, ink, a material of mass print culture, shed its nineteenth-century history on its way to becoming the twentieth-century material of the unconscious.

CHAPTER 4

"Dreaming True": Playback, Immediacy, and "Du Maurierness"

> What enchanted hours have we spent among the pictures and statues
> of the world, weeding them here and there, perhaps, or hanging them
> differently, or placing them in what we thought was a better light! . . .
> Nearest to our hearts, however, were many pictures of our own time,
> for we were moderns of the moderns, after all, in spite of our efforts
> at self-culture. There was scarcely a living or recently living master in
> Europe whose best works were not in our possession. . . . There were
>   Millais's "Autumn Leaves," his "Youth of Sir Walter Raleigh," his
>   "Chill October"; Watts's "Endymion," and "Orpheus and Eurydice";
>   Burne-Jones's "Chant d'Amour," and his "Laus Veneris"; Alma-
> Tadema's "Audience of Agrippa," and the "Women of Amphissa";
> J. Whistler's portrait of his mother; the "Venus and Aesculapius," by
>   E. J. Poynter; F. Leighton's "Daphnephoria"; George Mason's
>   "Harvest-Moon"; and Frederic Walker's "Harbour of Refuge," and,
>   of course, Merridew's "Sun-God." . . . The immortal "Moonlight
>   Sonata," by Whistler; E. J. Poynter's exquisite "Our Lady of the
> Fields" (dated Paris, 1857); a pair of adorable "Bimbi" by V. Prinsep,
> who seems very fond of children; T. R. Lamont's touching "L'Après
> Diner de l'Abbé Constantin," . . . "Le Zouave et la Nounou," not to
> mention splendid rough sketches by John Leech, Charles Keene,
>   Tenniel, Sambourne, Furniss, Caldecott, etc.
>
> —GEORGE DU MAURIER, *Peter Ibbetson*

One of mass culture's depressive affects is a mingled exhaustion and disappointment, resulting from the individual's failed efforts to consume it
comprehensively. There will always be too many books to read, films to
see, and songs to hear. If modernity is "an ongoing and perpetually mod-
ulating process that would never pause for individual subjectivity to accommodate and 'catch up' with it," then its subjects always find themselves out
of breath, running a race in which the finish line continually recedes.[1] But
what if one could seize the productive technology that drives modern mass
culture, and scale it to one's individual capacity? What if one could slow
down the accelerating proliferation of ephemera, capturing all of it, so that

none of it would ever be lost? What if one found a way to "play back" one's consumer experiences, mastering time and space, and re-inhabiting their memory itself at will? Such flights of fancy animate George Du Maurier's first novel *Peter Ibbetson* (1891),[2] which imagines a mental practice and technology called "dreaming true." By this technique, intangible sensory and affective qualities such as the "tender grace" of a day can be preserved and reexperienced during lucid dreaming (1:207). In this offbeat, sentimental novel, Peter and his lover, the Duchess of Towers, meet clairvoyantly, while sleeping, to relive their past experiences together, and to consume music, art, books, newspapers, food, and travel. They achieve such prowess that they can clairvoyantly connect with their ancestors and thus revisit the past. Du Maurier frames their clairvoyance as a mental media technology; it is a compensatory fantasy for the protagonist, who wishes to re-create his idyllic Parisian childhood before Haussmannization irrevocably altered the city. *Peter Ibbetson* thus engages the iconic urban rupture of modernity. The salve for the wound is incessant consumption: Under the guise of high art enthusiasm of the kind conveyed in the epigraph to this chapter, the novel shows how mass culture conditions subjects to consume even while asleep. This kind of passive consumption of experience transforms it into something resembling information and transforms memory into media storage. Experience can be collected, like ephemera, and replayed at will. When experience no longer requires embodiment, social exchanges no longer require mutual presence; when it becomes information, it can circulate through mass print, which becomes a visual medium of a new mode of sociability. Du Maurier's cartoons for *Punch* perfectly exemplify this thinner, flatter sociability. Reading these along with *Peter Ibbetson*, we see how Du Maurier presents "dreaming true" as a charming, harmless form of insanity. Readers and critics responded with enthusiasm, taking the novel to heart for its satisfying fantasy of finally catching up to modern mass culture.

By imagining the playback of past experiences, *Peter Ibbetson* also indulges in what we might call the technological paradox of presence. The desire for presence can never be fully gratified through mediated means, because it originates and culminates in a sensing, perceiving body that must be figuratively superseded by the technological prostheses that would obtain its object—in this novel, technologically enhanced memory. The occult mental technology of "dreaming true" disembodies its protagonist, since his visitations to the past take place in the mental space he shares with the duchess, while his body remains asleep and still. This narrative of oddly disembodied consumption forms a modern origin of late twentieth-

and early twenty-first-century cultural fantasies of shedding the slow, fleshy human body to become the light and energy of electronic information media. An early part of this trajectory, Du Maurier's novel converts embodied experience into bodiless information. Imagining the mental bond between Peter and the duchess as the gateway to a metaphysical presence in which all people and things transcend the time and space that normally separates them, it cheerfully leaves behind traditional human traditions and limitations. Du Maurier's idea drew on recent media technologies such as the telephone, the phonograph, and composite photography, as well as the proliferation of mass print in the 1880s. Performing influential cultural work at the intersection of media technology, consumerism, and psychology, *Peter Ibbetson* cheerfully imagines media technologies enhancing, rather than destroying, conventional storytelling, history, and memory. The novel makes its technophilic interventions at the historical moment when scholars see elite literature beginning to position itself against popular media technologies.[3]

It is no surprise that Du Maurier wrote such a beloved cultural dream of mastering mass culture. As a cartoonist for *Punch* from 1865 to 1891, he was trained in the production of ephemera and in turn shaped an enduring mass visual idiom. Nineteenth-century scholars often use *Punch* cartoons to index late Victorian middlebrow attitudes to topics of the day such as Aesthetes and New Women, yet they rarely interrogate their form and circulation as ephemera. Because they feature recurring characters, lengthy dialogue, and omniscient narration, Du Maurier's cartoons have been discussed as an apprenticeship to his novel writing, which he took up in the last years of his life.[4] But the emphasis works both ways: The novels can also be seen as elaborated cartoons—especially since Du Maurier illustrated them himself. Indeed, they veer between the literary density required to convey psychological and social detail, and—in their illustrations, song lyrics, mispronunciations, glossolalia, untranslated French, and catalogue-like lists—the immediacy of visual and aural forms, clamoring to be seen and heard. By the 1880s, print was undergoing technical advances, such as halftone printing; generating new genres, such as the celebrity interview and feature story; and seeking cheaper markets, such as the *Daily Mail's* address to newly literate, lower-class women.[5] Traditional cartoons multiplied, and some began to morph into comic strips, with their new mix of brevity, seriality, and humor. At the same time, the success of the telephone, phonograph, and wireless telegraph were opening up imaginative horizons, as people began to rethink the technologies, modes, and aesthetic and social forms of communication. In this chapter, I show how Du

Maurier's novels—primarily *Peter Ibbetson*, but also *Trilby* (1894), and *The Martian* (1896)—and his cartoons coalesce new desires and demands for immediacy, social connection, and the cultural mastery promised by increased access to information and broader publics. I call this distinctive aesthetic "Du Maurierness," after the je ne sais quoi of his most famous character, Trilby. As one commentator wrote, "Alas that we cannot invent a noun to express [Du Maurier] as 'Trilbyness' expresses Trilby!—He is French, chic, daring, sometimes vivid, sometimes unsatisfactory and irritating, but always and above all charming. He sings, dances the cancan, drinks and smokes with you."[6] Du Maurier's imagined sociable immediacy is the effect of a paradoxical fantasy of achieving presence through disembodiment, transparent media technologies, and hyperkinetic or superanimated motion.

The desire to master time is itself timeless, but Du Maurier was responding to a specific event that later became a crucible of modernity, the Haussmannization of Paris. The enchanting opening chapters of *Peter Ibbetson* drew on his childhood wanderings in the forest of the Bois de Boulogne, and the gardens and streets of Passy and St. Cloud. After a brief, unhappy absence studying chemistry in London, Du Maurier returned to Paris to learn painting, residing in Faubourg Poissonnière, and living the life that he would spin into the Bohemian plot of *Trilby*; he returned to Paris again in 1867 to see the Exposition universelle d'art et d'industrie, encountering the city's transformation. Later passages from the novel describe his personal disappointment in Haussmann's changes: the cleared slums, broadened boulevards, sewers and gaslight, and centralization of administrative and financial power. The immense speed and scale of the effort disoriented not only Parisians and the French but observers around the world. In his memoirs, Haussmann mythologized his efforts as a radical break with utopian reforms of the 1830s and 1840s, and they later came to emblematize the rupture of modernity.[7] Historians and theorists influenced by Walter Benjamin's unfinished histories of Paris, *The Arcades Project* and *Charles Baudelaire: Lyric Poet in an Age of High Capitalism*, also have positioned Haussmannization as a decisive split from a past scaled to individuals and smaller communities, to a future dominated by the large, anonymous forces of global capital.[8] *Peter Ibbetson* registers the anomie that followed these sweeping changes and an optimism that its dream technology could surmount them. Appearing at the same time that "Haussmannize" came into common parlance, it is the most significant nineteenth-century literary response in English to the transformation of

Paris in the Second Empire.[9] It thus belongs in an ongoing critical conversation about modern memory in the industrial age.

I turn to *Peter Ibbetson* here because it offers, in literary form, an enthusiastic reflection on the relationship of ephemera to the dreaming mind from the perspective of a mass media practitioner, theorist, and fantasist. From the early 1890s, it looks back on a century of Romantic-inflected psychological writing about controlled dreaming and ahead to twentieth-century science fiction and cybernetic fantasies of mind uploading. And of course, it dwells in its own moment, responding to developments such as the phonograph and its attendant psychological phenomena such as earworms, developing a convivial ethos of trivial consumption that would culminate in Du Maurier's *Trilby* (1894) a mere three years later. Above all, the cheerful, sociable immediacy, the contagious affect so often associated with Du Maurier, seen in both his novels and his cartoons, demonstrates a lost Victorian enthusiasm for mediated modernity. Rather than dwelling in individual psychic depth, this counter-aesthetic spreads the self out thinly, dispersing it into a social network, and accentuating its immediacy and ephemerality.

Life on Demand: Playback and Mastery

Commentators early and late took *Peter Ibbetson* to their hearts. A contemporary reviewer for the *Atlantic Monthly* called it "the sort of book which one reads and decides to keep, and does not lend to everybody," and in the twenty-first century, Hélène Cixous has rhapsodized it as "a cherished book . . . goodness itself for us. The absolute friend. The first and the last. It promises and lives up to what it promises."[10] Henry James referred to it as "a love story of exquisite intensity and fantasy" and "my most particular pleasure."[11] John Masefield, writing in 1947, called the plot "a romantic thing of beauty," noting that "the effect of it upon [its] generation was profound."[12] The novelty of its clairvoyant plot, combined with nostalgia and sentiment, made *Peter Ibbetson* a minor success in England; it met with more enthusiasm in the United States, and sales increased everywhere after the phenomenon of *Trilby* several years later.[13] In 1915, John N. Raphael adapted it for the stage, developing the dramatic effects of Peter's and the duchess's visitation of themselves as the children Gogo and Mimsey.[14] It was adapted as an opera by Deems Taylor in 1931. It was twice adapted as a film: *Forever* by George Fitzmaurice in 1921 and the more critically respected *Peter Ibbetson* by Henry Hathaway in 1935. André

Breton described the latter as "a triumph of surrealist thought."[15] Current critics such as Jill Galvan and Nicholas Daly have revived attention to the novel's relation to technologized modernity.[16]

The novel consists of Peter's diaries, which tell of his idyllic Parisian childhood, miserable English adulthood, and remarkable ability to "dream true," or transport himself, during sleep, back into his happier past, when he was known as Gogo. This psychic travel is taught to him by a society acquaintance, the Duchess of Towers—who, he discovers, is also his beloved former childhood playmate Mimsey Seraskier. The dreamers may visit that part of the past they have already experienced, or together, visit each other's past experiences; but at first, they must not try to touch the past: This causes the vision to blur and become an ordinary, chaotic dream. Peter's nocturnal experiences with the duchess are the only way he may spend time with her: For much of the novel he is imprisoned for killing his uncle, Colonel Ibbetson, when he learns that, having extorted sex from his mother, the colonel is really his father. Peter's true dreaming is a respite from such repugnant realities, and the novel oscillates between his painful melancholy and his deeply pleasurable escape from it. Indeed, it seems like an endless holiday of "enchanted hours" as he and the duchess attend every gallery, theater, opera house, zoo, and botanical garden that she has ever visited (2:125). Moreover, because they can travel to any place she has visited in real life, they spend a pleasant hour "on the deck of a splendid steamer, as it cleaves its way through a sapphire tropical sea, bound for some lovely West Indian islet . . . and then, half smothered in costly furs, [were] whirled along the frozen Neva to a ball at the Winter Palace" (2:132–35). Some days, however, they merely delight in champagne and lobster salad (2:106–7). In this way, the novel's clairvoyant conceit permits an orgy of consumption in high bourgeois style. Because one or the other of them has done these things already, and because they repeat these experiences many times together over a span of thirty years, Du Maurier lards the novel with indulgent representations of fetishistic, figuratively mediatized consumption.

The novel's fantasy of excessive consumption reflects the reburgeoning commodity culture of the 1890s and, in particular, its aggregate spectacular component, phantasmagoria.[17] Du Maurier's novels reflect a new address of subjectivities—those of characters and readers—by visual media and printed ephemera such as illustrated advertising. *Trilby* famously launched a transatlantic orgy of consumption, from ham and ice cream to high-heeled shoes and hearth brushes.[18] As critics such as Jonathan Freedman and Barbara Hochman have noted, the novel and its ephemera are objects of a middlebrow consumption that mimics haute bourgeois taste.[19] Du Maurierness is keyed to this phenomenon: All three novels' joking, dancing, affable, amiable narrators conjure a rapport with readers, inspiring them to keep consuming even after reading, as if at a "big London party" at which a charming host pleasantly adjusted one's taste.[20] Du Maurier thus updates Charles Dickens's Pickwickian ethos of gregarious sociability and spinoff consumption, recasting it as a middlebrow aesthetic.[21] Du Maurier's characteristic narration inculcates a mode of fashionable reading as "a sexier, more social, more active process."[22] That this frenetic activity happens while Peter is sleeping suggests that consumption has penetrated this human respite from commerce and sociability. Jonathan Crary has argued that "sleep poses the idea of a human need and interval of time that cannot be colonized and harnessed to a massive engine of profitability, and thus remains an incongruous anomaly. . . . The stunning, inconceivable reality is that nothing of value can be extracted from it."[23] In *Peter Ibbetson*, Du Maurier rewrites this reality altogether, weaving a tale in which sleep offers an enchanted realm of untold opportunities for exciting, sociable consumer experiences.

Du Maurier creates a frame for the narrative that disingenuously implies that Peter may be insane. It consists of a preface narrated by his cousin Madge Plunkett, serving as the editor of Peter's diaries, which he composed while imprisoned in "——Criminal Lunatic Asylum," to which he had been transferred from ordinary jail, after "a sudden and violent attack of homicidal mania (which fortunately led to no serious consequences)" (1:1). Du Maurier's characteristic charm appears as he refers to violent insanity only to immediately reassure readers that it was of the trivial variety. Similarly, Madge acknowledges Peter's "dreadful deed" of killing Uncle Ibbetson, but absolves him of moral culpability by claiming that it had "long been condoned by all (and there are many) who knew the provocation he had received and the character of the man who had provoked him" (1:2). In this way, Du Maurier foreshadows the novel's violent, sensational events, while domesticating them; this strategy cultivates sympathy for his unusual protagonist. Readers are comforted by Peter's gentility and incapacity to prevaricate; moreover, even his insanity is dubious: "At the risk of being thought to share his madness—if he *was* mad—I will conclude by saying that I, for one, believe him to have been sane, and to have told the truth all through" (1:6). Du Maurier's opening piques interest, establishing a hero tinged with craziness that is mitigated by understandable circumstances. Creating an aura of insanity, violence, and the paranormal, Madge's frame narrative quickly tames such wild topics, making them easy to consume.

In the offbeat but harmless world of Peter's mind, the reconsumption of memory refashions the brain as media storage. Du Maurier writes, "Evidently our brain contains something akin both to a photographic plate and phonographic cylinder, and many other things of the same kind not yet discovered; not a sight or a sound or a smell is lost, not a taste or a feeling or an emotion" (2:30–31). Here, media apparatuses proliferate in the brain's unplumbed depths, coalescing the technological speculations of psychic research. Such notions of total recall are linked to popular entertainment media: "It was something like the 'camera-obscura' on Ramsgate pier: one goes in and finds one's self in total darkness; the eye is prepared; one is thoroughly expectant and wide-awake" (2:18). Camera obscuras were rooms with lenses and mirrors mounted in the roof that projected images onto tables below; one was installed in the Crystal Palace after it moved to Sydenham in the 1870s; they could also be visited at seaside destinations such as Margate, Swansea, and Weston-Super-Mare.[24]

Du Maurier's technologically sophisticated model of mind surpasses experience and memory, since it captures and reproduces even those things that go unnoticed: "Unconscious memory records them all, without our even heeding what goes on around us beyond the things that attract our immediate interest or attention" (2:31). These layers of mediation enfold experiencing subjects in processes and techniques of automatic perception, storage, retrieval, and presentation, creating immediacy. "Not a detail is missed. . . . And what colour it is! A painter's despair! It is light itself, more beautiful than that which streams through old church windows of stained glass" (2:18–19). The verisimilitude of "dreaming true" amounts to the virtual reality of "a life within a life—an intenser life—in which the fresh perceptions of childhood combin[e] with the magic of dreamland" (2:37). Original experience and its repetition are transposed, and paradoxically, it is the mediatized repetition that is more direct, detailed, and seemingly unmediated.

In this figuration of the mind as camera obscura, Du Maurier updates the Romantic concept of the palimpsest mind that records all experience. Samuel Taylor Coleridge famously refers to his mind as storing poetry that he nonetheless cannot consciously recover, when writing *Kubla Khan*, and elsewhere, to "the palimpsest tablet of my memory."[25] In *Biographia Literaria*, he recounted the story of the illiterate German servant who, in a delirious fever, recited Hebrew; a medical investigator discovered that she had been raised by a Hebraist uncle who recited passages in the language in her presence. Coleridge concludes, "All thoughts in themselves are imperishable"; if human body and spirit could be optimally organized, then "the collective experience of its whole existence" could be brought before each human soul."[26] Thomas De Quincey, echoing Coleridge, gave an equally strong account of the mind's recording abilities: "There is no such thing as forgetting possible to the mind . . . whether veiled or unveiled, the inscription remains forever." This declaration culminated his story of an acquaintance who, as a young girl, almost drowned but recovered, and recollected that when near-death, "she saw in a moment her whole life, in its minutest incidents, arrayed before her simultaneously as in a mirror; and she had a faculty developed as suddenly for comprehending the whole and every part."[27] This idea of having one's life flash before one's eyes became a piece of conventional lore in Western culture in the nineteenth century.

So too did the notion that the mind retains everything in crystal-clear visions that could be recovered using special techniques. E. S. Dallas and William B. Carpenter each invoked photography to describe this retention. "Absolute as a photograph, the mind refuses nought. An impression once made upon the sense, even unwittingly, abides for evermore," wrote Dallas in *The Gay Science*.[28] Likewise, in *Principles of Mental Physiology* (1874), Carpenter claimed that memories could be "revived again in full vividness under certain special conditions,—just as the invisible impression left upon the sensitive paper of the Photographer, is developed into a picture by the application of particular chemical re-agents."[29] As discussed in chapter 3, Wilkie Collins's *The Moonstone* (1868) developed a plot on this model of visual repetition: under the "certain special conditions" re-created by the psychologist Ezra Jennings, Franklin Blake is able to reenact his apparent theft of the diamond for others' viewing, if not his own memory. For all of these writers, the past inhered in images that could be restored by metaphorical technologies. Du Maurier's true dreaming goes further than these writers: Visual memories are far more available than only at the point of death. They can be lucidly re-created—not just visually, but with sound, feeling, smell, and lifelike scale and verisimilitude, on demand. In this fantasy, all of life's perceptions and experiences, and the facts to be drawn from them, create an archive of information from which the living mind can constantly draw. The personal mastery Du Maurier imagines is tremendous: If the review of life events offered the solace of insight just before life ends, "dreaming true" suggested that such insight into the meaning of one's life could be constantly available.

Du Maurier's concept of dreaming true also builds on nineteenth-century theories of ordinary dreaming and practices of its lucid control.[30] Dreams had fascinated Romantic writers, only to be dismissed by positivist thinkers as meaningless brain activity; hence the significant late-century writers on dreams tended to be belated Romantics who in turn influenced Freud and Carl Jung. "Dreaming true" resembles lucid dreaming, in which dreamers can control the images and sensations of the dream. Significantly, nineteenth-century dream research also suggested an overlap between dream images and memories, a key aspect of the novel. In his influential *Philosophy of Sleep* (1830), Robert Macnish had declared, "I believe that dreams are uniformly the resuscitation or re-embodiment of thoughts which have formerly, in some shape or another, occupied the mind. They are old ideas revived either in an entire state, or heterogeneously mingled together."[31] Henry Holland wrote that vague impressions that cannot be assigned to specific memories "are not improbably the shades of former dreams."[32] This was also the conviction of Alfred Maury in *Sleep and Dreams* (1861).[33] In these contexts of nineteenth-century theories of dreaming, *Peter Ibbetson* emerges as a fantasy of lucidly controlling one's own memories through the technical mastery of one's dreaming mind. The practice resembled a kind of personal consumerism. The psychologist James Sully characterized dreaming as absorptive entertainment, "a more perfect state of illusion than when we half lose ourselves over a novel or before the stage of a theatre"; he described dreaming as a "nocturnal phantasmagoria" to which one could "repai[r] . . . as a source of preternatural delight."[34] Du Maurier develops this model, imagining a habitual recourse to visions of the past as an entertainment technology producing exquisite imagery.

In his book *Dreams and the Means to Direct Them* (1867), Marquis Hervey de Saint-Denys described thirty years of his increasing prowess at mastering his dreams until he is able to direct them completely. Henri Ellenberger proposes Hervey de Saint-Denys's text as an inspiration for *Peter Ibbetson*, whose protagonist similarly must practice the technique to master it, and the connections between the two books are suggestive.[35] Like Saint-Denys, Peter spends thirty years practicing the techniques of dreaming true—or as Saint-Denys puts it, "pure dreaming," in which external factors such as one's digestion and temperature have no relevance.[36] Saint-Denys also describes viewing an album of watercolors and gouaches with crystalline clarity, which may have inspired the virtual art gallery Peter visits; and like Du Maurier, Saint-Denys uses photographic metaphors to describe the mind's storage of images. The most salient resemblance, however, is both books' emphasis that dreams are memories. For Saint-Denys, dreams of people we have not met, or places we have not visited, are merely memories, for example of artworks, which the imagination has distorted. Our memories are populated by direct and mediated experience:

> The people we meet, the surroundings we live in, the shows we see, the paintings and albums we look at and even the books we read—all provide a multiplicity of images which are stored away in our memories. In a dream, what was originally the work of an artist may take on the solidity and appearance of reality, so that we effectively dream of imaginary people. (27)

The imagination works over memories of all experience, both direct and mediated, reproducing them as dreams. Moreover, we can control our dreams: Saint-Denys's answer to the question, "Does sleep take away free will?" is no: One can master one's dreams, so that "the same phenomenon that sometimes forces us to experience distressing visions under other circumstances enables us to dream the fulfillment of desires" (163). Saint-Denys's Romantic blend of art, dream, memory, and imagination likely appealed to Du Maurier, but the most attractive theme of his book, replicated in *Peter Ibbetson*, was surely satisfaction of desire through controlled dreaming.

Peter Ibbetson takes not only imagery but sound as the crux of mental control and mastery. Peter's total recall of music prefigures his total recall of experience. Du Maurier, riffing on Carpenter's well-known concept of "unconscious cerebration," or cognition below the threshold of consciousness, calls it "unconscious musical cerebration": "I am never without some tune running in my head—never for a moment; not that I am always aware of it; existence would be insupportable if I were" (1:109). The idea of music replaying constantly in "some useless corner [of the brain] full of cobwebs and lumber" furthers the notion of the brain as media storage (1:110). It also resembles the contemporary concept of an earworm, a tune stuck in one's head; Mark Twain described the misery of such an obsession in his essay "A Literary Nightmare" (1876). In that story, "a relentless jingle" takes "instant and entire possession" of the narrator for days, until he manages to foist it off on a companion. Written one year before Thomas Edison revealed the phonograph, "A Literary Nightmare," as its title suggested, is keyed instead to print. The narrator catches the virus from the newspaper; and though he warns his readers to avoid it, he also begins his story by quoting it.[37] Before the era of recorded music, the catchy tune replayed to the point of mental nausea is a minor pathology of mass print, especially when its consumption goes awry, spoiling one's pleasure. Written after the phonograph appeared, *Peter Ibbetson* omits the print dimension. Yet Peter still catches earworms: When he wants to recite poems by Alfred, Lord Tennyson and William Cullen Bryant to himself, "all the while, between the lines, this fiend of a subcerebral vocalist, like a wandering minstrel in a distant square, insists on singing, 'Cheer, Boys, Cheer,' or 'Tommy, make room for your uncle' (tunes I cannot abide)" (1:110). Fortunately for Peter, he possesses a degree of mastery over these intrusive popular songs and is able to smother them by whistling other melodies in other keys. He can also compel "this never still small voice" of "ghostly music" to imitate other singers (1:111). Like a dream, the tune shifts mercurially: "Now it is one tune, now another; now a song *without* words, now *with*; sometimes it is near the surface . . . sometimes to make sure it is there I have to dive for it deep into myself, and I never fail to find it after a while, and bring it to the top" (1:110). Peter's lucid ability to control these interior recordings suggests a level of psychic mastery of his brain's archive of music. Moreover, his psychic space is imagined as uniformly filled with music. Du Maurier uses a depth-surface model, but the deeps are not more fraught than the shallows. His mastery helps him control the influx of auditory stimulation: He can drown out "Cheer, Boys, Cheer" with "J'ai du Bon Tabac."

Because repetition is the formal fabric of music, the ability to repeat music itself takes on a special kind of status and mastery in Du Maurier's conceit of true dreaming. Repeating music certainly becomes the figurative fulcrum between the experience of reality and mediated consumption in the novel. Du Maurier dwells on the dreamers' enraptured acts of listening. Since the duchess is an avid concertgoer, keen to bring such experiences to the imprisoned Peter, the duo drive "to an exquisite garden concert in Dresden, or . . . ro[w] in a gondola to a Saturday Pop at St. James's Hall" (2:119). Peter's chief pleasure is to "rehear it together, again and again, and da capo" (2:123). Daniel Cavicchi has described how such a desire to hear music led to its mass institutionalization and commodification throughout the second half of the nineteenth century.[38] Peter and the duchess exemplify the next phase of such a burgeoning longing, since they replay the live performances, "encor[ing] any particular thing that pleases them" (2:123). In this way, "dreaming true" turns live music into a kind of occultly recorded music. Addressing renowned singers such as Clara Schumann and Piatti—"all of whom I know so well, but have never heard with the fleshly ear!" Peter taunts them: "How we have made you, all unconscious, repeat the same movements over and over again, without ever from you a sign of impatience or fatigue!" (2:124). Such control resembles Svengali's technique with Trilby. Trilby's body is, as Fiona Coll has said, a human singing machine, and thus marked by gender, sexual transgression, and compelled labor.[39] Such fault lines are less evident in *Peter Ibbet-*

son, which presents listening as repeated bouts of media consumption that abstract and dematerialize the commodity, as if music required no laboring bodies. Indeed, the only body parts of interest are the dreamers' hungry ears: "It was for music we cared the most, and I think I may say that of music during those three years (and ever after) we have had our glut" (2:123). The novel's depiction of excessive, absorptive listening models a new kind of consumption for its readers—one that relies on technologized repetition beyond the point of satiety. Before *Trilby* gave readers a stylish female icon of musical spectacle, *Peter Ibbetson* offered them a dream of aural desire that seemed tantalizingly realizable.

Such gorging on music suggests a new mode of endless listening that constantly gratifies hearers' demands; but Du Maurier had already featured the idea in his cartoons. In 1877, he had drawn two, one that represented music stored like wine in a cellar, with the names of famous singers such as Nilsson, Patti, and Trebelli as labels; another, that depicted a hostess instructing her servant to turn on music stored on tap for the evening's entertainment.

Commercial telephones had appeared in the 1880s; before the telephone became used for point-to-point communication, it was briefly used to broadcast music.[40] The caption of the first cartoon explains that by telephone, sound is converted into electricity and brought out in wine bottles for parties. Du Maurier is engaging the popular imagination of electricity as a cheap thrill akin to drunkenness, as seen in descriptions of accidental shocks as delivering the sensations of ether or chloroform, or the brief fad of the "electrical cocktail" in which electricity was used to burn sugar.[41] But to this association he adds music, so that the image suggests the pleasure and delirious transport of its sociable consumption. The fantasy of storing music as electric wine means that music itself may be intoxicating, but its repeatability certainly is. Always accessible, it can be shared as the perfect complement to a dinner party. In the second cartoon, the lady of the house consults a concert schedule in the newspaper, instructing her servant boy to turn on musical taps at different times during the evening's festivities, and warning him to turn off one tap before turning on another, to avoid the cacophony of overlapping songs. Novel and cartoons celebrate a technological triumph over music's temporality by imagining the mastery of sound archivization; this storage of experience permits it to be pleasurably reactivated as a sociable mode of consumption. Media consumption and sociability enhance each other, producing Du Maurier's distinctively convivial ethos. Here we can refine the imprecise claim that Du Maurier was thoroughly opposed to Aestheticism: He shared its ideals and only

BY THE TELEPHONE SOUND IS CONVERTED INTO ELECTRICITY, AND THEN, BY COMPLETING
THE CIRCUIT, BACK INTO SOUND AGAIN.   JONES CONVERTS ALL THE PRETTY MUSIC HE
HEARS DURING THE SEASON INTO ELECTRICITY, BOTTLES IT, AND PUTS IT AWAY INTO BINS
FOR HIS WINTER PARTIES.   ALL HE HAS TO DO, WHEN HIS GUESTS ARRIVE, IS TO SELECT,
UNCORK, AND THEN COMPLETE THE CIRCUIT ; AND THERE YOU ARE !

Figure 12. Detail of "The Telephone." *Punch*, December 14, 1877.

disdained what he regarded as its public posturing.[42] The conceit of
psychically replayable music is a solution to Walter Pater's notion of the
awful brevity of existence and the consequent priority of "getting as many
pulsations as possible into the given time."[43] Like Pater, Du Maurier idealized music and theorized its ephemerality, although his musings took
the route of cartoon speculation rather than academic philosophy.

Du Maurier's fantasies of archiving and playing back music were timely:
Edison's phonograph had appeared in 1877, the year of his cartoons; and

Peter Ibbetson was published between Emile Berliner's revelation of the gramophone in 1888 and his marketing of it in 1895. The phonograph recorded sounds onto tinfoil sheets on cylinders rotating on a spindle; the gramophone, onto flat disks rotating horizontally, with the sound emerging from a curved bell. In the social history of recorded sound, the phonograph is also associated with do-it-yourself home recordings, the gramophone, with the commercial sale of prerecorded music discs. The phonograph had memorial functions: Families could record their loved ones' voices and play them back after their deaths. Though it is less discussed, they also had a creative function. In Du Maurier's novel, Peter's inner musical voice "would warble little impromptu inward melodies of my own composition, which often seemed to me extremely pretty, old-fashioned, and quaint; but . . . I had not the means of recording them, as I had never learned the musical notes. What the world has lost!" (1:111). The phonograph could record such compositions even if the composer lacked musical literacy. Like the mind, it could capture every sound; unlike the mind, it could presumably play them all back on demand. John Picker observes that "unlike the telegraph and telephone, the phonograph was specifically designed for archival purposes and also ultimately to function without a specially trained and designated operator."[44] Its original scenes were private, domestic ones of amateur production; it afforded homemade media similar to Victorian scrapbooks, albums, and crafts. As Jonathan Sterne contends, the transition from phonograph to gramophone indexed a shift away from Victorian parlor life and toward consumerist culture; away from homemade objects toward mass-produced ones; and away from the insular family sphere toward public connectedness.[45] Du Maurier's cartoons, and the representations of "unconscious musical cerebration" and "dreaming true" in *Peter Ibbetson*, help effect this shift. Using their mental technology, Peter and the duchess act like early record collectors, curating, organizing, and revisiting their musical experiences with gusto. Their mastery is of their own minds, but also of the new mass culture of music.

Reproduced singers' and speakers' voices were more abstract than living ones, yet more embodied than printed song lyrics and reported speech.[46] In the 1890s, they inhabited the uncanny realm of a new medium that inevitably drew comparison with the mass print that had elicited the desire for closer representations of human performances. In *Peter Ibbetson*, Peter and the duchess's pleasure in listening to their mental records captured a precise historical moment, at the end of a Victorian era of live musical performance and printed sheet music and lyrics, and on the cusp of the twentieth-century music industry. The end of the era of music's fundamental ephemerality meant that listeners would no longer require an organic memory for it. "Dreaming true" simultaneously signifies such lost nineteenth-century mental skills of complex recall and imagines a future in which musical memory is exteriorized—not in the phonograph, but in its fictional and esoteric analogue, the technology of clairvoyant relations.

Surmounting Shock, Achieving Presence

The stakes of *Peter Ibbetson* are higher than just reflecting the incorporation of new consumer technologies into everyday bourgeois life. The incessant consumerism, especially while sleeping, fundamentally alters the nature of memory and experience. The novel tills the psychic soil that fertilizes the desire to replay—and indeed, to relive—one's past; and because this aspect of the novel was so beloved, it suggests that Du Maurier was gratifying a cultural demand. The long opening chapter, a lyrical love letter to Paris, has been judged Du Maurier's most effective writing, "*caviare*" to the masses who glutted themselves on *Trilby*.[47] In a familiar cultural narrative, artists, cosmopolites, and intellectuals arrive in Paris as young adults, but Du Maurier's exquisite love for the city kindled at the tender age of seven, when his family moved there from Boulogne. Paris seized his young imagination so fiercely that the memories poured out of him when he began writing novels in his mid-fifties. Drawing on his childhood memories of Passy, it offers a sensual feast of sound ("the clanging chimes, the itinerant street cries, the tinkle of the *marchand de coco*"), vision ("innumerable distant windows reflected the blood-red western flame" of sunset), and olfaction ("it required a nose both subtle and unprejudiced to understand and appreciate and thoroughly enjoy that Paris") (1:64–66). A tiny flaneur, Peter glories in his rambles: "It is something to have roamed over [Paris] as a small boy . . . curious, inquisitive, indefatigable; full of imagination; all his senses keen with the keenness that belongs to the morning of life" (1:66). Crucially, the field of these sensory explorations is old Paris—"not the Paris of M. le Baron Haussmann, lighted by gas and electricity, and flushed and drained by modern science" (1:66). Haussmann redesigned Paris with long boulevards that accentuated perspective, but Peter worships "pathetic little tumble-down houses, all out of drawing and perspective, nestled like old spiders' webs" (1:61). Like Du Maurier, Peter passes a miserable interlude in London, where the streets of "desolating straightness" resemble Haussmann's boulevards, limiting Peter's adventures by leading only "to a dreary square and back again, and nowhere else for me" (1:9). By contrast, Paris of the early 1840s highlights the exuberance and spontaneity of a perception that brims within its dynamic architectural, geographical, and social forms. This quivering vitality finds its opposite in the cadaverously straight lines of modernized Paris and its counterpart, London.

Elaborating on his own sad year studying and practicing chemistry in Pentonville, Du Maurier exiles Peter to England, where existential loneliness pushes him to suicidal contemplation. Longing for Paris, and for female companionship, and yet soured on himself and all those around him, Peter trudges the streets: "I loathed the very sight of myself in the shop windows as I went by; and yet I always looked for it there, in the forlorn hope of at least finding some alteration, even for the worse. I passionately longed to be somebody else; and yet I had never met anybody else I could have borne to be for a moment" (1:142). He is viewing his reflection in the glass, and yet this enduring urban experience also suggests the search for personal identity within mass consumer culture. He tries to escape in books and in sleep, but nothing avails. When Peter returns to Paris, he almost begins to feel happiness again—but is startled out of his dawning delight by the sight of his beloved Bois de Boulogne. As a child, he had spent hours in this enchanted wood, "a very wilderness of delight ... where beautiful Nature had reasserted her own sweet will, and massed and tangled everything together as though a Beauty had been sleeping there undisturbed for close on a hundred years" (1:17–19). Now, this fairy-tale forest had been "cut up, demolished, all parceled out into small gardens, with trim white villas, except where a railway ran through a deep cutting in the chalk" (1:200). Louis Napoleon, admiring Hyde Park, had directed Haussmann to convert the Bois de Boulogne into a similarly ordered public space in 1852. A railway, later destroyed in the Siege of Paris, had been installed, and a train suddenly materializes Peter's crushing realization: "A train actually roared and panted by, and choked me with its filthy steam. ... If that train had run over me and I had survived it, it could not have given me a greater shock" (1:200). The roar, choke, and blow represent the physical disorientations of Haussmannization, and nineteenth-century urban development more generally. The forces of modernization hack through tree and rock, slicing the natural landscape into units for sale. The train, that iconic symbol of mechanized life, infects Peter with its diseased respiration.[48] Even the human inhabitants resemble automatons: Children are "on their best behavior, discreetly throwing crumbs to the fish" (1:206). The occupants of modernized Paris are straight, narrow, and in perfect perspective, in keeping with their bourgeois manners and privilege. A new model of French citizenry, they contrast with Peter's shabbier English rowdiness. Occurring at the mid-point of the novel, this moment of shock reveals the crux of *Peter Ibbetson* to be a visceral confrontation with and rejection of Haussmann's Paris. Du Maurier's unique solution, "dreaming true," requires him to redefine memory itself.

Peter's agonizing desires to cure his malaise and reexperience his happy childhood with Mimsey in pre-Imperial Paris inspires the novel's esoteric media technology, which cures the deficiencies of human memory. Sitting and seething in the sterile new park, Peter discovers the limits of desire and will, which cannot erase the passage of time and the material changes to the Bois de Boulogne. In the novel's most important passage, the realization of these limits leads him to reimagine the nature of memory:

> Oh, surely, surely, I cried to myself, we ought to find some means of possessing the past more fully and completely than we do. . . . Memory is but a poor, rudimentary thing that we had better be without, if it can only lead us to the verge of consummation like this, and madden us with a desire it cannot slake. The touch of a vanished hand, the sound of a voice that is still, the tender grace of a day that is dead, should be ours forever, at our beck and call, by some exquisite and quite conceivable illusion of the senses. (1:207)

No longer mere mental recollection, memory becomes instead a failed materialization of the past. Rather than depending on temporal change, it is vanquished by it. Since memory cannot defy the changes wrought by time, Peter, along with his creator Du Maurier, proposes abandoning it altogether. Playback should be available for experience in its totality. The failure of ordinary memory to make the past present can be corrected by new forms of visual and aural media: finely produced sensual mirages that Peter—and Du Maurier—found quite imaginable. They correspond to a cultural fantasy associated with the Victorian novel's early response to the phonograph, "of perfectly capturing, representing, and *writing* the human voice."[49] Du Maurier's enthusiasm for the technologized archivization of sensual experience aligns him with this historical formation. Rather than identifying media consumption's complicity in the acceleration of modern temporality and the fragmentation of experience, the novel alights upon it as the solution to the eternal problem of the brevity and finality of experience, as described by Pater and numerous others.

An unacknowledged trade-off attended this solution: the thinning of experience into simulation. Its replayability meant that it could be mastered rather than endured, suffered, or just lived. Peter becomes impervious to that great nineteenth-century psychic menace, shock, but his memory, as information storage, also becomes overorganized and sterile. Before he learns how to dream true, Peter experiences shock, first, as he surveys Haussmann's destruction of the Bois de Boulogne, and second, when he discovers that his vile Uncle Ibbetson had raped Peter's mother, and is actually his father. The novel exposes him to such shocks in order to motivate the clairvoyant cure. Imprisoned for justifiably killing his evil uncle, Peter achieves such proficiency in true dreaming that he can access memories before they are even formed. Returning to an evening in the drawing room when his childhood self "was absorbed in his book," Peter listens to his parents' conversation, and learns that his uncle had also caused his father's financial ruin: "Every word that had passed through Gogo's inattentive ears and his otherwise preoccupied little brain and been recorded there as in a phonograph, and was now repeated over and over again for Peter Ibbetson, as he sat unnoticed among them" (2:58). The child's aural perception can be replayed later, when the adult Peter can recognize the value of the secret that has been belatedly overheard. Accordingly, no shock attends the revelation, either in the past or in the present. As a consequence of selective memory, experience and history become dubious categories; as Bernard Stiegler enigmatically writes of such industrial-era, mediated memory, "What takes place only takes place in not quite actually taking place."[50] These radical revisions also expose the disunity of Peter's character. Referring to himself in the third person, using his convenient childhood nickname Gogo, he displays his psychic fragmentation, a consequence of never being fully present.

On the one hand, the novel's conceit of the repeatability of experience updates the rigorously organized, instrumentalized model of memory that Nicholas Dames finds in popular midcentury fictional autobiographies such as Charles Dickens's *David Copperfield* (1850) and W. M. Thackeray's *Pendennis* (1850). On the other, by dwelling so lavishly on the details of the protagonist's past, the novel resembles the modernist version of aleatory memory exemplified by Marcel Proust's *mémoire involontaire* in *Remembrance of Things Past* (1913–27). In *Amnesiac Selves*, Dames demonstrates how midcentury fictional autobiographies represent memory as consolidating a static self through a repetitive habituation to experience, forcing a revision of the concept of self-development central to the bildungsroman.[51] For example, in *Pendennis* memory renders the self so immutable that no experience can alter it. *Peter Ibbetson* intensifies this formation. It suggests that this ordinary midcentury configuration of experience, memory, and self has become so attenuated by the 1890s that it requires facilitation by an outlandish plot of occult media prostheses. Yet the very techniques of figurative media consumption deployed to shore up a psychically disaggregated self warp and limit it instead: Peter endlessly repeats his own childhood, and lives Mimsey's life, rather than his own adulthood. Memory is so organized and repetitive that it eliminates spontaneity and organic growth. In tension with this instrumental model of memory are the novel's evident similarities to Proust's *mémoire involontaire*, "the immense edifice of memory" that lies dormant, and is reactivated in the present.[52] Peter's quaint Parisian childhood, with its wealth of sensual and perceptive detail—his mother's physical presence, the little wheelbarrow in his garden, his dog Médor, his illustrations of Byron's poems—resembles the de-plotted, sensually vivid texture of *Remembrance of Things Past*. Sara Danius reframes Proust's writing as a document of the new perceptions and sensations brought about by novel technologies such as the telephone and the cinema—a reorientation that brings his work into dialogue with *Peter Ibbetson*.[53] Thus *Peter Ibbetson* amazingly resembles novels as disparate as *Swann's Way* (1913) and *David Copperfield*. It does so by producing the illusion of richly sensual, immediate experience, but never letting it change a self who is only ever half-present at its coordinates. As an appeal to the cultural middle that stylizes technology, *Peter Ibbetson* occupies an intriguing place in literary history.

A critical difference between Du Maurier and Proust clarifies *Peter Ibbetson*'s specific response to industrial-era memory. In Proust's work, the wealth of remembered detail cannot be precisely controlled because it arises unpredictably, through the body and from the unconscious. By contrast, in Du Maurier's novel, Peter's reactivation of the past does not happen randomly, prompted by a trivial sensual act such as tasting a madeleine; it is rather a stop on an itinerary and the result of a craft. Benjamin posited a dialectical relationship between the auratic experiences of *mémoire involontaire* and the technological retraining of the human sensorium by media such as photography.[54] By making experience something to be replayed and mastered, Du Maurier offers an antidote to Benjamin's complaint that experience atrophies with the consumption of modern information media such as the newspaper and under the industrial regime of shock. Benjamin laments that the self's deep or long experience (*erfahrung*) cannot be reconciled with the fluctuating value of constantly expiring information. The plot of *Peter Ibbetson* resolves this conflict by converting experience into information and endlessly producing it. The narrative of dreaming true becomes a chronicle of replayed events and lists of musical performances and paintings, for example, as Peter recites the titles of paintings on view in their virtual art gallery: "Millais's 'Autumn Leaves,' his 'Youth of Sir Walter Raleigh,' his 'Chill October'; Watts's 'Endymion,' and 'Orpheus and Eurydice'; Burne-Jones's 'Chant d'Amour,' and his 'Laus Veneris'" (2:126). As the narration gives itself over to these lists, it becomes a consumer media guide, imparting cultural information to readers; at the same time, it creates the effect of a whirl of events as the dreamers consume and re-consume the entire catalogue. The effect is of hyperactivity and immediacy, as if the dreamers have been listening, viewing, eating, and traveling in fast-forward. Such an antic, disembodied self can dodge the shocks of modern life that Benjamin laments.

True dreaming does not insulate Peter from shock; rather, it obviates all need for insulation. For example, because the discovery of Uncle Ibbetson's swindling his family is never experienced directly, it requires no soothing; it has simply and seamlessly been assimilated by Peter as information-processing machine. Thus the novel models true dreaming not as an exploration of the unconscious understood as a region of deep subjectivity, but as a method for compartmentalizing, indexing, and reproducing experience that is already mediated, consumable information. We saw the beginnings of this model of the unconscious as information storage in chapter 2, in Collins's *The Moonstone*. When Franklin Blake discovers his name inked on a paint-smeared nightgown, evidence suggesting that he is the diamond thief, he receives a shock—but it is more of a narrative surprise than an affective jolt. Collins's characterization in that novel is self-consciously flat; he deliberately positions Blake as a hero without psychic depth. The nascent genre of long-form serial detective fiction, with its emphasis on narrative propulsion and the hermeneutics of suspicion, demanded the constant collection and comparison of information, precluding affectively rich moral transformation. Without the same generic and narrative pressure, Du Maurier creates similarly simple characters, as a fantasy of a self so busy bodilessly consuming—media, information, his own past—that he becomes impervious not only to shock but to most affect.

As I show in the following chapter, *Peter Ibbetson* shares a preoccupation with the psychological effects of mass media consumption with its contemporary, Oscar Wilde's *The Picture of Dorian Gray* (1891), a novel that also depicts a subjectivity thinned out by its attempt to accumulate, archive, and master experience. As I argue there, Dorian's predicament is that of the media consumer of the 1890s, attempting to fashion himself from the available mass media types. He becomes entranced by Lord Henry's book, recognizing himself in its pages. And he actively engages in remaking it, decorating it in covers of different colors. In the infamous chapter 11,

Dorian further experiments with taste and style, and although his enthusiasms are drawn from classical history and high art, they are crucially mediated through middlebrow print culture. Wilde recycled some of those long descriptions, for example of lace and perfumes, from pieces he wrote or edited for *Woman's World*, and they mimic the new forms and genres of lifestyle and feature journalism. Although Dorian experiments with the more porous, intersubjective self associated with mass culture, he ultimately retreats into an older, aristocratic model of personhood linked to elite rather than mass or middlebrow art. In that ultimately fatal, historically vanishing mode, he refuses to allow Basil to exhibit the painting, effectively censoring it by preventing its circulation. Far from simplistically suggesting that mass cultural consumption generates thin subjectivity, Wilde makes the counterintuitive argument, that the elite, privileged subjectivity associated with artistic patronage and highly controlled curation, is the flatter model of personhood that experiences a far smaller range and depth of affect. The crux of the novel, the notorious chapter 11, derives its density and opacity from its task of mediating between the two models of mass and elite cultural consumption. Playing the role of the cultural historian, Wilde writes this chapter to document a shift between two epochs and their psychological effects. His long, Decadent lists of Dorian's sensual consumer activities are meant to induce the accompanying affects of pleasure, nausea, stimulation, and boredom in the novel's readers. By contrast, Du Maurier's long lists—such as the one that forms the epigraph to this chapter—lack such complex motivation. Instead, they are meant lightheartedly to raise readers' taste levels. The souvenir industry associated with *Trilby*—all the shoes, hats, and ice cream—proceeds straightforwardly from the enthusiasm for consumption depicted all across Du Maurier's oeuvre, including *Peter Ibbetson*.

Wilde's novel demonstrates that media consumption can either open the self to the mass or insulate it from others; Du Maurier's suggests that the fantasy self that can replay its experiences requires no insulation at all. The lack of a need for insulation permits us to pause and readjust a common conceptualization of all media consumption as buffer, solacer, or narcotic—a poor substitute for experiences thought to be more sensual, direct, and real. In twentieth-century media theory, this notion can be traced to Marshall McLuhan's quasi-phenomenological observation that "we have to numb our central nervous system when it is extended and exposed, or we will die."[55] Susan Buck-Morss elaborates McLuhan's sketch, claiming that the phantasmagoric, synaesthetic system of distraction, having overexposed the human organism, goes into an anaesthetic mode: "Its goal is to *numb* the organism, to deaden the senses, to repress memory."[56] Such formulations have the disadvantage of universalizing the human body and its sense perceptions as the origin of their media theories, a strategy that ignores the politics of embodiment. Moreover, media only figuratively and phantasmatically extend the human senses. By focusing on the discourse as a historical phenomenon—of which *Peter Ibbetson* is a part—we discover that such extension does not require numbing, because the fantasy itself is conditioned by disembodiment. Peter's sleeping body remains inert throughout the dreaming-true portion of the novel; he and the duchess travel only in their minds. Because such dreams dispense with the body, they also erase the unconscious. Benjamin had cited Freud's *Beyond the Pleasure Principle* (1920) for its theorization of consciousness as the protective, insulating destruction of painful memory traces, rather than their preservation.[57] But where experience has converged with information, memory has become selective and mediatized, and human bodies have become media appendages, there is no unconscious. In contrast to Freud's *The Interpretation of Dreams* (1899), which figured dreams as censored material that consciousness had unwittingly permitted to surface, in *Peter Ibbetson*, Du Maurier imagined them as consciously directed pseudo-experiences. In Peter's psyche, there is no repression. Since he is using his sleeping hours to revisit his past, he lacks the psychic space and time for an unconscious.

The novel thus diverges precipitously from the parallel paths scholars have traced of nineteenth-century novels and Freudian psychoanalysis.[58] Along with *The Moonstone*, *Peter Ibbetson* suggests a counter-aesthetic and an accompanying alternative psychological model that will develop in twentieth-century speculative fiction and discourses that regard the mind as a computer designed for information storage. Peter's disembodied media consumption anticipates subsequent cultural fantasies of "becoming media" by shedding the body and freeing the mind to interact directly with information technologies. This fantasy of physical transcendence perpetuates the paradox of presence that I described at the outset of this chapter: as "extensions of man," to use McLuhan's phrase, media promise to achieve presence despite immutable conditions such as the passage of time, death of loved ones, and so on; but because media are not fully part of the human organism, presence remains an effect rather than a reality.[59] *Peter Ibbetson* pinpoints an iteration of this abiding fantasy specific to the 1890s. Its belated Romanticism proposes dreaming, an irrational state of mind, as the platform for the more Victorian, rationalist, intellectual values of archiving, collecting, and curating—activities by which one attempts to master time and space.

The narrative also clearly belongs to a post-Darwinian moment: Du Maurier has Peter express shockingly atheistic ideas, tempered by Madge Plunkett's judicious editing; yet he also leaves open the possibility of an afterlife when Mimsey returns to speak to Peter after her death. In the realm she now inhabits, her transcendent body heightens and unifies all sense perception; compared to this state of being, human eyes seem like pathetic "little bags of water"; humans "can't even smell straight" (2:203–4). Moreover, "Nothing is lost—nothing! From the ineffable, high, fleeting thought a Shakespeare can't find words to express, to the slightest sensation of an earthworm—nothing!" (2:209). Echoing the model of the mind as storage device, the universe records all events of all life; moreover, it joins them in a metaphysical presence that forms a secular, Romantic version of a Christian heaven. In this way, Du Maurier stages the ultimate bodiless fantasy of no mediation at all. In the 1890s, mass print culture was intensifying and expanding once again, but at least three generations had also already experienced what John Plunkett and Andrew King have evocatively called "being in print."[60] Innovations such as the phonograph began to push the imagination of how humans might inhabit new media. Du Maurier's cartoons, such as the ones imagining the telephone (Figure 12), and the often-discussed "Telephonoscope," actively participated in such speculation.[61] In *Peter Ibbetson*, the prosthetic media extension is so vast that the presence it is meant to effect becomes correspondingly evanescent.

This tendency takes place across Du Maurier's oeuvre: Several characters are simultaneously manically expressive and psychologically flat, such as the Laird and Taffy in *Trilby*, or Barty Josselin in *The Martian*. Once exteriorized, their feelings disappear, as if their emotions were all motion, flickering past readers in a whirl. This aesthetic logic underlies James's description of Du Maurier's fiction as having been hyperkinetically performed, while remaining essentially bodiless—in his prose, the subjects of all the dancing, joking, and smoking remain unspecified, even phantomlike. I discuss this peculiar mode of animation further below. In this glimpse of "Du Maurierness" as a media effect, we see individual psychology dispersed to a surface of social relations rather than rooting down into an individual, stratified, embodied psyche. Oddly superficial, Du Maurier's characters experience changes of mood more often than they do moral transformation. Peter's transformation is from feeling depressed to feeling euphoric.

Clear instances of this disembodied consumption animate representations of Haussmannization in all three of Du Maurier's novels. Proust's sensual, memory-laden madeleine differs significantly, for example, from the one Taffy eats when he, the Laird, and Little Billee return to Paris in midlife in *Trilby*. There, the three friends, older, wiser, and—most importantly—wealthier than in their early Bohemian days, stroll along smoking cigars and drinking rum, breathing easily in the new "atmosphere of banknotes and gold." The passage of time from Bohemia to the Second Empire is paved with pastry: "Taffy a Madeleine, the Laird a Baba, and Littlee Billee a Savarin."[62] Bodily appetites are as irrelevant here as they are to Peter's true dreaming, so no verbs are needed to describe the treats' physical consumption. Like lobster salad, "Laus Veneris," and all the other comestibles and consumables of *Peter Ibbetson*, these sweets are neither utterly random nor specifically motivated; they do not evoke unique, physically or emotionally dense memories. Though they appeared in the earlier part of the novel, they were part of the narrator's instruction in taste: "You must begin with the Madeleine, which is rich and rather heavy; then the Baba; and finish up with the Savarin, which is shaped like a ring, very light, and flavored with rum. And then you must really leave off" (58). No detailed realism or symbolism links the sweets to their different characters, and they cannot plausibly be interpreted as compensatory pleasures for the passage of time and the loss of Trilby. As literary elements, they correspond to Elaine Freedgood's metonyms that have "frozen into fetish form" and missed their metaphorical connections.[63] As a menu of confections still popular in the Second Empire, they advertise the luxurious delights of Haussmannized Paris to readers "eavesdrop[ing]" on bourgeois culture.[64] In all Du Maurier's novels, the characters' flat subjectivities clear the space for the communication of taste to readers. Joseph Bristow describes the trio's revisitation of Paris as wistful—a kind of "meandering melancholia"—but it is not traumatic.[65] For it to be truly so, the characters would have to possess the deep, differentiated subjectivities of which the body and the unconscious are constitutive parts.[66]

In each of Du Maurier's novels, the drive toward mediatization and consumerism reframes or eludes the modern shocks of Haussmannization and revolution, and it draws on early experiences consuming print. The critique of Haussmannization comes from a quasi-royalist rather than a left or Marxist standpoint. As a child Peter had enjoyed rambling through the slums and marveling at the grotesque "gutter imps," "jovial hunchbacks," and "mendicant monsters" constructed for him by the fiction and illustrations of Honoré de Balzac, Victor Hugo, and Gustav Doré (2:60–63). He also enjoyed the oral storytelling of "Major Duquesnois," one of Napoleon's inner circle who, during the July Monarchy, was on parole at a boarding house in Gogo and Mimsey's neighborhood. Duquesnois tells the children "a new fairy tale . . . every afternoon for seven years," even comically insisting that the English had lost at Waterloo (1:24). The major embodies a long and volatile swath of French history, but as Du Maurier represents it, it is not one of false starts and incomplete revolutions, but of romance, adventure, and grandfatherly intimacy—a history measured out for boyish ears. Peter's passing references to Louis Philippe suggest a reverence for the deposed king; he also dotes on the equestrian statue of Henry the Fourth, who ruled France from 1589 to 1610, and even Louis le Hutin from the early fourteenth century. Peter relishes French history as a series of delightful stories of noble people. He never aligns himself with French workers' demands because his Parisian romps kept the poor and proletarians at the distance of spectacle. As if reading "a chapter from Hugo or Dumas," he ogles "strange, delightful people in blue blouses, brown woollen tricots, wooden shoes . . . gay, fat hags, . . . precociously witty little gutter imps of either sex; and such cripples!" (1:62–63). Since French fiction guided Peter's flânerie, his Parisian rambling was already determined by bourgeois interest in the poor and disabled as grotesques. Later in the novel, when he learns to "dream true" and return to the Paris of his youth, he substitutes psychic for print technology. Dreaming true mimics his childhood reading; both are modes of media consumption. Having learned early to understand the city as a series of piquant sights, Peter never feels the solidarity that would come from engaged, embodied relationships with Parisians. Thus his outrage at the commercialization and sterilization of the Bois de Boulogne is not on behalf of any of the inhabitants, but rather at the loss of his own visual mastery, mobile freedom, and rights of occupation. Returning to Passy and finding that no one remembers him or his family, he laments, "We had left no trace. Twelve short years had effaced all memory of us!" (1:203). Peter takes Haussmann's urban planning as a personal attack. Dreaming true compensates him accordingly.

The same sensual delight and thrilling excitement graces the adult Peter and Mimsey's psychic historical tourism, undertaken when the narrative revises the rules of clairvoyance, so they can revisit their ancestors' experiences, which are stored in their own minds as "antenatal memories." These operate according to the same media fantasy as bourgeois consumption governing all of their true dreaming: "Then, presto! Changing the scene as one changes a slide in a magic-lantern, we would skip a century, and behold!" (2:166).[67] Since they are related to enough people who witnessed the Revolution, Napoleon's reign, and even the court of Louis XIV, they attend the taking of the Bastille "(several times!)" with Carlyle in hand; the sage's accuracy suffering in comparison (2:181). History becomes repeatable on demand, and improves on its print renditions. Print created the childhood demands for romance and adventure, which the mental technology of dreaming true satisfies as an adult. The past becomes available for reanimation because it never was a collective formation, but only ever existed as material for Peter's individual consumption. Peter really learned to dream true by consuming print as a child.

The Martian follows a similar strategy of sentiment and satire in its passing representation of the Revolution of 1848 and its comments on Haussmann. Du Maurier was attending boarding school at Pension Froussard between 1847 and 1851; his family moved to a less expensive neighborhood to afford his and his brother Eugene's fees.[68] Fictionalizing his schoolboy delight and terror as that of his narrator Robert Maurice, Du Maurier wrote, "One night we had to sleep on the floor for fear of stray bullets; and that was a fearful joy never to be forgotten—it almost kept us awake!"[69] Alarm over stray bullets was "a fearful joy never to be forgotten"; being frisked for cartridges was "entrancing"; and "the subtle scent of gunpowder was . . . the most suggestive smell there could be" (61). The destruction of Paris becomes a child's spectacle: "Peering out of the school-room windows at dusk, we saw great fires, three or four at a time. Suburban retreats of the over-wealthy, in full conflagration; and all day the rattle of distant musketry and the boom of cannon a long way off, near Montmartre and Montfaucon, kept us alive" (61). Protected by the royalist forces, the narrator enjoys watching Paris explode, being frisked for cartridges, and smelling gunpowder—all with a boy's lack of understanding. To balance this merriment, he briefly acknowledges the reality of dead and injured soldiers: "And then one's laugh died suddenly out, and one felt one's self face to face with the horrors that were going on" (62). In general, however, French struggles for democracy held for Robert the same charm as Major Duquesnois's embroidered histories of Napoleonic conquest did for Peter in *Peter Ibbetson*. Du Maurier represented these armed conflicts in his signature mixed idiom of fondness and mockery.

His detached pose links Du Maurier's attitude to recent French history to his direct comment on Haussmann's Paris in *The Martian*, which opens by muddling the name of the Parisian street in which Robert's school lies. "There is not much stability in such French names, I fancy; but their sound is charming, and always gives me the nostalgia of Paris—Royal Paris, Imperial Paris, Republican Paris! . . . whatever they may call it ten or twelve years hence. Paris is always Paris, and always will be, in spite of the immortal Haussmann, both for those who love it and for those who don't" (5). Du

Maurier's politic characterization of Haussmann remains inoffensive to all readers. The changeability of place-names serves not to mark specific armed political conflicts, but to cast Paris paradoxically as the space of modern change itself, and as an eternal constant. In this way, Du Maurier's text helps deterritorialize Paris, converting it from lived space into information overload: "Rondpoint de l'Avenue de St.-Cloud; or, as it is called now, Avenue du Bois de Boulogne; or, as it was called during the Second Empire, Avenue du Prince Impérial, or de l'Impératrice; I'm not sure" (5). Priscilla Parkhurst Ferguson claims that the continual changes in Parisian street names politicized everyday life, but such flux also suggested the phantasmagoria of modern consumerism, in which novelty and variety reigned.[70] By acknowledging that not everyone adores Paris, Du Maurier makes consumer taste the abiding criterion of judgment, referencing the city itself as commodity. In *The Martian*, thick layers insulate Paris from readers: not only the veils of memory of Robert's retrospective narration, but the celebration of boyhood stories, and the casual attitude to Haussmannization as the expression of Paris's modern changeability. Thus from *Peter Ibbetson* to *Trilby* to *The Martian*, a trajectory of trauma to ambivalence to caprice characterizes Du Maurier's engagement with modern Paris.

THE MAMMOTH.

Figure 13. "The Mammoth." In *Peter Ibbetson* by George Du Maurier (1891; London: Osgood, McIlvaine, 1892).

In the oddest example of the novel's consumerist flattening of history, Peter and the duchess's historical jaunts culminate with a visit to prehistory itself, when, channeling the visual memories of their distant ancestors, they glimpse a woolly mammoth. Averaged together, the perceptions of intervening generations make the sight "blurred and indistinct like a composite photograph" (2:185). Composite photography, devised by Francis Galton in the 1880s, superimposed photographic portraits onto the same plate, creating putatively natural types within various racial, criminal, and degenerate taxonomies. In Du Maurier's fanciful appropriation, bodies have been reduced to eyes and configured together as a living photographic apparatus. One of the consequences of this technologization and reduction of the body is a eugenic message: Peter warns readers not to reproduce if they are unfit. If they do, they will be reanimated in the future by ever more biologically flawed, miserable descendants. Eugenics and racism are found throughout Du Maurier's novels, from the anti-Semitism of Svengali's characterization in *Trilby* to Marta's otherworldly superiority, occultly communicated to Barty in *The Martian*; one can also see it in the Hellenic profiles and statures of his cartoon figures. In *Peter Ibbetson*, it is a consequence of Du Maurier's valorization of technologized media and its annexation of the human body: Kinship becomes a media extension of which the individual human sensorium is merely a part.[71] Moreover, this kinship is ahistorical: People are related as parts of an apparatus that can be reanimated, or switched on, at any time. Genealogy, the grounding logic of the structure, disappears. Since this mystical technology is so highly contrived and implausible, it suggests, despite itself, eugenics' status as a demented dream.

Du Maurier rewrites French revolutionary history, as well as natural history, to make it a dreamlike simulation, consumed by beguiled media spectators rather than agents of history. This phenomenon resembles Thomas Richards's account of the way Queen Victoria's Golden Jubilee kitsch commodified and thus trivialized collective life by making commodities into "the validated repository of historical memory."[72] In Du Maurier's fictional world of disembodied, psychologically shallow characters, history cannot be the collective, physical action of revolution, only visual content for consumption. However, the inability to participate in monumental history is also a condition of modernity, even for psychically embodied, whole people and their literary analogues.

Having offered a critical reading that exposes the losses incurred in Du Maurier's fantasy of disembodied, technologically assisted consumption, I would like to suggest its reparative side through a closer engagement with the experience of mass culture that he represents. Du Maurier's literary and visual production also depicts and fulfills desires for more intensive sociability, conviviality, and belonging—that characteristic immediacy of "Du Maurierness,"—which compensates for the other apparent losses of modernity. By the extension of the self into mass media networks of print and clairvoyant dreams as a social world, the consumer activates a broad, if thin, network of relations and the cultural information that forms its currency. The cartoon was the aesthetic form that best conveyed this cultural turn.

Cartoons, Immediacy, and "Du Maurierness"

When all of experience is a beautiful dream, lucidly controlled, archived, and repeated at will, when people experience only with eyes and ears, and without the rest of their bodies, when memories assume the character of information and thus become transferrable to others, then the nature of social experience changes too. Rather than being composed of events at which multiple people are fully present and spontaneously engaged in mutual activities without predictable outcomes, it becomes the consumption and reproduction of information-bearing images—the exchange of social information. Paradoxically, however, this highly mediated experience has the air of immediacy: the lack of mediation and the quick spontaneity of social closeness. The cartoon as aesthetic and social form coalesces the immediacy of "Du Maurierness" and the lived realities of mass culture.

The happenstance of physical infirmity turned Du Maurier from the old medium of painting to the new print media of illustration and cartooning. His understanding of and talent for visual and textual modes of mass print began forming when partial blindness forced him to give up painting.[73] He became an illustrator, furnishing imagery for Elizabeth Gaskell's *Cranford* (1864), Mary Elizabeth Braddon's *Lady Audley's Secret* (1866), Wilkie Collins's *The Moonstone* (1868), and Thomas Hardy's *A Laodicean* (1881), among others. From illustration, he came to cartooning. Perhaps, within an all-powerful visual modernity, being blind in one eye suited him to a medium not dominated by verisimilitude and detail, a medium of bold, swift strokes and quick observations made to elicit laughs and be forgotten. Illustration, conceived of as giving life and motion to people trapped within lines of text, helped him develop animatedness as his affective and aesthetic mode—one key to cartoons. Sianne Ngai has described animatedness as "one of the most basic ways in which affect becomes socially recognizable in the age of mechanical reproducibility"; it is the most "minimal of all affective conditions: that of being, in one way or another, 'moved.'"[74] Du Maurier's friend and obituary writer Henry James described this manic quality, which he saw in the form of Du Maurier's novels; it was "almost anything, almost everything but a written one. I remember having encountered occasion to speak of it in another place as talked, rather, and sung, joked and smoked, eaten and drunk, dressed and undressed, danced and boxed, loved and loathed, and as a result of all this, in relation to the matter, made abnormally, triumphantly expressive."[75] James was getting at the illusion of liveness developing in the mass print culture of the 1890s, and of which Du Maurier, as cartoonist and illustrator, was already a master. David Kunzle, who disdains the English style of humorous illustration compared to the rapid quality of continental caricature, notes Du Maurier's flirtation with the genre, its "sketch-like thinking," and its resemblance to modern comic strips.[76]

Indeed, Du Maurier's novels can be seen as extended cartoons, with their brief, caption-like sentences and paragraphs, characters who are more social types than individuals, visual tableaux, and illustrations. In addition to sketchlike characterization, Du Maurier also relied on caricature, including racism, in cases such as Svengali from *Trilby*. In *Social and Pictorial Satire* (1898), his posthumously published review of his forebears at *Punch*, John Leech and Charles Keene, Du Maurier championed cartoons as "little pictures in black and white, of little every-day people like ourselves, by some great little artist who knows life well"; these cartoons "can be taken up and thrown down like the book or newspaper."[77] Here, Du Maurier adds a sense of exclusive intimacy—"like ourselves"—to Charles Baudelaire's declaration of the ephemeral modernity of beauty in Constantin Guys's sketches of Parisian types.[78] Du Maurier's cartooning career spanned the shift from wood-block engraving to pen and ink drawing, but the new mode retained the same boldness of line, impression of speed, and quick delivery of the human figure as type. Like Guys's, Du Maurier's rendering of the fashions, morals, and feelings of the present for a wide audience was a classed transaction that succeeded on its consumers' recognitions—and misrecognitions—of themselves as such types. Well aware of the self-consciously historical character of these identifications, Du Maurier predicted the afterlife that his cartoons have assumed as indexes to late nineteenth-century mores.[79] The cartoon form may have been reductive and occasionally pernicious, but it also amused and enchanted. Satirical drawings performed a special kind of humorous, modern immediacy unachievable by the more technologically sophisticated photograph, with its static, overdetailed imagery, which began to appear in periodicals in the 1890s.[80] The rambunctious intimacy of hand-drawn cartoon satire offered an older visual aesthetic point of contrast, humor, and critique regarding newer, technologized media developments, while remaining amenable to the airier, abbreviated New Journalism that was also transforming the texture of mass print.

As in his illustration of the woolly mammoth in *Peter Ibbetson*, several of Du Maurier's cartoons reframe kinship and social communities as the mechanical reproduction of visual media; these are emblematic of his signature idiom of gentle satire. For example, "Photographing the First-Born" depicts a line of six adults attempting various ridiculous poses in order to coax a smile from the stoic child on whom the camera lens is trained. As they clap, wave flags, and flap umbrellas, the adults both extend the apparatus and become themselves the spectacle for the cartoonist's more widely ranging eye. The humor comes from the recognition of the new difficulty of producing and maintaining, on the apparatus's schedule, the infant smile. The unpredictable, organic spontaneity of the tot foils the precision of visual reproductive technology. Yet we can also read the image as the witty deconstruction of modern kinship itself: It redeploys the visual trope of the line of descent as a media technology that produces the sentimentalized image, rather than the physical being, of the child. The cartoon displaces the affective ties of family with a broader appeal to a public familiar with the chore of posing for photographs.

Likewise, in "Disastrous Result of Beautymania," tuxedoed guests at a party are amused to enter a drawing room and find their dates all lounging in the same pose; the caption explains that "the last new beauty, having an innocent cast of countenance, has been painted, sculptured, and photographed with her head on one side, sucking her thumb." Du Maurier mocks bourgeois women's identical physical self-fashioning after old and new media models.[81] The cartoons identify what is amusing and charming in image-conscious bourgeois modernity: Social mores are now technologically mediated. The consequence of consuming media images, whether photographs of children or publicity photos of the latest celebrity, is their active reproduction, in place of a putatively more original expression. In consuming media, one is consumed by it. Companionate love must accept the modern burden of apparently interchangeable partners. Nicholas Daly has proposed that *Peter Ibbetson* critiques the emergence of image culture, but the novel, as well as these and others of Du Maurier's cartoons, share a bemused recognition and celebration of it.[82] The characteristic immediacy of Du Maurierness is on display here, not only by the cartoon form's witty brevity, but because the satire on technologized social life itself implies that its own communicative act is somehow fresher, more direct, and unmediated.

Figure 14. "Disastrous Result of Beautymania." *Punch*, May 3, 1879.

The idiom of Du Maurierness is satire, but it is also sentiment. People are obliged to reproduce the mediated images they have consumed, but they also desire to do so, as a way of being together. The best-loved instance of a form of kinship revitalized by technologized culture in *Peter Ibbetson* was the romance between Peter and the duchess. Readers enthusiastically responded to Du Maurier's depiction of intimacy unfolding, over decades, through the obsessive consumption of mass media. In addition to replaying music, revisiting history, and reviewing paintings, the lovers also mentally process newspapers together: During her waking hours, the duchess "merely glanced through them carefully, taking in the aspect of each column one after another, from top to bottom"; but at night, with Peter, "she was able to read out every word from the dream-paper she held in her hands—thus truly chewing the very cud of journalism!" (2:128). This episode recalls Peter's eavesdropping on the conversation at which Gogo was present but inattentive. Once again, media consumption entails reproduction, although here it is presented as a sentimentalized delight. This paranormal but strangely bureaucratic scanning and conversion of visual to auditory information reverses the iconic figuration of the married couple divided by screenlike newspapers and novels. Leah Price has interpreted novelistic and visual representations of alienated conjugal reading as an empty defensive gesture, but Peter and the duchess's liaison is energized by this shared media consumption, which replaces the eroticism and intimacy missing from a necessarily disembodied relationship.[83] The activity also produces a more equal relationship; it may even explain the duchess's comparatively strong role in the narrative as Peter's clairvoyant mentor. Yet the duchess functions both as the medium through which Peter remembers his past and as the repeatable content of it. Peter never falls in love with her: She is lovable because she is the mature version of his lost childhood companion, Mimsey. Accordingly, the duchess is an icon, like Du Maurier's tall, statuesque, classically Greek profiled figures from his *Punch* cartoons, La Svengali at her most mesmerizing, and Marta, the eponymous, otherworldly psychic presence of *The Martian*.[84] Like the replica of the Venus de Milo that Du Maurier kept in his studio for inspiration throughout his career, she was beloved, by Peter and by readers, as an ideal.[85]

In Peter and the duchess's romance, we glimpse a new kind of affect that mass print media can produce by exerting pressure on existing kinship structures. Peter, by conventional measures of literary heroes, is the most inactive, inert protagonist in all of Victorian fiction: He spends thirty years sleeping, dreaming, being trained by a woman in esoteric psychic arts, and replaying the same scenes and sounds in his head—many of which are not his own. But such judgments issue from norms of rationalist, sovereign, productive subjects and the masculinities they support. By contrast, what struck readers, then and now, was the possibility of intense togetherness— the communal affect—that the clairvoyant plot imagines. Du Maurier's cartoons share this intersubjective imagination, in which originality, authenticity, and individual sovereignty are no longer paramount. Although his representations of shared mental space also accommodate pernicious ideologies such as eugenics, they also generally loosen preexisting kinship structure and social norms, creating room for more progressive configurations. In this space, for example, the duchess's more complete mastery allows her to become Peter's mentor, a rare relationship in Victorian fiction. Where immediacy is the most desirable goal, and—paradoxically— new mental and other media technologies are the means to attain it, the forms of social relations come second. It is in this vein that Hélène Cixous valorizes what she calls the "telepathic" connection between Peter and the duchess; she titles her homage to the novel *Philippines* in reference to the duchess Mary's, term for their bond: "Like twin kernels in one shell ('Philipschen,' as Mary called it), we touched at more points and were closer

than the rest of mankind (with each of them a separate shell of his own)"
(2:146).[86] Here, the dream of collective affect we saw in chapter one is sentimentalized within the telepathic romance plot.

Hathaway's film *Peter Ibbetson* seized on the novel's sentimentality, while
preserving its interest in media by foregrounding its own special effects.
Michael Atkinson called it "a lush, straight-faced Hollywood weeper that
beats down all comers in the mad-love department"; and on the surface it is
deeply conventional.[87] But its special effects also held the interest of cine-
philes. Peter (Gary Cooper) walks straight through prison bars and past
nonexistent guards to join Mary (Ann Harding). Indeed, the film suggests
that cinema itself operates as a kind of "dreaming true" that can supply
prohibited desires, when Peter introduces Mary to the castle he has designed for her with the invitation, "Would you be good enough to look?"
and when Mary references the sound track as a piece of music she brought
him from her waking life.[88] The castle—a literalized castle in the air—
spectacularly explodes and sparks an avalanche when it is hit by lightning,
because Peter and Mary grow afraid of its splendor. The trick to realizing
dreams is to command oneself to keep believing in them. Despite such Hollywood platitudes, one can see how Breton admired the features of the film
that made the story seem drily Freudian: Peter's obsession with his childhood playmate, the repetitions of dialogue and scenery that enact their
reunion, the symbolism of crumbling castles. Mary's declaration that
"Who is to say what is real and what is not real? We're dreaming true! A
dream that is more than a dream," certainly supplied the subversive brief of
Surrealism. Like that movement, it reframed mass culture as a collective,
ephemeral dream.

Peter Ibbetson looks forward to cinematic technology, but also backward
to older media. Because they seem unable to support sociable immediacy,
two older media forms—books and painting—become casualties of Du
Maurier's surface affects and aesthetics. Having led active modern lives,
neither Peter nor the duchess ever had much time for solitary, contemplative reading, so they do not clairvoyantly reread, and in the zone of true
dreaming, they have no means of acquiring new books. Hence, their books
are few, and they limit themselves to "the true bibliophilous delight of gazing at their backs, and taking them down and fingering them and putting
them carefully back again" (2:129). Such fondling is their only way to enjoy books together—briefly, as visual and tactile material, rather than as
the extended, solitary interpretive decoding of sustained reading. Throughout the century, "printed matter in general was becoming just another
'novelty' to be devoured or consumed as fast as fashions changed"; by the

1890s this transition was producing novels in fewer volumes, short fiction, and genre fiction, all attempting to compete with other media spectacles.[89] *Peter Ibbetson* itself, after having appeared in *Harper's Monthly Magazine* from June to December 1891, appeared the same year in two volumes and then in one from the publisher James Ripley Osgood and his subsidiary Osgood McIlvaine.[90] The library in *Peter Ibbetson* portends the book's diminished status in a faster age of more ephemeral print. The duchess even dusts the virtual books with care, having "arranged that dust shall fall on them in the usual way to make it real" (2:107). The fake dust emphasizes the collectible book's status as old media corpse, a kind of premature memorial to contemplative reading. Equally, since the grimy, unread books resemble the trompe l'oeil libraries of dummy spines, they reveal a desire to display rather than merely to store: the middlebrow anxiety to acquire cultural knowledge and reproduce it as if spending social currency.

The same affective pull to display oneself before a community is activated by an anomalous moment of ennui about the virtual picture gallery, the Palace of Art, where the duchess and Peter collect all the paintings they have ever seen. "Then suddenly . . . we felt that a certain something was wanting. There was a certain hollowness about it; and we discovered that in our case the principal motives for collecting all these beautiful things were absent. 1. We were not the sole possessors. 2. We had nobody to show them to. 3. Therefore we could take no pride in them" (2:127). To read this as a straightforward bourgeois complaint about the loss of the aura and the prerogatives of ownership in the age of mechanical reproduction is to miss the ways it might also resonate for middlebrow readers who sought such social privilege by acquiring photographs, lithographs, and engravings of famous paintings. Owning a painting and displaying it privately, in one's home, does not allow the aspirant to reproduce the special knowledge it confers. In *Social and Pictorial Satire*, Du Maurier disparaged paintings as "wall-furniture, in which we take a pride . . . but which we grow to look at with the pathetic indifference of habit."[91] *Peter Ibbetson* complexly frames this insight for middlebrow readers, because Peter and the duchess treat paintings as if they were such cartoons, viewing them whenever the caprice strikes them. Unlike paintings adorning an actual bourgeois home, those in the clairvoyant gallery never become tiresome because they can be glanced at on a whim; meanwhile, they retain their elite status as desirable cultural artifacts. They are more like the reproductions that decorated actual working- and lower-middle-class homes. The brief moment of complaint, then, expresses a middlebrow anxiety that once acquired, the cultural knowledge conveyed by aesthetic forms can merely be possessed—not reproduced and displayed to enhance social status. As the fin de siècle became the age of the mass image, cultural information that failed to circulate could not realize its value. To be sure, this passage exemplifies an ethos of conspicuous consumption, but it also registers the way mass culture reorients affect more broadly, toward a larger social field in which the primary communicative mode is display.

The hand-drawn image's reflectivity, grabbability, momentary charm, and disposability suggested both the quicker acts of recognition required of late-nineteenth-century mass media culture and the timelessness of one of the oldest models of visual representation, drawing itself. This historical positioning of Du Maurier's cartoons within and before their moment redound upon *Peter Ibbetson*'s representation of old media's transposition into newer formats. As books, paintings, and music become media objects to be stored, collected, displayed, replayed, snatched, thrown, fingered, and appreciated for their surfaces, they convey the lightness and caprice of Du Maurierness. They also perform the middlebrow cultural work characteristic of Du Maurier—that of rekeying bourgeois aesthetic contemplation to the petit-bourgeoisie's fragmented leisure time, interest in style, and increasing self-consciousness.[92] In an ever more disposable culture, self-fashioning was becoming an intensive task of trivial significance, but it also occasionally celebrated itself as such. This concession to image culture was the dynamic underlying the "big London party" of Du Maurier's cartoons and fiction.

Such celebrations index the bonhomie of Du Maurierness, as well as its intensive expressivity. Du Maurier registered the shocks of modernity—the mediatization of experience, the fragmentation of time and space by Haussmannization, and the acceleration of consumption attending everyday bourgeois life—but responded with a mixture of amusement, wonder, speculation, and optimism. Although his aesthetic dwelt on the surface of life, in minor habits and customs of consumption, and the new affective modes that they fostered, his literary and visual work offered a faith that a central problem of nineteenth-century self-consciousness could be solved: Technological mediation and the proliferation of phantasmagoria could preserve the freshness and immediacy of experience—especially social experience—rather than threatening its authenticity. Unlike thinkers such as Pater, Benjamin, and Freud, Du Maurier found the truth of experience not in its putative limits—its uniqueness, unrepeatability, embodiment, and solipsism—but in its fanciful possibilities for extension, repetition, and transcendence. His last planned, unwritten novel was to depict a couple who could fly.[93]

CHAPTER 5

"A Form of Reverie, a Malady of Dreaming": *Dorian Gray*, Personality, and Mass Culture

What does it mean to be lost in a book at the fin de siècle? I have been focusing on other print forms and material practices, but even in the hyperactive print market and among the proliferating new media technologies of the 1890s, books remained a central focus for theorizing the relationship between mass print media and altered states of mind. Indeed, this milieu inspired book designers to reflect on the long history of the book as a consumer object. Oscar Wilde's 1891 novel *The Picture of Dorian Gray* famously describes the antihero's obsessive consumption of a book lent to him by his friend Lord Henry, as well as his absorption as he gazes at his self-portrait, assembles his notorious collection of art objects, and becomes enchanted with an actress. The novel's most culturally resonant term for this sort of absorption is "reverie," which it characterizes using the language of intoxication: "It was a poisonous book. The heavy odour of incense seemed to cling about its pages and to trouble the brain."[1] This pleasurable, sensual toxicity induces "a form of reverie, a malady of dreaming" that enraptures Dorian, who points out to Lord Henry that he doesn't merely like the book—rather, it fascinates him (121). Wilde places Dorian's "poisonous book" as the centerpiece of seductive aesthetic forms—

oil painting, objets d'art, and theater—that were intuitively understood as the "old media" of the 1890s, because they were elite and not machine-driven. Yet he uses Dorian's reveries in them to observe the psychological and social effects of the emergence of mass culture in the preceding decades. Within this project, the toxic book reveals a new relation to print, still the preeminent mass medium of the 1890s. Print dominated the dilemma of mass media consumers, who had to find their authentic selves by perusing models fabricated by others. I turn to Wilde's novel to conclude this book, because it answers a century-long cultural question: How does one find oneself within mass-mediated modernity?

In didactic readings of the novel, the poisonous book infects Dorian with Lord Henry's Decadent ideology; acting recklessly under its influence, he loses himself. Rather, Wilde deconstructs such cheap moralism, foregrounding instead the historical emergence of demands for authentic selfhood within a mass culture that makes the assumption of alternative identities seem even possible. Wilde resurrects an older, masculinist Victorian view, that "all influence is immoral" to satirize it. He assigns to Lord Henry the speech that skewers its animating individualist ideology of supreme self-sovereignty, reenergized by Aestheticism: "To influence a person is to give him one's own soul. He does not think his natural thoughts, or burn with his natural passions. . . . He becomes an echo of someone else's music, an actor of a part that has not been written for him. The aim of life is self-development. To realize one's nature perfectly—that is what each of us is here for" (20). For Wilde, influence cannot denaturalize an individual's thoughts, passions, and virtues; rather, influence—always grounded in media, materials, and people—is the means to self-expansion and realization. Wilde recognized that echoing others' ideas, styles, and even emotions was inevitable in a mass-mediated age. Thus, though he suggested that Joris-Karl Huysmans's *À Rebours* (*Against Nature*, 1884) was the secret identity of the addictive book, I am less concerned to interpret its content than to postulate broadly the imagination of reading, viewing, and collecting as mad, absorptive experiments with mass culture. A new quest to experience one's true self propels such fascinations. Nancy Armstrong, keying the process of self-identification to fiction, photography, and realism, suggests that they "produce[d] subjects whose formation begins with an identification with an image and involve[d] them in a lifelong attempt to maintain that relationship."[2] Similarly, Audrey Jaffe identifies the painting as the fulcrum of Dorian's desire to have an identity that will make his social group whole and, in this way, embody culture.[3] Extending this critical trend, this essay reveals the novel's subtle argument: Getting lost in a book, painting, or performance does not reflect a naïve consumerist relationship to art, but a pleasurable, critical exchange. In Wilde's novel, reverie evokes the ambivalence of the modern media consumer, compelled to sort through and try on an array of personalities.

In fashioning a reparative argument about mass culture, Wilde belongs in a critical conversation about media history; particularly, he can be placed in dialogue with Walter Benjamin. In "The Work of Art in the Age of Its Technical Reproducibility," Benjamin famously argued that the "aura" of an original work of art, the elusive effect of its own time and place within ritual, withered in the age of its mass reproduction.[4] By contrast, Wilde's novel suggests that he instead saw original artworks and their mechanically reproduced copies in a dialectical relationship, which enhanced rather than eroded the mystical power Benjamin associates with the aura: It is only in an era of mass media reproduction that originals begin to seem magically special. This synergy shines through in the interdependent relationship between Dorian and the painting: the novel playfully transposes original and copy, showing how they energize each other. Accordingly, the novel also consistently balances Dorian's high art interests with low aspects of mass culture: Dorian creates his own private gallery to stare at his portrait, but he also frequents Sibyl's shabby theater; he breathes the rarefied air of high culture, but he also frequents docks populated by prostitutes and opium addicts; he plays alone at arcane enthusiasms, but he also sets iconic fashion trends. The coterie media forms and high society milieu of the novel become a comic ground for new media and low manners. For example, the novel features aristocrats, but their quipping, posturing, and scandal-mongering index mass culture's new regime of middle- and working-class social relations, which rely on the ability to circulate information, and commodify one's self as a personality. Wilde thus charts a historical shift observed by Niklas Luhmann: Mass media transpose the traditional order of taste, so that now the upper orders imitate the middle class.[5] Wilde's success as a dramatist, writer, and a media personality hinged on his exploitation of this development. Inverting the dynamic of mainstream middle-class culture, which was haunted by the specter of the mass, in Wilde's oeuvre and in his own mediated performance, the haute figure of the dandy operated as the unconscious of mass culture.[6] As critics have recently observed, Dorian's portrait functions in tension with Lord Henry's seventeen photographs of him; and Sibyl Vane, had she lived only a few years more, might have been seen in the very same theater as a silent cinema star.[7]

What affects attend self-fashioning through mass culture? We can approach this question by attending to "reverie," a key term in Victorian culture and in Wilde's oeuvre. Reverie, with its unstructured, spontaneous, ostensibly uncoerced contemplativeness, offered a space for the transmission of affect within mass culture. In its first section, the chapter will show how Wilde links reverie's characteristically unsystematic thinking to a pleasurable, even intoxicating kind of media consumption; surprisingly, by attaching it to criticism, he generates a democratizing, populist version of that concept akin to entertainment, which is not mere passive consumption but active self-making. The infamous chapter 11 forms the novel's crux: When it describes Dorian's succession of new enthusiasms, it draws on Wilde's experience editing *Woman's World* to incorporate new journalistic idioms that blend historical esoterica with sensationalism and lifestyle reportage. At the same time, it stages affective play as a series of engagements not merely with the material culture of Dorian's collections, but with the print culture through which he learns about them.

Whereas reverie's openness encourages a range of affect and social engagement through mass media consumption, paranoia is a defensive affect that seeks to protect the self as monad. Chapter 11 is the crux of *The Picture of Dorian Gray* because it represents Dorian's reveries shutting down as they turn to paranoia. The second section of this chapter demonstrates how, in Wilde's darkly comic novel, Dorian's efforts to fashion his personality from cultural materials founders under the weight of the old disparagement of influence, leading him from critical intoxication into addiction and its corollary, paranoia, and from the new media of the 1890s back into the old, aristocratic medium of yesteryear, oil painting. Mass media consumers reproduced the images, styles, and tropes they had consumed in their own personalities, for example, the dandy or the actress. But the inability to filter mass media appropriately could leave one trapped inside, and attempting to defend, an artificial personality. Dorian suffers accordingly—not because he has leaped wholeheartedly into a superficial image culture, but because he is unable to do so. Retreating to an aristocratic, elite position of patronage and censorship, he meets his end.

Eve Sedgwick has associated paranoia with homophobia in relation to *The Picture of Dorian Gray* and indeed, modern Western epistemology as a whole.[8] Dorian's paranoia that his unspecified sins will be detected, and Basil's anxiety that the public might see his love for Dorian in the painting, generate critical discussions of influence and aesthetic abstraction that, in her view, elide the novel's gay desire. Yet by focusing on the novel as a cultural object with a production and consumption history, and as a media object with affordances, we can unify these two interpretive strands. Of mass culture, Luhmann writes, "Every individual finds himself to be someone who has yet to determine his individuality or have it determined according to the stipulation of a game 'of which neither he nor anyone else back to the beginning of time knew the rules or the risks or the stakes'" (*Reality of the Mass Media*, 59–60). Every mass media consumer plays this game; at stake for some in the 1890s was gay desire and identity. If the novel describes the new freedoms and terrors of the media subject, who loses and finds himself in imaginative reverie, constantly producing and reproducing his personality, then it also queers that process. The game of self-fashioning can never be won, but no one can stop playing it, either. The chapter concludes by showing how this dynamic worked for the novel's gay addressees.

Reverie: Form, Genre, Affect

We should beware of the nature of the reveries that fasten on us. Reverie has in it the mystery and subtlety of an odor.... You may poison yourself with reveries, as with flowers. An intoxicating suicide, exquisite and malignant.... Reverie attracts, cajoles, lures, entwines, and then makes you its accomplice. It makes you bear your half in the trickeries which it plays on conscience. It charms; then it corrupts you. We may say of reverie as of play, one begins by being a dupe, and ends by being a cheat.

VICTOR HUGO, *The Man Who Laughs* (1869)

In his *Essay concerning Human Understanding* (1689), John Locke briefly defined modern reverie: "When Ideas float in our Mind, without any reflection or regard of the Understanding, it is that which the French call *Reverie*; our Language has scarce a name for it."[9] Locke describes reverie as a kind of conscious dreaming, in which judgment and cognition recede, permitting ideas and imagery to play. We could call this Enlightenment description the standard definition of reverie, as evanescent mental activity detached from systematic ratiocination. Jean-Jacques Rousseau's *Reveries of the Solitary Walker* (1782) developed its associations with mental wandering, solitary meditation, and nature, while also reviving an obsolete sense of wild revelry. Noting that his aging mind no longer ignites with inspiration, Rousseau writes, "I become less intoxicated by the delirium of reverie."[10] For Rousseau, reverie suggested both serene contemplative reminiscences and frenzied mental chaos, a combination of great appeal to Romantic writers. In *Zoonomia* (1794), Erasmus Darwin had defined it as "an effort of the mind to relieve some painful sensation," linking it to convulsions and insanity.[11] Reverie became a quintessentially Romantic state of mind, akin to dream and imagination.[12] Rousseau's *Reveries*, never meant to be published, were conversations with himself, sequestered from his persecutors—a glimmering of antisociability and paranoia that Wilde would develop in *The Picture of Dorian Gray*, as I shall later demonstrate.[13] Rousseau's *Reveries* were written in pencil on playing cards during his walks in meadows and woods, and although themes emerge, they reflect his desultory thoughts. Yet Rousseau organized and rewrote them into a manuscript, self-conscious acts that reframe the original experiences. In reverie, we "experience our own experience; we have a sentiment of our own existence. [But] because of this indeterminacy, our experience . . . might have anything as its object."[14] These three qualities of reverie—self-consciousness, randomness, and discontinuity—have been described by critics from Charles Baudelaire to Benjamin and beyond as the hallmarks of modern experience. Victor Hugo, in a description that we shall hear Wilde echo in his novel, gives reverie the distinctive sheen of a modern consumerism that inveigles the erstwhile independent dreamer in a pleasurable snare of his or her own making.

Driven by self-consciousness and the cultivation of randomness, "reveries" quickly became a self-consciously shapeless literary genre; indeed, its leveling tendency makes it a metaphor for all of print media. By 1825, its aleatory qualities were parodied by "Paul Ponder" as *Noctes Atticae; or, Reveries in a Garret*, an updated commonplace book or encyclopedia uniting topics as diverse as "acting and declamation" and "false ornaments in gardening."[15] Since the imagination could alight on any topic and by turning it over, make it interesting or boring, then drop it for a new one, "reveries" referenced this uncommitted activity in the guise of literary form. Throughout the long nineteenth century, the term "reveries" prefixes the titles of many genres, from poems (W. B. Yeats's *Reveries over Childhood and Youth*, 1916) and travel writing (Lafacadio Hearn's *Out of the East: Reveries and Studies in New Japan*, 1896) to lower genres such as joke collections (Mary Wilson Little's *A Paragrapher's Reveries*, 1904) and comic sketches about deliberately boring middle-class household fixtures such as andirons (Ashbel Green Vermilye's *Stray Reveries*, 1897). Reveries also came to be synonymous with memoirs, as in Theodore Sedgwick Faye's *Dreams and Reveries of a Quiet Man* (1832), Donald Grant Mitchell's *Reveries of a Bachelor* (1851), and Helen Davies Tainter's *The Reveries of a*

Spinster (1897). Both the individual titles and the whole literary profusion reflect the deflation of Romantic imaginative mobility into mundane Victorian archiving. Since the same print that dignifies ephemeral thoughts also debases the soul's sublime poetry, the publication of private, uncontrolled thoughts unleashes a new form of self-conscious, instrumental reading. "Reveries" could advertise themselves as frivolous sedation or ironically challenge that expectation; in either case, they conceptualized reading as consumer entertainment, an effect of mass print culture. Moreover, the spontaneous, effortless appearance of reveries suggested that published writing need not be crafted or insightful. As Walter Benjamin observed of one effect of the emergence of mass print culture, "At any moment, the reader is ready to become a writer."[16] Wilde himself mocked the phenomenon: "In old days books were written by men of letters and read by the public. Nowadays books are written by the public and read by nobody."[17] "Reveries" epitomized this leveling.

Just as reveries gestured toward a social openness, so too did the experience of reverie open itself to an array of affects generated in response to mass print entertainment. Under an overarching framework of dreamy contemplation or introspection, reveries could accommodate a great variety of moods and feelings. The quicksilver changeability of reveries as they flitted from topic to topic meant that their accompanying affects might also swiftly morph. George Henry Lewes, likening reverie to dreaming, described it as uninterrupted visual consumption: "We do not pause on certain suggestions, do not recur to them, and reflect on them, but let one rapidly succeed another, like shadows chasing each other over a cornfield." Moreover, this speed resembled that of print transporting its consumers across the world: "In reverie the mind passes instantaneously from London to India, and the persons vanish to give place to very different persons, without once interrupting the imaginary story."[18] Reverie reflected the random juxtapositions of the print medium, as one kind of story followed seamlessly on another. Its affective coordinates were accordingly difficult to map. But the everyday middle- and working-class activity of reading reverie increasingly became the time and space of affect. Whatever these affects may have been—excitement, sentimentality, delight—they were keyed to mass print as a mode of entertainment. We have already seen this cultural formation in the desultory reading of leisured smokers, who whiled away time saturating their minds with printed words and images. If these observations seem overly broad, it is because reverie signified a newly mobile, restless psychology that mirrored the new speed, volume, and range of mass print.

If "reveries" permit any humble experience to be published, then they conversely suggest that things printed can be experienced. This suggestion propels the midcentury novel that famously indicts the reverie induced by mass print, Gustave Flaubert's *Madame Bovary* (1857). Emma Bovary, primed by her compulsive novel reading, desires to transcend her mundane life; she embarks on an affair, falls into debt, makes herself ill, and ultimately kills herself. Though Flaubert uses "reverie" to describe several of the characters' mental states, Emma is its principal subjective focus, a distracted daydreamer whose habitation of simulated worlds ruins the real one. Emma personifies Flaubert's critique of Romantic desire, which morphs too facilely from spirituality to sensuality, resembling mass-produced, alienated experience.[19] Reverie describes the fantasizing that takes place after reading, when Emma dreams of fulfillment through imitation, confronts contrary realities, and fails: "And Emma tried to find out what exactly was meant, in real life, by the words 'bliss,' 'passion,' and 'ecstasy,' words that she had found so beautiful in books."[20] Flaubert's novel serves as a significant precedent for Wilde's. Jeff Nunokawa observes the dialectic relationship of affective boredom and desire rooted in Wilde's characters' weary bodies, a dynamic clearly at work in *Madame Bovary*.[21] Both texts measure the distance between mediated and everyday life; both protagonists come to grief by miscalculating it. "Reverie" invokes their misguided attempts to imitate media constructions. Yet a difference distinguishes the two novels: Flaubert critiques Emma Bovary's consumption of lower, feminine novel genres that are clearly bested by the supreme realism of *Madame Bovary* itself. For Flaubert, mass culture is reverie's focus. Wilde, by contrast, represents Dorian's reveries moving from a liberating openness that includes mass media to a paranoid, exclusive, censored, closeted realm of high art or old media. Though both novelists are writing from within the alienation of post-Romantic mass culture, Wilde manages to preserve, via his appropriation of Walter Pater's ideas, vestiges of Romantic desire.

Wilde drew extensively on Walter Pater's *The Renaissance* (1873) for *The Picture of Dorian Gray*. Paterian Aestheticism had transfigured Romanticism in part by reinvigorating reverie as a state of mind both refined and commonly available. Pater posited reverie as a finely perceptive attention to life and art: "any stirring of the senses, strange dyes, strange colours, and curious odours, or the work of the artist's hands, or the face of one's friend."[22] Kate Hext writes that Pater "struggles between his desire to know and his Romantic sense that things are essentially unknowable and beautiful because of their mystery."[23] The tension is intellectual, but also sensual, aesthetic, and affective. The Aesthetic premium on psychological strangeness licenses reverie and its affects as the self seeks transcendent experience in small details, fleeting moments, and contained forms. Aestheticism was a bourgeois ideology, but it also possessed potential as a brief for mass consumption. On the one hand, *The Renaissance* emphasized canonical Western art as the elite source of Aesthetic experience; on the other, its commitment to appreciating the sensuality of everyday life lent it a universalizing openness. Pater associated reverie chiefly with the spiritual introspection or mysticism of the medieval period. But reverie transcends this time period and religious context; in Pater's famous rhapsody on La Gioconda, it exteriorizes affect and converts it into aesthetic value: "It is a beauty wrought out from within upon the flesh, the deposit, little cell by cell, of strange thoughts and fantastic reveries and exquisite passions" (*Renaissance*, 80). Here, reverie is deliberately obscure and elusive, a biological extravagance following the human life span, yet building over seemingly geologic spans of time. As in Basil's painting of Dorian, affective material creeps out, literally expressing itself in painted flesh. In its association with fantasy, abnormality, and luxury, reverie sounded affective deeps. Yet La Gioconda and Dorian are also not quite deep subjects— they are images alluding to depths. Paterian Aestheticism, quoted liberally by Wilde in the novel, also made art resemble advertising, most clearly in *The Renaissance*'s ringing conclusion that "art comes to you professing frankly to give nothing but the highest quality to your moments as they pass, and simply for those moments' sake."[24] From Pater, Wilde borrows a model of reverie that combines a depth model of psychic absorption with the momentary temporality of modern consumption. Like the literary genre of reveries, it oscillated between depth and surface, intensity and lassitude, absorption and distraction, elite and mass.

Having surveyed the historical, literary, and Aesthetic contexts of reverie, I now examine how Wilde represents it in *The Picture of Dorian Gray*: as something like entertainment, yet more complex than the caricature of mindless consumption to which we may be used. Rather than suggesting the wholesale imprinting of Decadent ideas onto Dorian's blank mind, he characterizes Dorian's absorption as a dynamic exchange with the print medium:

> After a few minutes he became absorbed. It was the strangest book that he had ever read. . . . Things that he had dimly dreamed of were suddenly made real to him. Things of which he had never dreamed were gradually revealed. . . . The mere cadence of the sentences, the

subtle monotony of their music, so full as it was of complex refrains and movements elaborately repeated, produced in the mind of the lad, as he passed from chapter to chapter, a form of reverie, a malady of dreaming, that made him unconscious of the failing day and the creeping shadows. Cloudless, and pierced by one solitary star, a copper-green sky gleamed through the windows. He read on by its wan light till he could read no more. (*Picture of Dorian Gray*, 120–21)

Wilde describes the surface of the text as if it were a media object, likening its prose to music, and depicting its consumer's affect. Readers see an icon of civilization—a man reading through a lighted window—but at twilight, under a green sky and a violent star, as if an Enlightenment scene of study and edification were giving way to Romantic reverie-as-revelry. In this immersive act of consumption, Dorian acquires new dreams, and his own dreams, socially confirmed, become realities. The passage thus dramatizes entertainment, which, Luhmann says, "aims to activate that which we ourselves experience, hope for, fear, forget—just as the narrating of myths once did. . . . Entertainment reimpregnates what one already is" (*Reality of the Mass Media*, 58). Entertainment connects mediated to unmediated experience. Luhmann's odd construction, to make pregnant again, suggests both a Decadent pedagogy and a compulsive malady that mystifies Dorian's agency. To illustrate self-expansion and self-multiplication via media consumption, Wilde must represent Dorian's moral autonomy as slightly compromised but not fully undermined. In the nineteenth century, the old meaning of "entertainment" as "the cherishing of an idea in the mind," which captured Dorian's obsessiveness, combined with its newer designation of publicly performed amusements.[25] Entertainment, a category that cuts across aesthetic forms and increasingly suggested the overtaking of elite by mass culture, resides in this psychological and material structure of repetition and activation that compromises sovereignty by opening the self to mass media influences.

This lyrical scene establishes norms of media consumption. Readers observe Dorian incorporating the poisonous book's matter: The hero "became to him a kind of prefiguring type of himself. And, indeed, the whole book seemed to him to contain the story of his own life, written before he had lived it" (*Picture of Dorian Gray*, 123). Losing himself in the book, Dorian finds himself in the character type that it circulates; but this is merely another image or bad copy, not the truth of his self.[26] Wilde amplifies the point in "The Decay of Lying," in which a fascinating friend models herself after the heroine of a piece of serial fiction by eloping:

"She told me that she had felt an absolutely irresistible impulse to follow the heroine step by step in her strange and fatal progress, and that it was with a feeling of real terror that she had looked forward to the last few chapters of the story. When they appeared, it seemed to her that she was compelled to reproduce them in life, and she did so."[27] This tidbit satirizes the phenomenon of self-fashioning through mass media. The compulsion to consume a melodramatic and suspenseful story was familiar from critical complaints about sensation fiction in the 1860s, but in Wilde's exaggerations, Dorian and the woman literally reenact such plots. Their over-the-top imitations exaggerate the partial, insidious ways in which readers assumed media figures as models. The novel alludes to Narcissus as a classical antecedent for Dorian's self-obsession, but his fanatical relationship to media suggests an opposite formation. Rather than projecting himself everywhere he looks, he compulsively patterns himself after models he finds elsewhere—in the book, the painting *Tannhäuser*, and indeed, all of literature and history (130).

Wilde is keener to describe self-fashioning through mediated reverie than to condemn it. Indeed, in "The Critic as Artist," he rhapsodizes the assumption of someone else's thoughts, feelings, and ideas as the basis of criticism itself. There, he offers a long description of the pleasure of entering others' minds through the intoxicated reading of books such as the *Divine Comedy* and especially *Les Fleurs du Mal*:

> Let its subtle music steal into your brain and color your thoughts, and you will become for a moment what he was who wrote it; nay, not for a moment only, but for many barren moonlit nights and sunless sterile days will a despair that is not your own make its dwelling within you, and the misery of another gnaw your heart away. Read the whole book, suffer it to tell even one of its secrets to your soul, and your soul will grow eager to know more, and will feed upon poisonous honey, and seek to repent of strange crimes of which it is guiltless, and to make atonement for terrible pleasures that it has never known.[28]

Using the tropes of music and poison to describe the assumption of another's perspective and ideas, the passage strikingly resembles Dorian's reverie with the seductively sweet book, as well as Hugo's description of reverie in *The Man who Laughs*. As we shall soon see, it also resembles his exhaustive consumption that dominates chapter 11 of *The Picture of Dorian Gray*, when "he would often adopt certain modes of thought that he knew to be really alien to his nature, abandon himself to their subtle influences, and then, having, as it were, caught their colour and satisfied his intellectual curiosity, leave them" (127). Such consumers immerse themselves in books, fictional spaces, and the miniature worlds of collections, moving from one to another. They assume others' identities and affects, then cast them off again. Temporarily abandoning oneself to such influences becomes the characteristic behavior of media consumers, whose identities fluctuate according to their choices of object and degree of engagement. But, according to Wilde, this behavior is also the habit of critics.

The difference between Dorian's fetishistic, immersive rereading and the connoisseur's or critic's rational rereading cannot be demarcated. Their overlap suggests that rational aesthetic communication relies on the delirious, irrational, more obviously pleasurable reverie associated with mass media. What strikes twenty-first-century readers as the language of addiction likely connoted selfish pleasure to late-nineteenth-century readers. Proposing a model of critical pleasure, Wilde collapses high and low culture into undifferentiated media consumption. Dorian and the woman who lives out a serialized novel are thus not the naïve readers they may at first seem. Although they err, their practices are part of a new mass culture in which such self-dissolution and reformation has become possible on wider, deeper scales. With cheap editions, Wilde could exhort the masses to lose themselves in Dante and Baudelaire; if excessive identifications ground critical judgments, then they could produce aesthetic reason. Reverie, affording both experiences, produces this radical result.

When media consumers fashioned themselves, they also materially remade mass media objects. Wilde reflects this phenomenon in Dorian's preoccupation with the book's materiality:

> For years, Dorian Gray could not free himself from the influence of this book. Or perhaps it would be more accurate to say that he never sought to free himself from it. He procured from Paris no less than nine large-paper copies of the first edition, and had them bound in different colours, so that they might suit his various moods and the changing fancies of a nature over which he seemed, at times, to have almost entirely lost control. (123)

Within the rhetoric of influence and self-mastery that Wilde has already satirized, the book seems to control Dorian, and yet Dorian also controls the book, dressing it, curating it, multiplying it into a collection. On its surface, this passage describes the bourgeois masculine connoisseurship of Aestheticism, but it also recodes feminine, juvenile, and middle- and working-class engagements with printed and domestic objects.[29] Dorian's play with the book also refigures an extensive cultural practice of women's crafts, one of the ways that middle- and working-class people engaged and remade mass-produced objects. As Talia Schaffer notes, "Bookbinding involved some of the most popular handicraft skills: gilding, incising, molding, and scorching decorative patterns into scraps of leather or cloth."[30] In Leah Price's account of the bourgeois ideology of reading, after 1850 such material engagements with print indicated a refusal of print's abstraction, and thus intellectual weakness and psychic shallowness.[31] In Dorian's reverie with the book, and in particular, his material remaking of it, Wilde countered this dominant view.

Dorian may be in the book's thrall, but he also uses it to express his moods, and imposes aesthetic order on it. Such agency is not the fictive, absolute control of the self as monad, but the porous agency of a mass media consumer. This porosity impinges on an account of the aura. Frankel describes Dorian's bookbinding as a process that "fuse[s] the book's very touch and look with the aura of something sacred"; yet his production of multiple copies "drain[s] the novel of any 'aura' that might have attached to it considered as something unique."[32] Both descriptions apply because the aura does not disappear when media consumers engage and remake mass-produced objects. Rather, if the aura inheres in the affective space of reverie itself, then it represents a negotiation between unique self and mass-produced object. Joseph Bristow has charted the gulf between the cheap, conventional version of the novel published in *Lippincott's Magazine,* and the handcrafted, avant-garde look of the book edition; this contrast manifests the negotiations Wilde, and his readers, made as they moved between cultural cliché and exquisitely deep subjectivity.[33]

The well-known opacity of chapter 11 of *The Picture of Dorian Gray* represents modern reverie as refraction of print-media consumption, in its relation to *Woman's World,* the journal that Wilde edited from 1887 to 1889. Dorian takes up a variety of enthusiasms in order to freshen "the same wearisome round of stereotyped habits" that have begun to bore him. This cycle of ennui and fascination is linked to the gothic imagination, which appeals to "those whose minds have been troubled with the malady of reverie" (127). Dorian's interests in mysticism, Darwinism, perfumes, world music, jewels, stories about jewels, embroideries, tapestries, textiles, and ecclesiastical vestments involve print media, since Dorian can learn about these topics only by consuming them. Even further, chapter 11 is like a digest of many issues of this periodical, with each item seeming to encapsulate the gist of an entire article:

And so he would now study perfumes, and the secrets of their manufacture, distilling heavily-scented oils, and burning odorous gums
from the East. He saw that there was no mood of the mind that had
not its counterpart in sensuous life, and set himself to discover their
true relations, wondering what there was in frankincense that made
one mystical, and in ambergris that stirred one's passions, and in
violets that woke the memory of dead romances, and in musk that
troubled the brain, and in champak that stained the imagination . . . of
spikenard that sickens, of hovenia that makes men mad, and of aloes
that are said to be able to expel melancholy from the soul. (129)

Each element of this list points toward an untold story, like a line in a periodical table of contents or index that may tickle the fancy and cause the
reader to flip to the appropriate page. For this passage, Wilde drew on
avant-garde and middlebrow sources: both Huysmans's *Au Rebours*, whose
protagonist Des Esseintes studies perfumes, and Anne Hathaway's piece
"Scents and Scent Bottles," which Wilde published in *Woman's World*.[34]
Thus, though Dorian's "psychology of perfumes" sounds like an avant-
garde experiment in materialism, it also reads like a list of feature articles
in a middlebrow magazine, which has spun natural and cultural history into
entertaining and edifying trivia.

Dorian is not pictured actually collecting specimens of these plants or
perfumes, but rather acquiring information about them. The chapter mines
historical texts by Marco Polo, Procopius, Philostratus, and many others,
pulling out teasers to be whipped into frothy ephemeral content: "In the
romantic history of Alexander, the Conqueror of Emathia was said to have
found in the vale of Jordan snakes 'with collars of real emeralds growing
in their backs'" (*Picture of Dorian Gray*, 131). Finding such literary historical oddities and compressing them into tidbits, chapter 11 resembles New
Journalism trends that would survive well into the twentieth century. One
is the manufacture of bizarre content from obscure historical and natural
historical sources. The adventurer William Seabrook, writing for the
Hearst Syndicate in the 1920s, described reading through back issues of
Nature and the *Lancet*, as well as the prayer book Anne Boleyn gave to
Henry VIII "just before he cut off her head, and other deep-dyed ancient
manuscripts" unfamiliar to general readers, in search of weird reports and
anecdotes that he could spin into sensational feature stories.[35] Wilde's unearthing and compressing of European and classical aristocratic traditions
of natural oddities, violence, cruelty, and luxury read similarly. When
Seabrook and others recirculated tales of historical serial murderers such
as Elizabeth Báthory and Gilles de Rais for mass audiences a few decades

later, they were participating in the same late Victorian tradition Wilde imitated in chapter 11. A second durable New Journalistic idiom involved the modern rediscovery of folk wisdom for consumer purposes: Could one really treat sadness with aloe? Was ambergris an aphrodisiac? As folk remedies and knowledge clashed with and sometimes transformed into patent medicines, heightened claims found their way into journalism and advertising. In mass print media, information and entertainment blurred together, creating yet another aspect of reverie, the acquisition of facts that may or may not become useful for self-fashioning.

In this way, chapter 11's representation of Dorian's collections more plainly describes a relationship to information that resembles media filtering. It differs distinctly from consumers' relationship to temperance ephemera that I described in chapter 1: There, I showed how temperance medals, ribbons, and pledge cards memorialized the moment of drinkers' conversions. Given away at large rallies and meetings in which collective affect was brought to bear on individuals, these ephemeral tokens were meant to recall that intensity for the drinker in moments of crisis, keeping them on the temperance path. Wilde, keen to represent his protagonist's gradual, uneven moral transformation, does not freight individual ephemeral objects with the specific personal history of conversion. Rather, he has Dorian try on each new enthusiasm, to see which ones he wants to keep as part of himself. Dorian's filtering thus more closely resembles the working-class collection of tobacco cards for the acquisition of cultural capital. Just as the child or worker could learn facts about the world that might confirm his intellectual curiosity to others, so Dorian's acquisition of esoteric trivia is meant to produce a model to which he might conform. The most telling comparison, however, is between Dorian's collection of information and Peter Ibbetson's collection of memories in Du Maurier's novel, which I interpreted in chapter 4. Superficially, Du Maurier's long lists of all the paintings Peter and the duchess have seen, and all the concerts they have heard, resemble the density of Wilde's descriptions in chapter 11. There is also a similar sense of total mastery: Peter's technical ability to "dream true" helps him consume and re-consume these experiences whenever he wishes, just as Dorian's inexhaustible wealth and time allows him to pursue even the most recherché interests. But they are truly worlds apart. Whereas Peter's delight is in playing back his own past, Dorian is searching for novel experiences. And whereas Du Maurier's lists have the effect of raising readers' taste levels by informing them of all the paintings and pieces of music they should know, Wilde's self-consciously comments on such cultural transactions by imitating the genres of New Journalism.

In the slow transformation Wilde wishes to portray, chapter 11's jarring catalogue of successive enthusiasms or self-experiments represents an in-between stage. On the one hand, it is linked to mass print culture via its relation to *Woman's World* and New Journalism, and it shows Dorian's affective openness to new sources of the self. On the other, it represents the cusp of Dorian's emotionally inauthentic relation to mass culture, as he begins to turn back toward old, elite forms. Luhmann suggests that the rejection of mass culture as trivial leads consumers "to search (in vain) for authentic experiences . . . complement[ing] mass media information by means of tourism, museum visits, foreign dance groups, and suchlike. These kinds of 'supplements' in turn, however, only lead one into culturally aware, that is, staged worlds" (85). Chapter 11 begins to represent Dorian committing this error. Dorian's activities include just such sterile performances of culture, as he hires "mad gypsies," "grave yellow-shawled Tunisians," "grinning Negroes," "slim turbaned Indians," and others to play their instruments for him (*Picture of Dorian Gray*, 129). Taken together, these performances constitute an emphatically multicultural alternative to the vulgarization of the national cultural icon, Shakespeare, by Sibyl Vane's theater. The chapter marks Dorian's forays into world music, Asian and Indian textiles, and indeed, European history and Catholic ritual, as a "search for sensations that would be new and delightful, and possess that element of strangeness that is so essential to romance" (127). But these bourgeois fads never shed their self-consciousness, which is why Wilde describes Dorian's attitude to them as paradoxically both "curious indifference" and "real ardour" (127). Not only can Dorian never transcend the Aesthetic and Orientalist desire for "strangeness," he fails to see how his preference for the esoteric over the mass is itself a crass reduction and an ideological reaction destined to fail. Once we reframe his activities as part of a conversation with mass culture, we can read chapter 11 clearly as Dorian's effort to style himself using media materials that are middlebrow.

Woman's World and the fashions it featured form a significant source and context for chapter 11, and the novel as a whole, in ways that complicate gender. As Regenia Gagnier, Schaffer, and others have pointed out, the topics Wilde assembles in chapter 11 resemble the thick description of the articles on fashion, travel, and history in *Woman's World*.[36] Wilde even recycled his own review of a book about lace for this chapter.[37] Bourgeois women had been used to fashioning themselves via printed images and descriptions, so that the periodical's lengthy lists of the year's trends—in sealskin, striped silk, jewels worn in the hair, and so on—would have reflected their own practices; the similar descriptions in the novel may not have registered as utterly outré or boring, as they do to later literary critics. Laurel Brake has shown that when Wilde assumed the journal's editorship, modernizing the title from *The Lady's World*, he foregrounded articles on the woman question, relegating the long fashion rundowns to the back pages.[38] Such moves suggest Wilde's critical purpose in compiling chapter 11's catalogue, which frames from within Dorian's obsession with the book and painting. By linking Dorian's compulsive search for himself in those two works of art to voracious consumerist reading and viewing, Wilde may feminize Dorian, but he may equally reframe women's reading, long maligned as excessive, as actually more reasonable and relatable. The search for novelty, the sense of obligation to finish a boring article, the temporary allure of a new topic, all revolving around the question of how to fashion oneself as an inhabitant of modernity—these had been characterized as the trivial experiences of bourgeois women in the 1860s, but by the 1890s, they affected everyone. Following Baudelaire's lead in "The Painter of Modern Life," Benjamin invoked fashion to valorize ephemeral materiality from the perspective of historical materialism: "The eternal is in any case far more the ruffle of a dress than some idea."[39] Wilde implied something similar when he made the case for historically accurate costuming in new productions of Shakespeare's plays.[40] Each was recognizing fashion as a historical phenomenon that had been accelerated in modernity.

Basil's painting also redirects readers below its elite surface to mass print culture. By the 1890s, the 150-year discourse on women's addictive novel reading was beginning to wear thin, although it still surfaced in periodical pieces—and, remarkably, underwent a resurgence in oil painting.[41] Kelly J. Mays and Kate Flint have each described the discourse's durable metaphorical economy, which diagnosed female readers with disease and addiction, comparing them to animals, savages, and machines.[42] Herself the sort of sensation novelist whose works such critics decried, Mary Elizabeth Braddon had even rewritten *Madame Bovary* as *The Doctor's Wife* (1864), to point out the heroine's folly of daydreaming over novels. Painters in the second half of the nineteenth century enthusiastically depicted women's mediated reveries, in ways that have seemed disparagingly Flaubertian, but can also be read as celebratory. Garrett Stewart has described the genre of paintings of women reading as a hybrid between portraiture and still life.[43] Paintings such as Antoine Wiertz's *The Reader of Novels* (1853), Alfred Stevens's *A Reverie* (1853), and Julius Leblanc Stewart's *An Enthralling Novel* (1885) presented women's media consumption as erotic or sentimental folly.

Figure 15. Edouard Manet, *Woman Reading the Illustrated Magazine*. 1879–80. With the permission of the Art Institute of Chicago / Art Resource, NY.

Consider Edouard Manet's *Woman Reading the Illustrated Magazine* (1880). At first glance, the painting suggests cultural irony: The fashionable young woman consumes a fashionable new periodical, reproducing its style in her dress, makeup, and appearance at a café.[44] But the indeterminate contents of the periodical might confound such easy judgment by viewers, mirroring the woman's use of the magazine to protect and enjoy her anonymity in public.[45] Borrowing from both interpretations, I suggest Manet's blurred Impressionist facture conveys the fast pace with which media consumers had to keep up with mass culture; in the process, a static, plain sense of self gives way to a mobile, obscure one. The painting resembles the woman in "The Decay of Lying," who had imitated the heroine of serial fiction, resulting in an "entire vagueness of character."[46] Like Dorian in chapter 11, this figure rapidly switched enthusiasms: "Sometimes she would give herself up entirely to art. . . . Then she would take to attending race-meetings. . . . She abandoned religion for mesmerism, mesmerism for politics" ("Decay of Lying," 93). Manet's thick buildup of paint recalls the density of this chapter, literalizing the layers of mediation that stick to and fall away from the modern self as media consumer. Dorian's reveries with the book, musical instruments, and other objects of connoisseurship suggest an effort to surpass feminized and petit-bourgeois self-stylings; but such elite enthusiasms could never completely disconnect from the mass culture they repudiated. Nor could the old medium of oil painting escape the mass culture that was driving modernity, as *Woman Reading the Illustrated Magazine* demonstrates. Stewart interprets such paintings to express viewers' fears of unoriginality: "The new premium on fashion illustration in the popular press interpellates your mirror recognition, but with yourself (what there is left of it) as the duplicate of the pictured 'model.'"[47] Wilde mocks such a sentiment, opting instead to document the incorporation of media as a history of his own present. Satirizing both the static, sovereign self that permits no influence and the opposing model of an overinfluenced, multiplied self, he opens a space that crosses both—a paradoxical zone of critical pleasure.

Wilde goes further, suggesting the transposition of life and mass media. Addressing readers at the start of chapter 11, the narrator describes the return to everyday life after a gothic nightmare: "The flameless tapers stand where we had left them, and beside them lies the half-cut book that we had been studying, or the wired flower that we had worn at the ball, or the letter that we had been afraid to read, or that we had read too often" (127). Like the book,

> We have to resume [life] where we had left off, and there steals over us a terrible sense of the necessity for the continuance of energy in the same wearisome round of stereotyped habits, or a wild longing, it may be, that our eyelids might open some morning upon a world that had been refashioned anew in the darkness for our pleasure. (127)

This is how absorptive mass media pleasurably renew and transform reality. Wilde's passage could well be illustrated by Catalan painter Ramón Casas i Carbó's *After the Ball* (1895). Pausing in her reading of a magazine, playbill, or booklet, the subject's drapery radiates outward in a proto-abstract motif that reflects her reverie and announces the composition's modernity. The image was later used to advertise the periodical *Pèl & Ploma*, demonstrating yet another cycle of image appropriation.[48] Dorian's reveries with the book and painting, and his research on his arcane interests, participate in the same psychological economy of entertainment as Casas i Carbó's. Far from vapid, passive, uncritical incorporation, this mode of entertainment represents the exhausting work of self-fashioning.

Stewart has shown that as painting increasingly depicted people's mental lives—for example, by showing them consuming print—paintings also become texts to be read.[49] Wilde observes the phenomenon in "The Critic as Artist": "Since the introduction of printing, and the fatal development of the habit of reading amongst the middle and lower classes of this country, there has been a tendency in literature to appeal more and more to the

Figure 16. Ramón Casas i Carbó, *After the Ball*. 1895. Photo: akg-images.

eye, and less and less to the ear."[50] Just as visual art incorporated literature, so too the meaning of "reading" was converging with seeing. Thus
Dorian characterizes the painting to Basil as a text: "I keep a diary of my
life from day to day, and it never leaves the room in which it is written. I
shall show it to you if you come with me" (147). His self-scouring mode of
reading engenders in Dorian the mounting paranoia of self-surveillance.
"After a few years he could not endure to be long out of England," far from
the painting, and so gives up his homes in Trouville and Algiers that he
had shared with Lord Henry (135). In the midst of extravagant country
house parties, he "would suddenly leave his guests and rush back to town
to see that the door had not been tampered with, and that the picture was
still there" (135). Dorian's range of life reduces to the narrow, locked room
of his boyhood. His habit resembles the reflex or automatic response that
accompanies addiction—a decisively different experience than the intoxicating pleasure that accompanies critical, entertaining media consumption.
As with other addictive substances, enjoyment eventually disappears: "Once
it had given him pleasure to watch it changing and growing old. Of late he
had felt no such pleasure" (212). Had Wilde read Hugo's *The Man Who
Laughs*? In Hugo's description, the epigraph of this section, reverie turns
the tables on its subject; his language of addiction and gambling resounds
through Dorian's transformation. Wilde transposes women's "addictive"
novel reading to Dorian's obsession with the painting, suggesting that
rather than the mass medium of print, it is the old medium of oil painting,
long associated with aristocratic, commissioned portraiture, which facilitates narrowly addictive, paranoid relations.

It may be helpful to pause here and recall Wilde's attitude to addiction
in the novel, exemplified by Lord Henry's comments on smoking. Whereas
temperance writers tried to substitute tracts for the bottle, Wilkie Collins
modeled addictive reading for his readers, and cigarette cards provoked
"addictive" acquisition of trivial information, Wilde prefers to theorize
rather than enact addiction. He does this by ostentatiously substituting a
discourse of pleasure, which addiction cannot countenance. Take Lord
Henry's famous quip about cigarettes: "You must have a cigarette. A cigarette is the perfect type of a perfect pleasure. It is exquisite, and it leaves
one unsatisfied. What more can one want?" (77). One can want no more
than to continue wanting. In this way, Wilde speaks of pleasure, satiation,
and desire rather than compulsion. While subtly acknowledging the experience of tolerance—to an addict, one cigarette will never be enough—
he clearly rejects the traditional Victorian vocabulary of sin, temptation,
and moderation from which concepts of addiction and compulsive behavior

were emerging. Lord Henry tells Dorian with his next breath, "Yes, Dorian, you will always be fond of me. I represent to you all the sins you have never had the courage to commit"; he later says to Lady Ruxton, "Moderation is a fatal thing" (172). Wilde's lighthearted mockery of conventional wisdom, informed by the temperance movement, comes across as ribald and slightly wicked, but it makes the crucial point that living spontaneously and without calculation offers surer ground for ethical relations than conforming to norms of consumption to strike a pose—whether of moral rectitude or, in Dorian's case, recklessness. Taking tobacco smoking, as I suggested in chapter 2, as an icon of modern media consumption, we might note that virtually everyone in Wilde's novel smokes—not just cigarettes, but pipes, cigars, and even a cheroot. The practice represents a condition of modern life so common that it explodes and levels moral norms of consumption. As ubiquitous consumption becomes a condition of everyday life, it becomes forgivable in Wilde's moral economy—that is, if the individual can forgive himself or herself by adjusting to the new norm. Dorian, who cannot, descends into narrow, nearly inhuman confines where no pleasure lies.

Wilde's ingenious argument has proven to be too clever for many readers. Many assume that Dorian is poisoned by Lord Henry's advice and by the book as its extension and emblem. They take at face value the aristocratic characters' mockery of mass culture. My focus on reverie reveals instead Wilde's complex revaluation of elite and mass forms in a changing mass print media culture. Reverie, the time and space in which the modern self could be present with itself, was increasingly mediated, as shown in chapter 2. Wilde does not reject this present-day reality; rather, he examines its experiential contours and psychological effects, and contrasts it to the older model of elite art. His valorization of the new mode of seemingly superficial mass media consumption over the old one of classical art, static identity, and limited meaning seems counterintuitive only after a twentieth century in which "the media" became a byword for distortion and inauthenticity. The critical pleasure, the intoxicating imbibing of new ideas and representations, and the self's response to them, which characterize his representation of Dorian's reveries with the book, are contexts in which affect can move and, so to speak, breathe. Wilde is equally keen to show how this life and motion can slow into the rigid conformity of static notions of the self—the defensive mode of paranoia, and the limited affective range and focus of addiction. I will return to these topics as I move from reverie to the media consumer's characteristic reproduction of the material he has consumed in his "personality."

Personality: The Performance of Mass Culture

> A human being can only acquire the sort of personality you mean
> after a long experience of struggle and suffering and thanks to an
> inherent and powerfully developed disposition. Such a personality is
> very rare. Besides, you couldn't possibly already be the sort of person
> who's found a rational ground for her existence within herself and
> who, in all circumstances, maintains and develops her own individual
> and immutable nature and preserves it from all that's alien and
> negative, for everything in you is as yet unformed, unspoken and
> undeveloped. Although you're an adorable, infinitely adorable
> and enchanting young girl with an upright soul and a richly talented,
> frank and already self-assured person, you are still not a personality.
>
> GUSTAV MAHLER, letter to Alma Schindler, 1901

Gustav Mahler's letter to his future wife reveals the tensions structuring
the meanings of the term "personality" at the end of the nineteenth
century.[51] For Mahler, personality is both an inherent power and a quality
developed through the experience of suffering; it is both unchangeable and
capable of development; it preserves what is already there against external
influences, and yet its formation must take place through them. By the passage's end, his concession that Alma is an "enchanting young girl," seems
to reserve the status of personality for more established—or legitimate—
social subjects. Although the word *personality* sounds like an adverb that
might describe a way of being a person, one can be a person who is not a
personality—Alma's somewhat abject state. And yet having apparently
striven to achieve personality before her time, she suggests that Mahler's
opinions were not uncontested. Alma offers a productive point of reference for Dorian in Wilde's novel and for the questions Wilde asks about
influence and self-development in mass-mediated modernity. On the one
hand, personality offered a retrenched position of stability and selfhood
against what Georg Simmel called the "strangest eccentricities" by which
neurotic urbanites attempted to establish their difference from others; on
the other hand, precisely those superficial "extravagances of self-distanciation,
of caprice, of fastidiousness" seemed to suggest quite precisely ways of being
a person in modernity.[52]

Since around 1710, personality had meant "the distinctive personal or
individual character of a person, esp. of a marked or unusual kind."[53] With
the burgeoning of print culture at the turn of the nineteenth century, distinction overlapped with fame, and the social context that conferred it
became media consumption. As "personality" became synonymous with

"celebrity," Samuel Taylor Coleridge disparaged "the age of personality," complaining about the increased interest in the private lives of authors.[54] David Higgins notes that the turn toward "personality" and "celebrity" indexed a new interest in the private lives of authors as the source of their "genius" in literary self-expression.[55] This interest only developed rather than disappeared with the waning of Romanticism. Although personality thrived in social and mediated spheres, it also indicated an essentially private self-relation. In the latter half of the century it became the province of psychology, as the "conscious aspects of behavior" and "tantamount to an internal self."[56] Together, the social and subjective aspects of personality began to supplant the term "character."[57] Yet personality thrived in image culture, in which someone's appearance and attitude could be recognized at a glance. Paradoxically, the actor Henry Irving's electric personality seemed most authentic when most mediated by elaborate stagecraft.[58] In the 1890s, personality held in tension subject and society, privacy and publicity, genuineness and artifice. Moreover, these tensions influenced tacit understandings of affect as either an essentially private, solitary, contemplative mode, which I discussed in the first section as associated with reverie, or a public, social, embodied, energetic phenomenon, linked to personality.

Wilde was alive to this tension, and in *The Picture of Dorian Gray* and in his oeuvre generally, he uses personality in deliberately provocative ways, leveraging its private and public contexts. In "The Soul of Man under Socialism," it substitutes for and eclipses "soul" as the name of humankind's true essence: "It will be a marvelous thing—the true personality of man—when we see it."[59] In "The Critic as Artist," it becomes the social ground of art: "As art springs from personality, so it is only to personality that it can be revealed, and from the meeting of the two comes right interpretive criticism."[60] Yet in both that essay and in *The Picture of Dorian Gray*, "personality" is also trivial, a matter of self-reproduction that echoes mass production: "Is insincerity such a terrible thing? I think not. It is merely a method by which we can multiply our personalities" (137). The statement is the narrator's only first-person intrusion in the novel, though Wilde performs the multiplication of personality by concluding, "Such, at any rate, was Dorian Gray's opinion" (137). The joke draws on personality's Greek root as appearance or mask, emphasizing its changeability. Imbuing its social character with theatricality, Wilde offsets personality's association with unchanging character. The affects associated with more performative personalities may seem inauthentic, but they are really more finely attuned to social situations. Teresa Brennan draws attention to affect's formation in its transmission between people, rather than arising within the self-contained individual, as the Western individualist tradition formalized by Freud would have it.[61] Wilde too resists this dominant paradigm. In his exploration of personality and its intersubjective affects, he differs from Pater, for whom personality was "a thick wall" that cordoned off one's subjective experiences and impressions from others, and which no voice could pierce (*Renaissance*, 151). For Wilde, both the subjective and social contexts of personality suggest a mobile self, "permeated by otherness . . . generated and regenerated through a process of constant interaction with others."[62] The multiplication of personality indicates this dynamism; moreover, it figuratively opens it to the sphere of mass production.

Performance realized personality's figurative potential.[63] Throughout his writings, Wilde reconceptualized personality as performance; it shines through in the chapters of the novel that resemble his society comedies. By adapting the dandyism of the earlier part of the century to the media-saturated 1890s, he prompted a reading of the elite social sphere of aristocrats, drawing rooms, and country homes, as the wider sphere of mass culture. Several chapters of the novel, like his plays, foreground an economy of style, in which one aggregates personal value by building a reputation for wittiness, beauty, taste, and scandal; the sign of this value is ever-greater social circulation, whether in person or as the subject of gossip. The medium of this economy is conversation; characters strive to talk well and to be talked about; to look exquisite and to be seen. Paul M. Fortunato describes these efforts as a "spectrum of performance," likening them to a medium that reverses the base-superstructure model of self-expression.[64] Wilde's characters constantly spout their priorities within this economy. Lady Narborough laments never having had flirtations, since her husband "was dreadfully shortsighted, and there is no pleasure in taking a husband who never sees anything" (168). One of her guests is Lady Roxton, "who was always trying to get herself compromised, but was so peculiarly plain that to her great disappointment no one would ever believe anything against her" (168). When Gladys, the Duchess of Monmouth, says, "All good hats are made out of nothing," Harry responds, "Like all good reputations" (188). Such declarations described new, mediated social realities that organized middle- and working-class life. Scandal, gossip, reputation, and self-promotion had always operated locally within these classes, but when mass culture introduced new styles and attached new desires to them, self-image became a larger ongoing project and performance to be managed. Its affects became complexly tied to social experiences in ways that may seem superficial, but were merely new. Thus Wilde satirized the scene of self-commodification, generating humor from its incongruous setting among normally staid, upper-crust characters. Continually performing their personalities, they reflect the dilemma of how to be oneself—or just give up and become someone else—in a mass-mediated world.

Sibyl Vane struggles with this dilemma; she and her mother help build the novel's discourse of personality as performance. At first, they seem to fulfill the old notion of women as media addicts, so immersed in drama and fiction that they cannot see the truth: "But women never know the curtain has fallen. They always want a sixth act, and a soon as the interest of the play is entirely over they propose to continue it" (99). Mrs. Vane calculates the "theatrical picturesqueness" of the domestic scenes between herself and her children, and Sibyl invents adventure plots for James's sojourn to Australia, complete with gold fields, bushrangers, and an heiress (61, 64). Neil Hultgren has shown how Wilde revised the novel to include melodramatic incident while simultaneously destabilizing melodrama's moralizing tendencies.[65] Sibyl's nicknaming Dorian "Prince Charming" evokes the juvenile, scripted quality of her own sense of her experience, before she feels actual love. Dorian's attraction to her fulfills her script and his own. He clearly identifies her not as a talented artist, but as someone who has personality—indeed, as one who has successfully multiplied it: "She is all the great heroines of the world in one. She is more than an individual," he claims, advertising her to his friends. As with the objects of his other reveries, Sibyl draws Dorian in addictive terms: "I get hungry for her presence," he attests. "Every night of my life I go to see her act, and every night she is more marvelous" (54). Yet she is not a person he wants to know or for whom he cares. In Dorian's expostulation that Sibyl Vane is "sacred," and thus not for his sexual consumption, we see his desire for her as a disembodied image, replacing the conventional heteronormative narrative of sexual attraction (52). In his obsessive consumption of her performances, we see the beginning of fandom, and in particular, the early gay fandom of stage and screen actresses.[66] Ronald Thomas shows how theaters such as Sibyl's would showcase early cinema features a mere five years after the novel's publication.[67] When Henry describes Sibyl's death as "a wonderful scene from Webster, or Ford, or Cyril Tourneur," he hints at the regime of personality as mediated life (100). Dorian's claim that Sibyl "has personality," resonates as an early instance of the traditional show business phrase. A code for sexual charisma, it means one adeptly recycles mass cultural erotic signs.

Readers likely recoil at Lord Henry's callousness about Sibyl, because in between her fanciful immersion in fictional and theatrical worlds and her death, she had consciously and purposely rejected the stage in favor of her authentic feelings for Dorian. But Lord Henry's misogynistic comments about women's histrionic immersion in life as a series of scenes must be interpreted ironically, since he intends his insensitive remarks to prompt Dorian's self-exposure as an egotist. Sibyl's awakening begins to undermine the conventional notion that women only ever compulsively immerse themselves in, and construct themselves from, media images; Wilde also satirizes the accompanying idea that they exist only as media spectacles for masculine entertainment and delight. Indeed, it is Dorian who comes to conform to the satirized depiction of consumerist femininity. At first, his search for theory and practice and his desire to surpass his status as fashion plate recall the more serious female readership of *Woman's World*, which tried to ground its nascent feminism in modern thought. The "new hedonism" sounds like other new intellectual trends, such as the New Woman. Though Wilde moved the fashion rundowns to the back of the journal, he still had to cater to older and more appearance-obsessed women. Lord Henry wittily describes such consumers: "As long as a woman can look ten years younger than her own daughter, she is perfectly satisfied" (48). The quip feminizes Dorian's wish to remain young and recalls his obsessive relationship to the painting. Dorian may seem like women trying to replicate static media images, obsessing over tiny lines in his aging, reflected face.[68] Yet this similarity does not feminize Dorian; rather, it exposes women's ordinary beauty practices as defensive and paranoid. It also suggests that such self-image consumption is no longer the exclusive province of women. It is now the task of both sexes and different classes—the effect of an ever-expanding mass media literacy: "We live in an age that reads too much to be wise, and that thinks too much to be beautiful" (101). In the 1890s, media immersion ceases to be women's special defect, expanding its reach to become a force within a broader consumerist lifestyle. This shift opens room for Sibyl's love of Dorian to be both frivolously generated by sentimental mass media clichés and worthy of the respect of true feeling.

Like the female actress, the dandy embodies the dilemma of personality in a mass-mediated age. Though he seems to reject mass culture, it is actually the true ground of the dandy's self-fashioning. His novelty can emerge only as the refashioning or recycling of the status quo, in slightly different but nonetheless recognizable form. Dorian's dandyism, an echo of Wilde's, perfectly epitomizes this dynamic; moreover, the novel also registers the dandy's dependence on the mass. Although he takes pleasure in thinking of himself as a trendsetter, Dorian also frets that this status is too ephemeral and trivial. He "desired to be something more than . . . to be consulted on the wearing of a jewel, or the knotting of a necktie, or the conduct of a cane" (125). Rather, he wishes to found the new, Paterian hedonism grounded in sensual experience. Apparently marking this difference between aesthetic philosophy and everyday life, high and low culture, dandy and mass, Wilde really implies their dialectical pairing. As a dandy, Dorian constantly reinvents mass culture, emerging both as its type and exception: "Very young men . . . saw, or fancied they saw in Dorian Gray the true realization of a type" (125). Wilde's language is precise: The dominance of mass culture means that originality is no longer legible; rather, there are only preexisting types, which may be more or less truly manifested.[69] Gagnier describes this social logic when she claims the dandy as the "unconscious" of nineteenth-century mass culture; in other words, the dandy appears to defy mass culture while actually drawing on it. Wilde limns this exchange in "The Decay of Lying": "A great artist invents a type, and Life tries to copy it, to reproduce it in a popular form, like an enterprising publisher."[70] In the sentence, Wilde's imprecise "Life" grows clear as something like the social effects of mass communication, an idea's journey from the avant-garde to the masses; as a printing metaphor, the term "type" suggests this incipient reproducibility. Dorian is the "enterprising publisher." He never founds a new philosophy based on Lord Henry's maxims, but he disseminates elements of style to impressionable young men—the novel's stand-ins for mass consumers, who, enthralled with him, "copied him in everything that he did" (125). Tracing the circuits of media incorporation and resignification, the novel reminds us that in mass culture, the subject of mediated reverie also becomes available for others' reverie and imitation. Mass media triangulate social relations, replacing people with personalities.

Dorian's frustration reveals the new texture of social change that is driven by personalities. "He sought to elaborate some new scheme of life that would have its reasoned philosophy and its ordered principles, and find in the spiritualizing of the senses its highest realization" (125–26). Yet only trivial practices can be successfully imitated: "The young exquisites of the Mayfair balls and Pall Mall club windows . . . tried to reproduce the accidental charm of his graceful, though to him only half-serious, fopperies" (125). The Paterian rejection of theory and valorization of the senses cannot be mass-reproduced; only the signs of them can. Dandyism, whether of the earlier part of the century or in its Wildean resurgence, gestures against dominant styles and norms, but it exhausts itself in the assertion of its counter-aesthetics. Wilde, engaging Baudelaire's famous definition of art as half modern, half eternal, makes clear that fashion and dandyism are only partial measures in reshaping the world: "Fashion, by which what is really fantastic becomes for a moment universal, and Dandyism, which, in its own way, is an attempt to assert the absolute modernity of beauty, had of course, their fascination for him" (125).[71] Fashion and dandyism can do no more than fascinate, because they must cite the norms of mass culture to which they posit alternatives. They achieve universality only "for a moment": In asserting beauty's modernity as "absolute," they sentence their own gesture to quick obsolescence. Wilde could deploy the dandy, both in his own self-styling as a famous personality and as the figure of Dorian in his novel, to gain traction against the reigning model of Victorian aesthetics as morally edifying, and this itself amounted to a significant social change. But he knew that the next turn, of establishing a new creed, could not come about: When mass culture triangulates social relations, social change would always be indirect and unlooked for. The novel thus continues to expose Dorian's naïveté in his hope for a radically changed world.

The novel's dandy par excellence, Lord Henry, exemplifies the capacities and limitations of personality to create social change. Within the bourgeois economy of self-fashioning, he constantly creates new value through his witty, paradoxical reconfigurations of ideas. "Nowadays most people die of a sort of creeping common sense, and discover when it is too late that the only things one never regrets are one's mistakes" (42). "It is perfectly monstrous . . . the way people go about nowadays saying things against one behind one's back that are absolutely and entirely true" (170). Though the quips' sharp observations and critiques never build into social action, the tiny adjustment that reverses the entire meaning of the maxim causes it to implode, generates novelty and surprise. Though his witticisms rehearse the conventions they mock, they force consumers to see them in a new light. Dorian's error is to commit himself religiously to their singular influence rather than allowing them to be one of many influences— that is, to open himself to the tumult of mass-mediated modernity. By codifying Henry's impostures and pursuing them as a creed, he makes them as sterile and ridiculous as the hoary Victorian values they skewer. "Well, one evening about seven o'clock, I determined to go out in search of some adventure. I felt that this grey, monstrous London of ours, with its myriads of people, its sordid sinners, and its splendid sins, as you once phrased it, must have something in store for me. The mere danger gave me a sense of delight" (48). Dorian hits the streets looking for action, but he ends up at Sibyl's theater—a site of mass culture, with its tawdriness, vulgarity, and third-rate rendition of *Romeo and Juliet*. His romance with Sibyl echoes the play's by then hackneyed plot of cross-class love. The maxims of Aestheticism, put into action, merely recycle stereotyped popular stories. As a personality stuck within a mass-mediated culture, Dorian orbits what he imagines to be a more genuine or truer sphere of action, without ever joining it. The novel adds another instance of this consumption of personality when Lord Henry enjoys watching Dorian's develop.

Coleridge dubbed the turn of the nineteenth century the "age of personality"; Wilde identified his moment as another epoch in its history. Through Basil's brief lecture on the history of painting, the novel provides a theory of personality as an aesthetic medium that resembles performance. Basil claims,

> There are only two eras of any importance in the world's history. The first is the appearance of a new medium for art, and the second is the appearance of a new personality for art also. What the invention of oil-painting was to the Venetians, the face of Antinous was to late Greek sculpture, and the face of Dorian Gray will some day be to me. (13)

Basil turns out to be wrong, since his idealization of Dorian fundamentally mistook his motives, affections, and capabilities. But Basil also proposes a role for personality in a materialist, aesthetic history, by having it reside in the face. The novel constantly describes Dorian's face in mediumistic terms, its nostrils and lips both "chiseled." This metaphor invokes sculpture, an art not amenable to mass reproduction; but Dorian's face is also associated with photography, since it presumably appears in Lord Henry's eighteen photographs of him—evidence of the older man's own fascination with him. Traditional and mass art forms converge in Dorian as an image or mask rather than a self or psyche. For example, having just met Dorian, Lord Henry tells him that he might be the new symbol the century has been waiting for: "With your personality there is nothing you could not do" (25). This is clearly more of Wilde's satire, since Dorian—like Alma—is too undeveloped to have a personality that rationally grounds his existence. It is confirmed as such at the novel's end, when Henry praises him for never having done anything with his personality: "I am so glad that you have never done anything, never carved a statue, or painted a picture, or produced anything outside of yourself!" (207). For better or worse, Wilde implies, Dorian is the icon of an age that characteristically consumes and reproduces. Such an age typifies modern paralysis—the

inability to act in ways more obviously efficacious than through performance. One can hear the satire in the extravagant absurdity with which
Dorian's anonymous love letter writer—Basil himself?—claimed, "The
curves of your lips rewrite history" (210).

Yet Wilde is not indicting the superficiality or consumerism of the age,
but rather Dorian's rearguard response to it. This point can be difficult to
grasp given the common reading that Dorian's media immersion scram-
bles his moral compass, causing him to murder Basil and blackmail Alan
Campbell. I dispute this misreading. Consider instead Rachel Bowlby's
judgment, that "far from being poisonous, or an antidote to poison, the
morality plot functions more like a parody of the style of the 'sensational'
novels and tabloid newspapers of the period."[72] Charles Bernheimer sec-
onds this notion of parody: "Rather than embodying a lesson in ethics—if
you destroy your soul you kill yourself—it offers a sort of comic send-up
of this message." In his view, Wilde instead exposes "the mistake of imagining that life is anything other than art, that a soul is anything other than
a style of representation."[73] Bernheimer's insight about art applies to media. Dorian's mediated reveries and development of a hyperperformative
personality do not cause his crimes. His death, like Sibyl's, is the darkly
humorous consequence of his attempt to extricate himself from his historical moment of mass cultural immersion and reenter an unmediated
world—an environment that no longer exists. Despite his media consumer's reverie and reproduction of it as a "multiform" personality, Dorian fails
to multiply his personality: "I am too much concentrated on myself. My
own personality has become a burden to me. I want to escape, to go away,
to forget" (137, 195). If Dorian could effortlessly integrate himself with
mass culture, then he would adopt styles and poses that felt natural. Instead, having retreated from a dynamic self to a static one, Dorian has become mechanical, delusional, and paranoid. From the intoxicated, critical
pleasure of sampling others' ideas and identities, he has become a joyless
addict, leering at his opium before he hits the docks. The scene is motivated by the same mordant humor with which Walter Benjamin, in his
essay "Surrealism" described the ennui of addiction, not to the usual
substances, but to "that most terrible drug—ourselves—which we take in
solitude."[74]

If affect seems to have disappeared from the scene of personality, it is
not because personality is superficial and affect is deep. Rather, it is because
Wilde's satire cannot make a straightforward, visible case for a new model
of affect transmitted through social interactions. However, his novel
can, and does, mock the old, individualist model of affect as solitary and

self-contained. In the first section of this chapter, I demonstrated how reverie, especially the reverie associated with desultory reading, facilitated the transmission of affect between media consumers and mass culture. Wilde represented the space of this reverie as intoxicated, critical pleasure. When Dorian's intoxication turns to addiction, and his reverie to paranoia, Wilde begins to critique the self-contained model of affect more directly.

As the painting acquires the status of "the most magical of mirrors," the function of its supernatural exceptionality becomes clearer as a metaphor for its transfer from the realm of open to closed circulation, or mass to elite culture (103). As his own portrait, gifted by the artist, the painting has personal meaning; Dorian's wish that the painting would have an even more exceptional relationship to him exacerbates this rarefied social context. In this paranoid logic, the artwork's meaning for others is irrelevant, and there is no disputing its significance as being for Dorian only. Wilde satirizes this dynamic: His friend, from "The Decay of Lying," experiences "real terror" as she finishes the installment of the novel printed in a magazine, because she knows she must act out its script. Likewise, Dorian's self-discovery in the pages of the book and in the lines of the painting terrifies him. (Wilde, "Decay of Lying," 94). It registers his desire for a reduced field of media consumption, which limits the uncertainty and labor of self-fashioning. Following only a handful of guiding lights—the book, the painting, Lord Henry's paradoxes—helps Dorian evade not only the welter of mass media but also moral decisions and spontaneous action. The supernatural, gothic conceit encodes Dorian's paranoia, and with it, Wilde's realist account of the challenges of mediated modern life. The Faustian pact insulates Dorian from a meaningful encounter with an artwork that garners variable meanings by circulating through society. Literalizing the idea that "his own soul was looking out at him from the canvas and calling him to judgment," the novel invokes the supernatural to explain a contemporary social formation—the point at which intoxicated, mediated reverie turns into addictive, paranoid imitation of mass media models (116).

The novel's gothic idiom steers it between suspense and black comedy as it dispassionately studies Dorian's paranoia through its analysis of "suggestion." Assigning too much authority to the painting and the book, Dorian narrows his media consumption. Wilde lampoons his overattribution of agency to the painting in the scene just before he kills Basil: "Dorian Gray glanced at the picture, and suddenly an uncontrollable feeling of hatred for Basil Hallward came over him, as though it had been suggested to him by the image on the canvas, whispered into his ear by those grinning lips" (151). The painting's whisper is Dorian's paranoid projection. Gazing incessantly at the same painting, obsessively rereading the same book, and becoming fascinated with a stage actress are ways of fashioning oneself; but egoistically believing that they refer to oneself is a delusion that ignores the existence of mass culture. Wilde is mocking the specter of suggestion, which had long featured in conservative anxieties that mass media could impose its makers' wills on impressible publics the way mesmerists could implant hypnotic suggestions. In the 1890s, crowd psychologists would elaborate this notion of suggestion to explain the delusions and violence of the mass.[75] The idea that an artwork or mass media item could make a specific, directive suggestion—for example, to kill someone—is itself the delusion. Earlier in the novel, Wilde had given a more realistic model of how suggestion operates, when Basil tells Lord Henry that Dorian "is never more present in my work than when no image of him is there. He is a suggestion, as I have said, of a new manner" (14). Suggestion functions more plausibly here as an unspecific motive, inspiration. When a paranoid Dorian removes the painting from circulation and abandons his moral autonomy to it, Wilde reveals the exhaustion of aristocratic culture and its old media. Lacking self-detachment, humor, and pleasure, Dorian cannot adapt to mass culture, nor can he return to the static self of the high cultural past.

The Picture of Dorian Gray thus documents the new psychological terrain shaped by mass media: Although the process of losing and finding one's self within models found in mass media requires constant attention and alertness, the process also demands self-detachment. Whereas modern reverie had become mediated, taking place within the pages of print or in the moments of pause between their consumption, the premodern, obsolete version of wild, delirious revelry resurfaced in Dorian's paranoid intensity—just as it had flashed up in Rousseau's unwarranted fears of persecution. To reflect this oscillation between domesticated and untamed thought, Wilde chose the gothic idiom, claiming it as "the art of those whose minds have been troubled with the malady of reverie." Alive to its suitability for reflecting such challenging negotiations of identity, he described its "enduring vitality" as a mass cultural style (126). In chapter 3, I showed how the gothic furnished bourgeois deep subjectivity with a visual vocabulary taken from mass print media. E. T. A. Hoffmann's fantastic aesthetic, Victor Hugo's Romantic imagery, and Hermann Rorschach's eldritch inkblots set the iconography of the Freudian unconscious, which was thought to be distant from mass cultural cliché. In *The Picture of Dorian Gray*, Wilde deconstructed this cultural logic. The novel reflects instead this very play between depth and surface in describing personality in the age of mass media consumption. What better idiom than the gothic, so adept at embodying mass culture while seeming countercultural, for Wilde's masterful, darkly comic rendering of the media consumer's dilemmas?

Luhmann writes persuasively of the way that mass print culture inculcates a search for authentic personal identity within its consumers: "Individuals are encouraged to believe that . . . they must become even more real (or unreal?) than they already are" (114). This belief is not a symptom of false consciousness; Luhmann's is rather a neutral observation of the psychological effects of mass culture. As a mediated everyman, Dorian suffers from "the problem of modernity" that can be treated only by judicious, temperate image incorporation: "Too many images in the air; none in me. And yet some have lodged in me, but are they mine?"[76] Wilde sympathized with this dilemma; that is why he satirized the conventional Victorian view that "all influence is immoral." One of his many accomplishments, in *The Picture of Dorian Gray*, was to plot the pleasures and perils of losing oneself in media, over and over again.

Coda: Mass Culture and Gay Identity

What exactly happens when the painting survives Dorian's stabbing? Many critics focus on Dorian's corpse, but the "splendid portrait of their master as they had last seen him, in all the wonder of his exquisite youth and beauty" is also performing cultural work: It makes an argument against censorship (213). Wilde's preface intervened in the shifting scene of largely informal censorship in the period, as Barbara Leckie explores, by strategically proclaiming the autonomy of the aesthetic.[77] But taking Wilde at his word has never been a surefooted critical strategy. It is not merely that the painting, like all art, outlives its human makers and inspirations, but that it triumphs over efforts to hide it from the people—in this passage, from the gaze of Dorian's servants. The argument is for aesthetic autonomy, but it is also crucially—and less obviously—for the unregulated circulation of cultural productions through the mass market. As Jonathan Freedman notes, Wilde's Aestheticism disparages the market while making it work for him, "in the name of the mysterious, organic, and transcendent powers of art."[78] The unfettered operation of capital quietly powers the mass cultural system to which Wilde subscribes, in which subversive figures such as the dandy and the actress constantly replenish outworn cultural tropes. The system of mass cultural consumption and reproduction enacted through reverie and the performance of personality allows for constant self-fashioning. Structural protections for self-fashioning are vital to the generation of new identities—in this case, gay ones. Indeed, the argument against the censorship of art is inextricable from the defense of the gay desire that creates it. Basil invests his desire for Dorian into the painting: In the 1890 version, his "extraordinary romance"; in the 1891 version, his "curious artistic idolatry." He worries that "the world might guess it; and I will not bare my soul to their shallow, prying eyes" (14). Dorian reinforces this self-suppression when Basil confesses his desire to him, and his calculated response amounts to blackmail. His sequestration of the painting and his murder of Basil perform homophobic violence. As I stated above, Wilde is playing out Dorian's inability to integrate himself into mass-mediated modernity; this includes the circulation of gay desire and the art to which it gives rise.

But Wilde's gesture against artistic and sexual censorship works both ways, since it conversely suggests that Basil cannot remain in the closet, making art for no one but him and his beloved. Narrating to Lord Henry his first meeting with Dorian, Basil notes, "I believe some picture of mine had made a great success at the time, at least had been chattered about in the penny newspapers, which is the nineteenth-century standard of immortality" (10). Basil's offhand elitism reflects the older period of artistic patronage, an era on the wane. As Lord Henry, ever the proponent of commodifying one's experiences, rejoins later on, "Nowadays a broken heart will run to many editions" (14). The novel thus raises the possibility that the expansion of a disguised market for gay desire will push it into visibility. Long before Dorian stabbed the painting, Basil had meditated a violent attack on it, in order to prove his commitment to Dorian. But the novel's doomed artist and subject imply that art can no longer be created and destroyed in private drawing rooms, gardens, and attics, and among tiny coteries. Critics typically assume this aristocratic milieu as part of the novel's realist idiom, but Wilde invests his measured descriptions of it with the preciousness of the past. Marked by Decadent ennui, they are scenes that have outlived their own dramatic life.

In Sedgwick's foundational reading, *The Picture of Dorian Gray* deploys an "alibi of abstraction" to cover over the "'open secret' or glass closet" of gay desire with the "public rhetoric of the 'empty secret'" characteristic of modernism (*Epistemology of the Closet*, 164). This tendency in the novel can be seen in Basil's long speech to Dorian that begins with his confession of desire: "Dorian, from the moment I met you, your personality had the most extraordinary influence over me"; and narrates Basil's process of rationalization that concludes with modernism's antirepresentational brief: "Art is always more abstract than we fancy. Form and colour tell us of form and colour—that is all" (*Dorian Gray*, 111). For Sedgwick, this is the central tension within the novel, which has given rise to its teaching as an example of "the divided self" or "life and art" without any acknowledgment of its gay content (161). Refocusing our attention on Wilde's defense of mass culture as the historical reality of 1891 instead demonstrates that the two themes are as inseparable from each other as are mass and elite culture. As I've demonstrated, at the outset of the novel Dorian looks to mass culture to find his "real" self, but when he discovers the realities and possibilities of gay desire, he reacts by repressing them and censoring the painting as evidence of them. The force of mass media is precisely to make such desire visible, but at the same time, as open to interpretation—the "chatter" of the penny newspapers, which must now be taken seriously. Mediated reverie and the performance of mass culture as personality can be alienating and confusing, but they can also be reparative: They can affirm identifications and desires, fostering intersubjectivity and community. Luhmann had described the cultural demand that mass media consumers "become more real" (*Reality of the Mass Media*, 114). Feeling "more real" can repair the social damage done to those who are not already socially visible or validated. But Basil and Dorian cling to the old media model of aristocratic patronage, and their fear and homophobic paranoia close down the potential for gay visibility unleashed by mass media circulation.

The old, aristocratic gay male community had struck a certain bargain: It enjoyed permissive sexual privileges in exchange for public silence about them.[79] Mass print media began to dilute this social agreement even before Wilde's trials. Lee Edelman posits "homographesis" as the internal quality that forces visible signification of homosexuality; but this force is more plausibly attributed to the new operation of mass media self-fashioning than to any intrinsic gay quality.[80] The widespread practice of identification through mass print consumption helps confirm existing desires and build them into identities. As Dorian read and reread his favorite book, "Things that he had dimly dreamed of were suddenly made real to him" (*Dorian Gray*, 120). As Edelman correctly observes of the drive to recognition and visibility, it enacts a double operation of conservative policing and progressive destabilization.[81] That is, making gay desire visible blazes a politically liberalizing trajectory out of the closet and toward gay rights; but the new visibility operates within its own regimes of surveillance, indoctrination, and identification. When the novel participates in this doubled gesture, it defends mass culture against the class-based privileges of privacy. It tries to close a chapter in the history of closeted gay aesthetics and to open a new one grounded in mass media, which as we have seen, obliges consumption and reproduction of social norms. Through mediated reverie, identification, and the performance of personality, social change happens indirectly and almost imperceptibly, without elected leaders and organization. It is in this way that the actress, the dandy, and mass culture gradually reshape the social body.

As a mass media object, the novel itself underwent acts of censorship that returned it to the older, closeted model. As Nicholas Frankel and other scholars have shown, Joseph Marshall Stoddart, editor of *Lippincott's Monthly Magazine*, made numerous changes to Wilde's typescript to downplay Basil's sexual attraction to Dorian.[82] To return to Basil's long speech that culminates in the defense of artistic abstraction—perhaps the best-known example—the 1890 version has him confessing,

> [I] have worshipped you with far more romance of feeling than a man usually gives to a friend. Somehow, I had never loved a woman. I suppose I never had time. . . . Well, from the moment I met you, your personality had the most extraordinary influence over me. I quite admit that I adored you madly, extravagantly, absurdly.[83]

In the 1891 single-volume edition of the novel published by Ward and Lock, this confession becomes less sexual and affective, and more aesthetic:

> Dorian, from the moment I met you, your personality had the most extraordinary influence over me. I was dominated, soul, brain, and power by you. You became to me the visible incarnation of that unseen ideal whose memory haunts us artists like an exquisite dream. (110)

The well-known reason for Wilde's de-accentuation of Basil's desire was the furor in Britain over the homoeroticism in the *Lippincott's* version, which had even caused W. H. Smith to pull the publication from its railway racks. The *Daily Chronicle* infamously called it "a tale spawned from the leprous literature of the French Décadents—a poisonous book, the atmosphere of which is heavy with the mephitic odours of moral and spiritual putrefaction" (217). Coded reactions against the novel's gay content, including its "effeminate frivolity," "Wardour Street Aestheticism," and "wickedness or filthiness" abounded.

How might the revised, single-volume version have struck readers? Laurel Brake points out, "By 1887, homosexual discourse had begun to appear intermittently in periodicals largely read by men, and to be denounced as well."[84] The return from a more explicit to a more encoded gay desire makes identification with male-male attraction and affection more an act of imagination and less one of recognition. It puts reading on the slow, wandering path of reverie rather than in the quick consumption of familiarity. It challenges self-fashioning in a different way: Incipiently gay readers of 1891 might have been entranced by vagueness, as Dorian was with Lord Henry's book; whereas those of 1890 might be thrilled, or shocked, by representational clarity, and challenged to meet it. The return to the literary closet reflects the uneven transition to mass print media capacious enough to nurture gay representation. It also reflected the difference between a novel appearing serially in a magazine and one presented as an aesthetic whole in a single volume. We might more accurately call this "incipiently gay" cultural space a queer one, in order to acknowledge the potential of the indeterminate, in-between, backward- and forward-looking energies of the self-fashioning mass print consumer.

A second instance of Dorian's mediated reverie shows how the desire for media sedation and self-forgetfulness affects gay recognition from within queer possibilities. This act of consumption, from the latter part of the novel, charts Dorian's distance from his earlier self-fashioning through Lord Henry's poisonous book. I contextualized that earlier experience as one of intoxicating critical pleasure. Later, having become fully paranoid, closeted, and homophobic, Dorian attempts to treat his books not as specific, personal occasions, but as undifferentiated substances or anesthetic drugs. Having just murdered Basil, Dorian pulls Théophile Gautier's *Emaux et Camées* "at hazard" from his shelf, proceeds to read, and loses himself in its scenes of Venice—until they recall his own memory of visiting that city: "He remembered the autumn that he had passed there, and a wonderful love that had stirred him to mad, delightful follies. . . . Basil had been with him part of the time, and had gone wild over Tintoret. Poor Basil!" (157). Dorian had conceived of a book, and any book would do, as a drug to help him forget, since Basil's murder "was a thing to be driven out of the mind, to be drugged with poppies, to be strangled lest it strangle one itself" (156). Yet as an anesthetic to dull the senses and induce amnesia, Gautier's book fails to quiet Dorian's memories; rather, it broadens and deepens them, bringing back Basil, the anonymous Venetian love, and the book's giver, Adrian Singleton. The book binds each man to Dorian in homoerotic terms. Its own history makes it too specific to be consumed lightly, as entertainment. The tension between the two models can be seen in the book's materiality—its "Japanese paper," "Jacquemart etching," "citron-green leather" binding, and "a design of . . . dotted pomegranates" (156). As elite, handcrafted features, they are associated with the book's uniqueness to Dorian; but Dorian, looking for distraction and anesthesia, takes them as the showy phantasmagoria of an impersonal, anonymous mass culture. Yet neither model can dominate over the other. Mass media always fail to remain anonymous; they cannot help becoming personalized when consumed. Conversely, elite handmade artifacts cannot confine themselves to idiosyncratic, cloistered meanings: The rare edition's very efforts to set itself apart from mass media recall their relation, as the force of popularity created the space for outré, avant-garde niches. And, as Frankel notes, "Books were subject to the incursion of spectacular new technologies of production—photomechanical engraving, new dyes and materials for bookbinding, new means for the production of paper."[85] As a material and a style, the green leather may be less rarefied than it seems.

Dorian's paranoid turn to homophobic repression fits with a perspective on mass culture and sovereign selfhood in which books are undifferentiated substances to be used, not laboratories for self-experimentation. He attempts to fulfill a caricature of the mass media consumer as drugged nonthinker, but fails—as do all who attempt it. No individual can consume media as an anonymous "media consumer." These tensions recall those of *Peter Ibbetson*, in which media consumption increasingly depersonalized Peter by converting his experience into information. As I argued in chapter 4, Peter learns to "dream true," or consume media mechanically, to compensate for his real-life disappointments. Du Maurier and his readers were enthusiastic about this fantasy of psychological flattening. Wilde's view, by contrast, reflected greater psychological realism—perhaps because he was invested in challenging heteronormative culture by suggesting how mass culture might begin to spark gay identification.

Inevitably both singular and shaped by the mass, "the personal," in the form of personality, took center stage in Wilde's trials, both as the performance of mass culture and as an alibi for gay desire. In *Wilde v. Queensberry*, Wilde's ill-advised prosecution of the Marquess of Queensberry for libel, the defense attorney Edward Carson read aloud from Basil's declaration of attraction in the *Lippincott's* edition ("your personality had the most extraordinary influence over me"). Carson then asked:

> "Do you mean to say that the passage describes the natural feeling of one man towards another?"
> "It would be the influence produced by a beautiful personality."
> "A beautiful person?"
> "I said a beautiful personality. You can describe it as you like. Dorian Gray's was a most remarkable personality."[86]

Wilde's equivocation reveals the dilemma the term posed for gay self-expression. If "personality" reduces to "person," then it signifies plainly as gay sexual attraction. The novel's emphasis on Dorian's image and its generalized conceptualization of personality as one's self-image reproduced from media sources and circulated within social economies includes this component of visual erotic appeal. Yet avowing these meanings by allowing personality to equate to person would have constituted legal peril for Wilde. Instead, he insisted on Dorian's remarkable "personality," a move that de-corporealized personality as merely a queer image floating through mass culture, the desire for which, and influence of, could not be legally regulated. Ed Cohen has shown how the mass media coverage of Wilde's second trial produced his own personality as a medical and juridical type, akin to Foucault's notion of "the homosexual" as "personage."[87] Personality could increasingly be read symptomatically, in paranoid fashion, as Dorian reads his self-image in the painting. But it crucially covered an area that was not quite a person and not quite an act; it operated in a zone in between real people and the images they projected into their social world. In this way, it impinged on prosecution but escaped it. As a performance of mass culture, it was suggestive, but not definitive. Dorian Gray's absorption in the "poisonous" book and readers' absorption in *The Picture of Dorian Gray* meant more things than anyone could count; figurations of media consumption such as Wilde's emerged in response to the very vastness of that possibility.

Unknown Publics

In an amusing irony of literary history, the best-selling sensation novelist Wilkie Collins discovered the existence of mass-circulation ephemera: illustrated, unbound quartos sold by tobacconists and confectioners, filled with dull, unoriginal material and consumed by the millions for whom Alexandre Dumas's best-selling *The Count of Monte Cristo* (1845) would have been too challenging to read.[1] To illustrate the subpar intellectual condition of this "unknown public," Collins reproduces excerpts from "Answers to Correspondents" columns, in which kindly editors respond to ignorant and inappropriate questions. Collins knows his own middle-class readers will be shocked to learn that this abject public wants recipes for gingerbread, cures for gray hair, warts, and worms; that it doesn't know the meaning of the word "esquire," how to pronounce "acquiescence," the fact that Daniel Defoe wrote *Robinson Crusoe*, and the distinction between ancient and modern history. Collins cites this "inconceivably dense ignorance, inconceivably petty malice, and inconceivably complacent vanity" to make the point that these millions of readers, possessing literacy, but lacking education, culture, and taste, seek the simplest imaginable literary fare.

Collins's evidence bears a striking resemblance to the common questions addressed to Google, revealed when its search prediction feature autocompletes the field, based on a user's past searches, and on trending searches in one's area. "Is Toronto a state?" "Is toenail fungus contagious?" "Who is the next bachelor?" "Is Donald Trump Mexican?": Such questions reveal a similar ignorance of basic facts, an interest in common ailments, and a fascination with mass cultural narratives of romance and race. Web 2.0, the internet's second phase that emphasizes user interactivity rather than static websites, has revealed a twenty-first-century unknown public—one that strikes middle-class, educated consumers as ill-informed, crass, and politically repugnant or naive. Every time a media revolution takes place, the middle class rediscovers the masses who were really part of the public sphere all along. Like Collins, we may marvel at their ignorance, but we are obligated to try to understand its causes and conditions. This book has imaginatively re-created scenes from the long nineteenth-century revolution in print, studying its ephemera to gain a fuller picture of the first mass media consumers. By bringing temperance medals, cigarette cards, inkblot games, cartoons, and other material to our attention, I refocused critical attention on segments of Collins's unknown public, which anticipates our own.

Throughout the book, I described mass print consumers' affects, because their connection of mind to body, conjuration of quotidian life, and resistance to classification suggest the vast array of responses to the medium, while permitting a focus on specific ones that have hitherto escaped critical notice. Affect demarcates the friction—whether irritating, pleasurable, or compulsive—that results when a new mass medium repositions individuals in relation to the social. Affect updates and improves on the Marxist mystifications of Walter Benjamin, the broad phenomenological strokes of Marshall McLuhan, and the Lacanian structuralism of Friedrich Kittler. Web 2.0, social media, ubiquitous computing, and the upending of conventional media industries have all combined to compel new methods for understanding twenty-first-century media consumption. As the editors and authors of *Networked Affect* (2015) have demonstrated, affect offers a way to discuss distributed agency, an assemblage spanning individual computer users, networks and infrastructures, affordances, and interfaces.[2] In this regard, Web 2.0 generates telling comparisons to nineteenth-century print-related technologies: The rash internet post echoes the steel pen's encouragement of hotheaded expression (discussed in chapter 3), or the angry rejection of the temperance leaflet (mentioned in chapter 1). The cigarette card's scantily clad bicycle rider or boxing champion (treated in chapter 2) might arouse or relax, and could be collected and curated like internet porn. Dorian Gray's rebinding of Lord Henry's book in different colors (analyzed in chapter 5) is the same sort of aesthetic play that spans everything from choosing laptop covers and stickers to vidding, posting on Instagram, and sending text messages with complicated emojis. Paper, cardboard, ink, press, pamphlet, image, hand, fingers, pocket, cigarette, bodily temperature, position, and environment formed assemblages and scenes in which media consumers experienced themselves in new relations to the social body. Numerous modes of Victorian ephemera that I have not discussed, such as cartes de visite, trade cards, crossword puzzles, and postcards, would have evoked other incalculable affects.

One of these affective relations emerges in the figure of information addiction that I have been tracing throughout the book. In the nineteenth century, the Enlightenment dream of diffusing useful knowledge to the ignorant drove the expansion of older forms, such as commonplace books and encyclopedias, and the invention of new ones, such as the public lecture and trivia-based parlor games. Consuming information by reading printed material made one a well-informed person, an upstanding citizen, and a moral person. At the same time, print's plethoric quality meant that it recirculated inaccurate, outdated, and otherwise faulty information, necessitating readers' skepticism. As shown in chapters 2 and 3, detective fiction emerged as a genre partly to train readers simultaneously to crave narrative information and to verify it before accepting it fully. The spectacular visual entertainment of ink-gazing, adapted in Collins's novel *The Moonstone*, enacted an operational aesthetic in which audiences feasted on the knowledge of how enchanting illusions worked. Like print, the internet realized the publication of absurd amounts of useful and useless information and required new critical strategies to tell the difference.

With Web 2.0, information and misinformation alike began circulating from any point on the network, exacerbating the need to assess its provenance and validity. Although information consumption must be checked, it must also accelerate to keep pace with its incessant production and expiration. Information no longer merely crawls or flows: It cascades, snowballs, and avalanches, constantly threatening burial. In this situation, addiction has become an even more apt description of the never-ending crisis or double bind in which media consumers find themselves: Although they depend on mass-mediated information to function normatively, they are constantly disadvantaged by its partial, contingent, biased, and otherwise faulty nature. The language of addiction characterizes both the ailment, in advertising appealing to fixes, habits, and cravings, and the treatment, such as electronic "detox" retreats at which attendees are deprived of their smart phones or weaned off video games. "At the moment when information machines are becoming so powerful and seemingly lively . . . we *know* we are no longer fully in control," write the editors of *Networked Affect.*[3] Since complete disconnection from the information economy would lead to economic dysfunction and social isolation, the constant compulsion to check updated information becomes a chronic condition to be managed. Within it, consumers reexert agency by curating subsets of information and knowledge—creating Instagram displays, organizing RSS feeds to customize their news consumption, or choosing one app over another. Information addiction's affects oscillate between anxiety and enjoyment, suspense and satiation, abjection and mastery, depletion and fullness. "Yes, I have been using myself up rather too freely," said Sherlock Holmes, the original information addict, whom I discussed in chapter 2. This sense of over-self-consumption also characterizes a twenty-first-century networked affect.

This contemporary moment of information overload represents the later development of the nineteenth-century fantasy of infinite mental retention, in which the unconscious functioned to store all the information contained in print.[4] In this genealogy, the unconscious is operationalized, primed to convert experience and knowledge into memories that function as information. Nurturing unlikely dreams of disembodiment—for no ordinary body can hold so much information that is alien to it—this figuration produced the flattened affects of literary characters such as Franklin Blake (discussed in chapter 3) and Peter Ibbetson (described in chapter 4). Like computer programs, they followed rules for collecting, comparing, and storing information—Blake, when he conducted his informal detective work; Peter, when practicing the clairvoyant art of "dreaming true." Such figures form the opposite of the Romantic and twentieth-century models of bourgeois deep subjectivity roiled by conflicting drives and nurtured by psychoanalysis. As I showed in chapter 3, the two movements of this dialectic share the concept of psychological performance: In the rational and operationalized unconscious, it is a machine performance; in the psychic depth model, it is aesthetic. A traditional critical narrative of the nineteenth century, focused on John Ruskin and William Morris, emphasizes its definition of the human against the machine; more recently, scholars have begun to reconstruct a technophilic counterdiscourse in which nineteenth-century personhood resembled or emulated machine precision, efficiency, and regularity.[5] This motif emerges most distinctively in *Peter Ibbetson*, which, in its fantasy of disembodied information processing, presages the cybernetic model of personhood that N. Katherine Hayles cites as the cornerstone of posthumanism.[6] The twenty-first-century iteration of personhood as the virtuosic performance of unconscious information storage arrived slightly early, in the 1999 film *The Matrix*. The heroes of that film, like Peter, enter a truer reality while asleep; there, they mentally download and redeploy information without learning it. In transcendent moments of action, their bodies become data. Accordingly, their stolid affect—best exemplified by Keanu Reeves's wooden acting—reflects their personhood as never-ending series of operations to defeat their only slightly more affectless, programmed antagonists.

A third, related affective relation that I traced in this book is playback, the enjoyment of repeating mediated experiences, first through the phonographic imaginary of the 1870s, and subsequently, through a variety of other audio and visual formats and modes culminating most recently with the MP3. Playback builds on the figuration of the unconscious as media storage, as seen in *The Moonstone* and *Peter Ibbetson*, whose protagonists must reenact their memories to access stored information. Playback requires a lot of repetitive activity; we saw its manic quality in the zany clerk who copies and re-copies documents (in chapter 3), and in the overanimated aesthetic associated with Du Maurier's hyperactive, cartoonish characters (in chapter 4). These depthless subjects substitute incessant action for varied, spontaneous affect. Yet by making it repeatable, playback also transforms the nature of memory, converting it into information stored in files, and obscuring the differences in the moments and occasions of its repetitions. Wendy Hui Kyong Chun has described the most recent development of the regime of playback, in the context of software, which produces the illusion of permanence, in its constant activity of refreshing. This characteristic of "undead repetition" carries over to biological discourses, constructing the body as an archive and transforming it into a biopolitical tool.[7] Chun insists that memory and storage be differentiated, because by conflating them, information becomes a supercommodity, and subjects can be programmed to consume it (133–35). In the nineteenth-century novels I analyzed, we saw an earlier instance of this cultural formation, in which the ability to replay memories still seemed charming and exhilarating. Enamored by the possibility of replaying experience and thus mastering time, and of repeating acts of consumption at will, readers delighted in *Peter Ibbetson*.

This book also described the way print reorganized collective and solitary affects, through its representation of mass live events (discussed in chapter 1) and through Dorian Gray's rejection of mass culture and retreat into "old," coterie media, signified by Basil's oil painting (the subject of chapter 5). The two discussions form apt bookends to the project of demonstrating how print media repositioned self-fashioning in relation to the mass. I began this book by showing how the temperance movement pioneered two aspects of mass culture, cheap print, in the form of tracts, medals, cards, ribbons, and other giveaways, and the live event attended by tens of thousands of people. The strategies were complementary: Printed objects advertised, reviewed, and recalled to their possessors their commitments to the temperance cause as experienced among the mass of like-minded people. Paradoxically, a familiar discursive feature of temperance rhetoric was its self-confessed inability to convey the true power of the live experience; such protests of course enhanced the events' allure. The temperance movement was a political one, but twenty-first-century live mass events such as football games and rock concerts tend to be commercialized. The ephemera they produce are part of this commercialization, and the affects they mobilize necessarily take different cultural form than the aesthetics of sobriety. Yet a similar logic animates the relation of the live event to its mediation: While audio and video broadcasts achieve ever higher definition and fidelity, the sense remains widespread that they will never be able to capture the ineffable quality of proximity to the mass. The sound of the crowd to the naked ear, one's specific visual perspective from within it, the feel of other bodies surrounding one's own, the silly enjoyment of performing the wave or singing along, or the graver observation of the moment of silence—none of these is replicable by media. Nor, for that matter, are moments of jostling, drunken manners, or the smell of others' sweat, food, or marijuana. Though real, these experiences are only apparently unmediated. The proliferation of platforms for reproduction and circulation of mass live experiences, the sharing of video in real time, and the curation of online photo albums afterward intensify the feeling that "you had to be there." The event would lose its cachet if not hyped beforehand and afterward. The charismatic star performer who can focus the crowd's attention, energy, and affect, whether the temperance orator John B. Gough or Beyoncé, rises or falls in his or her ability to meet the extended mass audience's demands for authenticity and sincerity—demands that are negotiated in print or electronic media.

Although the live event offers individuals the opportunity to experience collective affect through seemingly unmediated experience, and thus to offer one kind of authenticity, another significant mode emerges in the smaller, more focused communities that form selectively through print and electronic media. We saw an early version of this phenomenon in chapter 5, in the narrative outcome that Wilde's novel did not realize for its eponymous character. When Dorian censors Basil's painting, removing it from circulation, he rejects mass culture to retreat into a private world of old media, art. This plotline contrasts with the real community of Wilde's gay readers, both of the *Lippincott's* and the single-volume versions of the novel, who refashioned themselves in relation to their emergent, mediated community. Dorian's earlier moment of absorption in the "poisonous" book, and his rebinding of it, suggested his openness to this kind of self-styling and mediumistic play. His reveries resemble absorption in any new medium that reflects something new about users back to themselves. Considering himself in a new light, he creatively restyles the book, in the same way that twenty-first-century media consumers interact with mass culture by writing fan fiction, vidding, isolating tracks, and engaging in cosplay.[8] Such activity may seem solitary, but it can also lead into online forums and communities that validate a host of alternative practices and identities that in turn extend into real life. Dorian's enthusiasms catalogued in chapter 11 were mediated, and some of them had social dimensions, but Wilde chose to satirize a different path through modern mass culture, based on Dorian's dandiacal self-commodification and ensuing paranoia. This path obeys the dictates of a different aspect of internet aesthetics, which Alan Liu has dubbed "the laws of cool." Contrasting older models of "the great public genres and style of affective experience— for example, tragedy, comedy, the beautiful, the sublime, and so on" to the feeling of information presented on websites, Liu notes that "there is so little feeling in cool feeling."[9] This coldness descends directly from the dandy's self-commodified coldness—the "latent fire which hints at itself, and which could, but chooses not to burst into flame."[10] Wilde places Dorian at a crossroads between two ways to engage mass culture, which are now effectively inextricable: the openness to shared affect and feeling and the coolness of style. He thus registered a dilemma that has only become more acute: how to feel authentically when engaging mass-produced materials. Wilde was prescient: In the 1890s, a decade noted for the burgeoning of print media, this was a new formation; the twenty-first century, Sarah Banet-Weiser writes, is "an age that hungers for anything that *feels* authentic, just as we lament more and more . . . that we are governed by superficiality."[11] At the same time, this tension has collapsed, into the idea that self-expression generates one's own personal "brand."

I withhold judgment about such developments. But the broad similarities this book proposes between nineteenth-century media consumption and our own should relieve our angst. We have seen it all before. Those who reactively dismiss new media developments, whether electronic newspapers and books, Twitter and Facebook, or the stranger forms of fandom, miss the deeper analysis that comes with engagement. Likewise, those who uncritically embrace them without understanding their histories play their role without a full understanding of their part. I wrote this book for both audiences. An academic work, its small sales will keep it aloof from mass culture. And yet like all elite production in a period of intensified media change, it will dwell in a niche directly connected to the mass, this time, by electronic reproduction and social media. Is such self-branding a terrible thing? I think not. It is merely the latest method by which we circulate our personalities.

ACKNOWLEDGMENTS

To write this book, I consulted several archives: the British Library, the Temperance Collection at Stanford University, the Arents Collection at the New York Public Library, and the Jay T. Last Collection at the Huntington Library in San Marino, where I owe thanks to David Mihaly and Krystle Satrum. At the University of California, Riverside, my detail-oriented graduate student researcher Lorenzo Servitje hunted down innumerable ink-related sources and found out exactly what kind of pipe Holmes smokes. Maria Mendoza, Janet Moores, and the staff at Interlibrary Loan kept me well supplied with primary and secondary sources.

At Fordham University Press, Richard Morrison approached the project insightfully and shepherded it through the approval process. I am also grateful to John Garza, Eric Newman, Ann-Christine Racette, and Katie Sweeney for their hard work producing this book.

Many generous colleagues helped me improve this book. I am especially indebted to Rachel Teukolsky and Richard Menke, who read long, chaotic early drafts of chapters. Other kind readers helped improve article versions and proposals, and supported grant applications: Heidi Brevik-Zender, Joe Bristow, Joe Childers, Simon Cooke, Adriana Craciun, Michael Cohen, Jennifer Doyle, Elaine Freedgood, Dehn Gilmore, Anne Goldberg, Rae Greiner, Devin Griffiths, Richard Kaye, Ivan Kreilkamp, Aaron Matz, Andrew Miller, Clare Pettitt, John Plotz, John Plunkett, Sarah Raff, Catherine Robson, Talia Schaffer, Dana Simmons, and Sherryl Vint. Numerous colleagues and friends helped and supported the project in other ways: Andrea Denny-Brown, Ian Duncan, Craig Dworkin, Lauren Goodlad, George Haggerty, Nancy Henry, Priti Joshi, David Lloyd, Roger Luckhurst, Helena Michie, Parama Roy, Stefanie Sobelle, Jim Tobias, and Amy Wong. I am especially grateful to the organizers and participants at the King's College London "Shows of London" workshop, especially Seb Franklin, Josephine McDonagh, Roger Parker, Clare Pettitt, and Mark Turner; the nineteenth-century working group at the City University of New York Graduate Center, in particular Anne Humphreys, Richard Kaye, and

Talia Schaffer; the University of California, Los Angeles, nineteenth-century working group, especially Jonathan Grossman; the Dickens Universe 2013, notably Jim Adams, Jim Buzard, and John Jordan; participants in the American Comparative Literature Association Conference 2016 seminar "Ephemera and Ephemerality," especially Sara Hackenberg and Priti Joshi: All interrogated the project and made it better. I am grateful to the graduate students at California State University, Long Beach, for inviting me to deliver an early version of chapter 1 as the keynote address at "Re/Inventions" in April 2015. I am also grateful to the organizers and audiences of the North American Victorian Studies Association annual conference from 2011 through 2014, who accepted my proposals and gave me invaluable suggestions. Audiences at the British Association of Victorian Studies (2013), the Modern Language Association (2013 and 2015), the Northeast Modern Language Association Convention (2011), the Victorians Institute Annual Conference (2012), and the Victorian Interdisciplinary Association of the Western United States (2014) stayed awake during my talks and asked helpful questions afterward.

At the University of California, Riverside, a Committee on Research grant from 2010 to 2012 relieved me of some teaching so I could develop this project. Working groups sponsored by the Center for Ideas and Society offered specific feedback and intellectual sustenance, including the Global Nineteenth-Century Group, the Science Studies Group, and the Transnational British Studies Group. A small working group sponsored by the center in winter 2014 afforded me the ongoing insights of Maudemarie Clark, John Kim, and Andrew Wiener. Graduate students including Brittany Carlson, Ann Garascia, Mackenzie Gregg, Kimberly Hall, Giulia Hoffmann, and Anne Sullivan offered helpful references and suggestions. Graduate seminar participants from 2011 through 2016 helped me think through key ideas in the book.

The project gathered momentum when I participated in a National Endowment for the Humanities Summer Seminar on Walter Benjamin and *The Arcades Project* at the University of California, Irvine, in 2011. I am grateful to all the seminar participants, especially Amy Sara Carroll, Ilka Kressner, Catherine Soussloff, and Christina Svendsen.

Chapter 2 is derived, in part, from "Holmes's Pipe, Tobacco Papers, and the Nineteenth-Century Origins of Media Addiction," published in the *Journal of Victorian Culture* 19, no. 1 (March 2014): 24–42; copyright Leeds Trinity and All Saints College, and reprinted by permission of Taylor and Francis Ltd. on behalf of Leeds Trinity and All Saints College. Several paragraphs first appeared in the short essay "Smoking, Reading, Daydreaming," in *Cabinet*, no. 51 (2013), 35–40. An earlier version of chapter 4, "'Du Maurierness' and the Mediatization of Memory," was published in *Victorian Studies* 56, no. 1 (2013), 31–57; and fragments of the chapter appeared in *George Du Maurier: Illustrator, Critic, Author: Beyond Svengali*, edited by Simon Cooke and Paul Goldman (Farnham: Ashgate, 2016), in an essay titled "Du Maurier's Paris: *Peter Ibbetson*, Haussmann, and Industrial Memory." A much abbreviated version of chapter 5, "'A Form of Reverie, A Malady of Dreaming': Dorian Gray and Mass Culture" appeared or will appear in *"The Picture of Dorian Gray" in the Twenty-First Century*, edited by Richard Kaye (New York: Oxford University Press).

INTRODUCTION: FROM PAPER TO PIXEL

1. A definitive account of Victorian ephemera remains to be compiled, but it constitutes a large portion of Maurice Rickards, *The Encyclopedia of Ephemera* (New York: Routledge, 2000).

2. See Richard Altick, *The English Common Reader: A Social History of the Mass Reading Public, 1800–1900* (Chicago: University of Chicago Press, 1957); Wolfgang Schivelbusch, *The Railway Journey: The Industrialization of Time and Space in the Nineteenth Century* (Berkeley: University of California Press, 1987); Kate Flint, *The Woman Reader, 1837–1914* (Oxford: Oxford University Press, 1993); and Sara Thornton, *Advertising, Subjectivity, and the Nineteenth-Century Novel: Dickens, Balzac, and the Language of the Walls* (Basingstoke: Palgrave Macmillan, 2009).

3. David Vincent, *The Rise of Mass Literacy: Reading and Writing in Modern Europe* (Cambridge: Polity, 2000), 16–22.

4. See, for example, Patrick Brantlinger, *The Reading Lesson: The Threat of Mass Literacy in Nineteenth-Century British Fiction* (Bloomington: Indiana University Press, 1998), 2–3; and Flint, *Woman Reader.*

5. See William B. Warner, *Licensing Entertainment: The Elevation of Novel Reading in Britain, 1684–1750* (Berkeley: University of California Press, 1998), chap. 5.

6. On this discourse, see Kelly J. Mays, "The Disease of Reading and Victorian Periodicals," in *Literature in the Marketplace,* ed. John Jordan and Robert Patten (Cambridge: Cambridge University Press, 1995), 165–94.

7. See James Mussell, "The Passing of Print: Digitising Ephemera and the Ephemerality of the Digital," *Media History* 18, no. 1 (2012): 77–92; and Laurel Brake, "The Longevity of Ephemera: Library Editions of Nineteenth-Century Periodicals and Newspapers," *Media History* 18, no. 1 (2012), 7–20.

8. Thomas De Quincey, *Confessions of an English Opium-Eater,* ed. Grevel Lindop (1821; Oxford: Oxford World's Classics, 1985), 69.

9. Forbes Winslow, *On Obscure Diseases of the Brain and Disorders of the Mind* (1860; London: Davies, 1861).

10. Wendy Hui Kyong Chun, "The Enduring Ephemeral, or The Future Is a Memory," in *Media Archaeology: Approaches, Applications, and Implications*, ed. Erkki Huhtamo and Jussi Parikka (Berkeley: University of California Press, 2011), 184–206: 184–85.

11. See Marshall McLuhan, *Understanding Media: The Extensions of Man* (1964; Cambridge, Mass.: MIT Press, 1994). On being-in-print, see Andrew King and John Plunkett, Introduction to *Victorian Print Media: A Reader* (Oxford: Oxford University Press, 2005), 2.

12. See Andrew Piper, *Dreaming in Books: The Making of the Bibliographic Imagination in the Romantic Age* (Chicago: University of Chicago Press, 2009).

13. On mobs and crowds, see Jon P. Klancher, *The Making of English Reading Audiences, 1790–1832* (Madison: University of Wisconsin Press, 1987); Caroline Sumpter, "The Cheap Press and the 'Reading Crowd': Visualising Mass Culture and Modernity," *Media History* 12, no. 3 (2006): 233–52; and *Crowds*, ed. Jeffrey T. Schnapp and Matthew Tiews (Stanford, Calif.: Stanford University Press, 2006).

14. See, for example, Nancy Armstrong, *Fiction in the Age of Photography: The Legacy of British Realism* (Cambridge, Mass.: Harvard University Press, 1999); and Niklas Luhmann, *The Reality of the Mass Media*, trans. Kathleen Cross (1996; Stanford, Calif.: Stanford University Press, 2000).

15. See Talia Schaffer, *Novel Craft: Victorian Domestic Handicraft and Nineteenth-Century Fiction* (Oxford: Oxford University Press, 2014).

16. Generally speaking, I follow Harry G. Cocks and Matt Rubery when they define ephemera as "everything printed that is not a book": Although I de-emphasize books, I do not entirely exclude them. "Introduction: Margins of Print: Ephemera, Print Culture, and Lost Histories of the Newspaper," *Media History* 18, no. 1 (2012): 3.

17. Although I share Alexander Galloway's method of historicizing the interface, I don't make it the key to aesthetics, ethics, politics, poetics, and truth. See Alexander R. Galloway, *The Interface Effect* (Cambridge: Polity, 2012), 25–53.

18. Brenton J. Malin, *Feeling Mediated: A History of Media Technology in America* (New York: New York University Press, 2014), 2.

19. Jonathan Crary, *Suspensions of Perception: Attention, Spectacle, and Modern Culture* (Cambridge, Mass.: MIT Press, 1999), 46.

20. This paradox informs the provocation that "Enlightenment is an event in the history of mediation." See Clifford Siskin and William Warner, eds., *This Is Enlightenment* (Chicago: University of Chicago Press, 2010).

21. See Jürgen Habermas, *The Structural Transformation of the Public Sphere: An Inquiry into a Category of Bourgeois Society*, trans. Thomas Burger

and Frederick Lawrence (1962; Cambridge, Mass.: MIT Press, 1991), 168–69.

22. See Michael Warner, *Publics and Counter-Publics* (Brooklyn: Zone, 2002), 51.

23. Lauren Berlant, *The Female Complaint: The Unfinished Business of Sentimentality in American Culture* (Durham, N.C.: Duke University Press, 2008), 5.

24. For a sketch of the various turns toward affect, see Gregory Seigworth and Melissa Gregg, "An Inventory of Shimmers," in *The Affect Theory Reader*, ed. Gregg and Seigworth (Durham, N.C.: Duke University Press), 6–8.

25. See José Esteban Muñoz, "Ephemera as Evidence: Introductory Notes to Queer Acts," *Women and Performance* 8, no. 2 (1996): 10.

26. Kathleen Stewart, *Ordinary Affects* (Durham, N.C.: Duke University Press, 2007), 1–2.

27. On the risks of tautological descriptions of affect, especially with respect to "intensity," see "Introduction: Networks of Transmission: Intensity, Sensation, Value," by Susanna Paasonen, Ken Hills, and Michael Petit in *Networked Affect*, ed. Paasonen et al. (Cambridge, Mass.: MIT Press, 2015), 11. For a cogent analysis of "affect" as a cipher that simply resists systematic thinking, see Eugenie Brinkema, *The Forms of the Affects* (Durham, N.C.: Duke University Press, 2014), xi–xvi.

28. See Eve Sedgwick, *Touching Feeling: Affect, Pedagogy, Performativity* (Durham, N.C.: Duke University Press, 2003), 123–52.

29. Teresa Brennan, *The Transmission of Affect* (Ithaca, N.Y.: Cornell University Press, 2004), 2.

30. Fredric Jameson, *The Antinomies of Realism* (London: Verso, 2013), 32. See also Malin, *Feeling Mediated*.

31. While seeking everyday experiences and vernacular theories of mental habits, I also build on the work of scholars who place Freud in a broader context, and who, in compiling histories of "the unconscious," accumulate material on related states of mind. See, for example, Lancelot Law White, *The Unconscious before Freud* (New York: Basic, 1960); Henri Ellenberger, *The Discovery of the Unconscious: The History and Evolution of Dynamic Psychiatry* (New York: Basic Books, 1970); and Rick Rylance, *Victorian Psychology and British Culture, 1850–1880* (Oxford: Oxford University Press, 2000).

32. See Nigel Thrift, *Non-Representational Theory: Space/Politics/Affect* (London: Routledge, 2008), 221.

33. Charles Dickens, *Our Mutual Friend*, ed. Adrian Poole (1865; London: Penguin, 1997), 28.

34. Altick, *English Common Reader*, 364. Valuable subsequent studies have modified Altick's model by fragmenting it sociologically. On women readers, see Flint; on working class readers, see Jonathan Rose, *The Intellectual Life of the British Working Classes* (New Haven, Conn.: Yale University Press, 2001); for convicts and other highly specific reading communities, see Adelene Buckland and Beth Palmer, *A Return to the Common Reader: Print Culture and the Novel, 1850–1900* (Aldershot: Ashgate, 2013).

35. See Leah Price, *Doing Things with Books in Victorian Britain* (Princeton, N.J.: Princeton University Press, 2011).

36. For an example of a quantitative psychological study of "ludic reading," see Victor Nell, *Lost in a Book: The Psychology of Reading for Pleasure* (New Haven, Conn.: Yale University Press, 1988). See also Martin Hewitt, *The Dawn of the Cheap Press in Victorian Britain: The End of the "Taxes on Knowledge," 1849–1861* (London: Bloomsbury, 2014).

37. Walter Benjamin, *The Arcades Project*, ed. Rolff Tiedemann et al. (Cambridge, Mass.: Belknap Press of Harvard University Press, 1999).

38. See, for example, "Experience and Poverty," in *Selected Writings*, vol. 2: *1927–1934*, by Walter Benjamin, trans. Rodney Livingstone et al. (Cambridge, Mass.: Belknap Press of Harvard University Press, 1999), 731–36.

39. Walter Benjamin, "The Work of Art in the Age of Its Technological Reproducibility," 2nd version, reprinted in *The Work of Art in the Age of Its Technological Reproducibility and Other Writings on Media*, ed. Jennings, Brigid Doherty, and Thomas Y. Levin (Cambridge, Mass.: Harvard University Press, 2008), 19–55.

40. Walter Benjamin, "Surrealism: The Last Snapshot of the European Intelligentsia," in *Selected Writings*, 2:207–21.

41. See, for example, Richard Menke, *Telegraphic Realism* (Stanford, Calif.: Stanford University Press, 2008); and Erkki Huhtamo and Jussi Parikka, eds. *Media Archaeology: Approaches, Applications, and Implications* (Berkeley: University of California Press, 2011).

42. Friedrich Kittler, *Gramophone, Film, Typewriter*, trans. Geoffrey Winthrop-Young and Michael Wutz (1986; Stanford, Calif.: Stanford University Press, 1999).

43. William Gibson, *The Ecological Approach to Visual Perception* (Boston: Houghton Mifflin, 1979), 18, 36.

44. Contrast their account of attention as highly regulated with Crary's more wayward one: "The required qualities of attention have become so familiar from other films and other culture products already known to him or her that they appear automatically. The power of industrial society is imprinted on people once and for all. The products of the culture industry are such that they can be alertly consumed even in a state of distraction."

Theodor Adorno and Max Horkheimer, *Dialectic of Enlightenment*, trans. Edmund Jephcott (1947; Stanford, Calif.: Stanford University Press, 2002), 100.

45. See *The Collected Works of Samuel Taylor Coleridge*, Vol. 5, Part 1: *Lectures 1818–1819*, ed. Reginald Foakes (London: Routledge, Kegan, Paul, 1987), 124; John Stuart Mill, *On Liberty*, 2nd ed. (London: John Parker and Son, 1859), 119; and Gabriel Tarde, *The Laws of Imitation*, trans. Elsie Clews Parsons (New York: Henry Holt, 1903), 84.

46. Brennan, *Transmission of Affect*, 17–18.

47. Hanno Hardt, *Myths for the Masses: An Essay on Mass Communication* (Oxford: Blackwell, 2004), 94.

48. Stuart Hall, "Popular Culture and the State," in *Popular Culture and Social Relations* ed. Tony Bennett, Colin Mercer, and Janet Woollacott (Philadelphia: Open University Press, 1986), 36.

49. Martin Conboy, *The Press and Popular Culture* (London: Sage, 2002), 8.

50. On this divide, see Andreas Huyssen, *After the Great Divide: Modernism, Mass Culture, Postmodernism.* (Bloomington: Indiana University Press, 1987), and John Carey, *The Intellectuals and the Masses: Pride and Prejudice among the Literary Intelligentsia, 1880–1939* (London: Faber and Faber, 1992).

51. Raymond Williams, *Culture and Society, 1780–1950* (New York: Columbia University Press, 1982), 289.

52. Henry Jenkins, *Convergence Culture: Where Old and New Media Collide*, rev. ed. (New York: New York University Press, 2008), 18. See also Henry Jenkins, Sam Ford, and Joshua Green, *Spreadable Media: Creating Value and Meaning in a Networked Culture* (New York: New York University Press, 2013).

53. For a description of this alternative critical path, see Simon Frith, "The Good, the Bad, and the Indifferent: Defending Popular Culture from the Populists," *Diacritics* 21, no. 4 (1991), 101–15.

54. See Trebor Scholz, *Digital Labor: The Internet as Playground and Factory* (New York: Routledge, 2013).

55. See Joel H. Wiener, *Papers for the Millions: The New Journalism in Britain, 1850s to 1914* (Westport, Conn.: Greenwood Press, 1988).

56. See Asa Briggs and Peter Burke, *A Social History of the Media: From Gutenberg to the Internet*, 3rd ed. (Cambridge: Polity, 2009), 105; Sumpter, "Cheap Press and the 'Reading Crowd'"; and Mary Hammond, *Reading, Publishing and the Formation of Literary Taste in England, 1880–1914* (Aldershot: Ashgate, 2006).

57. Reinhard Wittmann, "Was There a Reading Revolution at the End of the Eighteenth Century?" in, *A History of Reading in the West*, ed. Guglielmo

Cavallo and Roger Chartier, trans. Lydia Cochrane (Cambridge: Polity, 1999), 305.

58. William St. Clair, *The Reading Nation in the Romantic Period* (Cambridge: Cambridge University Press, 2004), 13.

59. See David Paul Nord, *Faith in Reading: Religious Publishing and the Birth of Mass Media in America.* (Oxford: Oxford University Press, 2004), 5; and Aileen Fyfe, "Commerce and Philanthropy: The Religious Tract Society and the Business of Publishing," *Journal of Victorian Culture* 9, no. 2 (2004): 166.

60. See James Hamilton, "Unearthing Broadcasting in the Anglophone World," in *Residual Media*, ed. Charles R. Acland (Minneapolis: University of Minnesota Press, 2007), 283–300.

61. See Patricia Anderson, *The Printed Image and the Transformation of Popular Culture* (Oxford: Clarendon, 1991); and Hewitt, *Dawn of the Cheap Press.*

62. See Nicholas Daly, *Literature, Technology, and Modernity, 1860–2000* (Cambridge: Cambridge University Press, 2004), 4; and Alain Corbin, *Time, Desire, and Horror: Toward a History of the Senses* (Cambridge: Polity, 1995), viii–x.

63. See, for example, Hall, "Popular Culture and the State"; and James Curran, "Media and the Making of British Society, c. 1700–2000," *Media History* 8, no. 2 (2002), 135–54.

64. Other recent accounts of print are similarly expansive. See, for example. Ann Ardis and Patrick Collier, eds., *Transatlantic Print Culture, 1880–1940* (Basingstoke: Palgrave Macmillan, 2008).

65. S. T. Coleridge, *Biographia Literaria*, vol. 1 (London: Rest, Penner, 1817), 115; E. S. Dallas, *The Gay Science*, vol. 1 (London: Chapman and Hall, 1866), 213.

66. See, for example, Daniel A. Novak, *Realism, Photography, and Nineteenth-Century Fiction* (Cambridge: Cambridge University Press, 2008), 118–45; and Ronald Thomas, "Poison Books and Moving Pictures: Vulgarity in *The Picture of Dorian Gray*," in *Victorian Vulgarity: Taste in Verbal and Visual Culture*, ed. Susan David Bernstein and Elsie B. Michie (Farnham: Ashgate, 2009), 185–200.

1. TEMPERATE MEDIA: EPHEMERA AND PERFORMANCE IN THE MAKING OF MASS CULTURE

1. They were likely bought by the middle class and distributed for free to workers. See Gary Kelly, "Revolution, Reaction, and the Expropriation of Popular Culture: Hannah More's Cheap Repository," *Man and Nature* 6 (1987): 154.

2. See Aileen Fyfe, "Commerce and Philanthropy: The Religious Tract Society and the Business of Publishing," *Journal of Victorian Culture* 9, no. 2 (2004): 166.

3. On the BFTS, see Brian Harrison, *Drink and the Victorians* (Pittsburgh: University of Pittsburgh Press, 1971), 108; on the ATS, see W. J. Rorabaugh, *The Alcoholic Republic: An American Tradition* (Oxford: Oxford University Press, 1979), 196.

4. David Paul Nord, *Faith in Reading: Religious Publishing and the Birth of Mass Media in America* (Oxford: Oxford University Press, 2004), 5.

5. See James Hamilton, "Unearthing Broadcasting in the Anglophone World," in *Residual Media*, ed. Charles R. Acland (Minneapolis: University of Minnesota Press, 2007), 283–300.

6. See Leah Price, *How to Do Things with Books in Victorian Britain* (Princeton, N.J.: Princeton University Press, 2011), 139–74.

7. See Peter Bailey, *Leisure and Class in Victorian England: Rational Recreation and the Contest for Control, 1835–1885* (1978; London: Routledge, 2006).

8. Richard Altick, *The English Common Reader: A Social History of the Mass Reading Public, 1800–1900* (Chicago: University of Chicago Press, 1957), 72.

9. See William St. Clair, *The Reading Nation in the Romantic Period* (Cambridge: Cambridge University Press, 2004), 308–10.

10. Historians refer to the temperance movement, which advocated the moderate use of alcohol, and the teetotal movement, which advocated total abstinence, together as "temperance." Where my argument requires it, I differentiate them.

11. William Lovett and John Collins, *Chartism: A New Organization of the People*, introd. Asa Briggs, Victorian Library (1840; Leicester: Leicester University Press, 1969), 6.

12. See John Mee, *Romanticism, Enthusiasm, and Regulation: Poetics and the Policing of Culture in the Romantic Period* (Oxford: Oxford University Press, 2003), 1–22.

13. On the gifted tract as burdensome social obligation, see Price, *How to Do Things with Books*, 148–64.

14. On the tea party, see Erika Rappaport, "Sacred and Useful Pleasures: The Temperance Tea Party and the Creation of a Sober Consumer Culture in Early Industrial Britain," *Journal of British Studies* 52, no. 4 (October 2013): 990–1016.

15. Performance studies has done much to combat the metaphysics of presence with nuanced accounts of presence's material traces. See, for example, *Art, Performance, and the Persistence of Being*, ed. Gabriella Giannachi, Nick Kaye, and Michael Shanks (New York: Routledge, 2012).

16. *Proceedings of the World's Temperance Convention* (London: Charles Gilpin, 1846), 7.

17. Klancher describes the cultural and literary evolution of this position in constructions of the "reading audience." See Jon P. Klancher, *The Making of English Reading Audiences, 1790–1832* (Madison: University of Wisconsin Press, 1987). For a representative example of this assumption in action, see György Markus's association of popular culture with folk, rural, pre-industrial, and "the lower strata of urban populations." "The Path of Culture: From the Refined to the High, from the Popular to Mass Culture," *Critical Horizons* 14, no. 2 (2013): 129.

18. Melissa Gregg and Gregory J. Seigworth, eds., *The Affect Theory Reader* (Durham, N.C.: Duke University Press, 2010), 1.

19. For a discussion of this enigma in terms of the uncanny, see James Mussell, "The Passing of Print: Digitising Ephemera and the Ephemerality of the Digital," *Media History* 18, no. 1 (2012): 77–92.

20. "The Farmer May Boast," in *Hoyle's Band of Hope Harmonist*, 4. Undated material in the Stanford Temperance Collection.

21. On the risks of contaminated water, see Tina Young Choi, "Writing the Victorian City: Discourses of Risk, Connection, and Inevitability," *Victorian Studies* 43, no. 4 (2001): 561–89.

22. Hamilton, "Unearthing Broadcasting," 290.

23. T. S. Arthur, *The New Juvenile Storybook for Boys and Girls* (London: Knight and Son, n.d.), 158.

24. Edward C. Delavan, ed. *Temperance Essays*, 4th ed. (New York: National Temperance Society, 1866), 15.

25. Rorabaugh, *Alcoholic Republic*, 196.

26. "New Publications," *Arthur's Home Magazine*, March 1869, 194.

27. "Self-Improvement: In Three Lessons: Lesson II," *Lancashire Temperance Messenger* 1, no. 9 (850): 135.

28. Ibid., 134.

29. See Alan Rauch, *Useful Knowledge: The Victorians, Morality, and the March of Intellect* (Durham, N.C.: Duke University Press, 2001).

30. The exception to this general rule is Percy Bysshe Shelley's abstinence from alcohol, which temperance discourse duly valorized. See, for example, "A Half Hour with Shelly [sic]," *Lancashire Temperance Messenger and Miscellany of Science and Literature* no. 2 (1849), 21–24. For a theoretical discussion of the deconstructed meanings of sobriety for Romantic writers, see Orrin Wang, *Romantic Sobriety: Sensation, Revolution, Commodification, History* (Baltimore: Johns Hopkins University Press, 2011).

31. Both quoted in Nord, *Faith in Reading*, 115–16.

32. *Report from the Select Committee on Newspaper Stamps* (House of Commons: July 1851), 1320–21. On Cassell, who went from being an itinerant temperance orator to a major publisher of temperance and other family-oriented newspapers, and a seller of tea and coffee, see Simon Nowell-Smith, *The House of Cassell, 1848–1958* (London: Cassell, 1958), chaps. 1, 2.

33. For a nuanced account of the adjustment of Evangelical publishing to the secular literary marketplace, see Candy Guenther Brown, *The Word in the World: Evangelical Writing, Publishing, and Reading in America, 1789–1880* (Chapel Hill: University of North Carolina Press, 1999), 19–20.

34. "Some Account of Himself, By an Irish Oyster-Eater," *Blackwood's Edinburgh Magazine* 45, no. 334 (1839): 781.

35. See Price, *How to Do Things*, 139–218.

36. Elaine Hadley, *Living Liberalism: Practical Citizenship in Mid-Victorian Britain* (Chicago: University of Chicago Press, 2010), 46–47.

37. See Harrison, *Drink and the Victorians*, 288.

38. Lilian Lewis Shiman, *Crusade against Drink in Victorian England* (New York: St. Martin's Press, 1988), 20.

39. Reynold Greenleaf, *Before and Behind the Curtain: A Queer Story about Drinking* (London: Tweedie, 1868), 21.

40. David S. Reynolds, "Black Cats and Delirium Tremens: Temperance and the American Renaissance," in *The Serpent in the Cup: Temperance in American Literature*, ed. Reynolds and Debra J. Rosenthal (Amherst: University of Massachusetts Press, 1997), 27.

41. "Temperance and Teetotal Societies," *Blackwood's Edinburgh Magazine* 450, no. 73 (1853): 394.

42. Shiman, *Crusade against Drink*, 22.

43. Ian Tyrell, *Sobering Up: From Temperance to Prohibition in Antebellum America, 1800–1860* (Westport, Conn.: Greenwood Press, 1979), 148.

44. Maurice Rickards, *The Encyclopedia of Ephemera* (New York: Routledge, 2000), 323.

45. "W. Tweedie's Catalogue of Publications," *Temperance Record*, no. 757 (1870): 491.

46. Amy Hughes, *Spectacles of Reform: Theater and Activism in Nineteenth-Century America* (Ann Arbor: University of Michigan Press, 2012), 51.

47. See Patricia Anderson, *The Printed Image and the Transformation of Popular Culture, 1790–1860* (Oxford: Clarendon Press, 1991), 20–21.

48. "Mrs. Burrage: A Temperance Romance," in *The Works of Thomas Hood in Six Volumes* (New York: Derby and Jackson, 1861), 5:438. See also "The Pope's Medal," *Punch; or, The London Charivari* 4 (January–June 1843): 66.

49. Harriet Martineau, *Biographical Sketches, 1852–1875*, 4th ed. (London: Macmillan, 1876), 302.

50. See the debate in "Are Bands of Hope, as at Present Constituted and Conducted, Generally Beneficial?" *British Controversialist* (London: Houlston and Wright, 1863): 363.

51. Shiman, *Crusade*, 19.

52. Harrison, *Drink and the Victorians*, 44.

53. Joseph Barker, *History and Confessions of a Man* (London: Chapman, 1846), 362.

54. Karl Marx and Friedrich Engels, *The Communist Manifesto*. 1848, in *Karl Marx: Selected Writings*, ed. David McLellan (Oxford: Oxford University Press, 2000), 267.

55. "Swallowing a Yard of Land," *Starlight Temperance Tracts* 1, no. 21 (London: S. W. Partridge, 1881): 1–2.

56. Quoted in Harrison, *Drink and the Victorians*, 395.

57. Tyrell, *Sobering Up*, 175–76.

58. John F. Quinn, *Father Mathew's Crusade: Temperance in Nineteenth-Century Ireland and Irish America* (Amherst: University of Massachusetts Press, 2002), 76.

59. Elizabeth Malcolm, *Ireland Sober, Ireland Free: Drink and Temperance in Nineteenth-Century Ireland* (Syracuse, N.Y.: Syracuse University Press, 1986), 125.

60. Quoted ibid., 132.

61. Quoted in Paul A. Townend, *Father Mathew, Temperance, and Irish Identity* (Dublin: Irish Academic Press, 2002), 97–98.

62. Review of *Father Mathew* in *Fraser's Magazine* 23 (January 1841): 99.

63. Martineau, *Biographical Sketches*, 306, 302–3.

64. Quinn, *Father Mathew's Crusade*, 115–17, 80.

65. For a reading of this phenomenon in the period, see Katie Trumpener, *Bardic Nationalism: The Romantic Novel and the British Empire* (Princeton, N.J.: Princeton University Press, 1997).

66. Teresa Brennan, *The Transmission of Affect* (Ithaca, N.Y.: Cornell University Press, 2004), 61–62.

67. Peter M'Teague, "Father Mathew," *Bentley's Miscellany* 8 (London: Bentley, 1840): 56.

68. Brian Massumi, *Politics of Affect* (Cambridge: Polity Press, 2015), 206. Further citations are to this edition and appear in parentheses in the text.

69. See, for example, Samuel Couling, *History of the Temperance Movement in Great Britain and Ireland* (London: Tweedie, 1862), and John Zug, *The Foundation, Progress, and Principles of the Washington Temperance Society of Baltimore* (Baltimore: John D. Toy, 1842).

70. Charles Dickens, *The Pickwick Papers*, ed. Mark Wormald (1837; London: Penguin, 2003), 439–44.

71. Glenn Hendler, "Bloated Bodies and Sober Sentiments: Masculinity in 1840s Temperance Narratives," in *Sentimental Men: Masculinity and the Politics of Affect in American Culture*, ed. Mary Chapman and Glenn Hendler (Berkeley: University of California Press, 1999), 127. See also Thomas Augst, "Temperance, Mass Culture, and the Romance of Experience," *American Literary History* 19, no. 2 (2007): 297–323.

72. Amanda Claybaugh, *The Novel of Purpose: Literature and Social Reform in the Anglo-American World* (Ithaca, N.Y.: Cornell University Press, 2007), 52–84.

73. Joseph Livesey, *Reminiscences of Early Teetotalism* (Preston: Staunch Teetotaler, 1868), 9.

74. Jabez Inwards, *Memorials of Temperance Workers* (London: Partridge, 1879), 272.

75. See, for example, the poem "Origin of the Word Teetotal": "Oh! What a very curious word / Is te-te-te-teetotal, / To some, forsooth, 'tis quite absurd— / A stalking ghost—teetotal; / Others there are who bless the hour / When first they felt its magic power, / Such benign blessings it doth shower / On those that are teetotal." Joseph Cooper, *The Temperance Reciter: Original Pieces in Prose and Verse* (London: W. Tweedie, 1856), 34–35.

76. Letter to Margaret Carlyle, 12 September 1840. Accessed 3/16/15 at Carlyle Letters Online, http://carlyleletters.dukejournals.org/cgi/content/full/12/1/lt-18400912-TC-MAC-01.

77. Sir George Head, *A Home Tour through the Manufacturing Districts of England in the Summer of 1835* (London: John Murray, 1836), 412–13.

78. Edward Grubb, "Memoir of Henry Anderton," in *The Temperance and Other Poems by the Late Harry Anderton* (Preston: W. and J. Dobson, 1863), xx.

79. Harrison, *Drink and the Victorians*, 129.

80. Edwin Paxton Hood, *The Book of Temperance Melody* (London: W. and G. F. Cash, 1854), xvii.

81. John B. Gough, *Autobiography*, 31st ed. (1845; Boston: Gould and Lincoln, 1852), 115.

82. Quoted in John W. Crowley, ed., *Drunkard's Progress: Narratives of Addiction, Despair, and Recovery* (Baltimore: Johns Hopkins University Press, 1999), 111.

83. Quoted in Rev. William Reid, *Sketch of Life and Oratory of John B. Gough* (Glasgow: Scottish Temperance League, 1854), 61–62. Further citations are to this edition and appear in the text in parentheses.

84. Gough, *Autobiography* (1845); headnote and appendix by "J.D.R.," 127, 148–49.

85. Tom F. Wright, "The Transatlantic Larynx in Wartime: John Gough's London Voices," in *Transatlantic Traffic and (Mis)Translations*, ed. Robin Peel and Daniel Maudlin (Durham: University of New Hampshire Press, 2013), chap. 2, Kindle edition unpaginated.

86. Lyman Abbott, "Snapshots of My Contemporaries: John B. Gough, Old Testament Christian," *New Outlook* 127 (1921): 257.

87. John Moon, "A Sober World, and No Compromise," "The New Reciter" (London: J. Moon, n.d.). [c. 1860], 8.

88. "Dissolving Views," *Lancashire Temperance Messenger and Miscellany of Science and Literature* 1, no. 9 (1850):131.

89. John B. Gough, *Sunlight and Shadow; or, Gleanings from My Life Work* (Hartford, Conn.: Worthington, 1883), 359.

90. Carlos Martyn, *John B. Gough: The Apostle of Cold Water* (New York: Funk and Wagnalls, 1893), 109.

91. Edward A. Rand, *A Knight That Smote the Dragon: The Young People's Gough* (London: James Nisbet, 1892), 150.

92. Gough, *Autobiography* (1845); headnote and appendix by "J.D.R.," 127, 148–49.

93. On this sense of performance, see Jon McKenzie, *Perform or Else: From Discipline to Performance* (London: Routledge, 2001). The application of the word *performance* to machines is first seen in the late eighteenth century but becomes a standard part of technological and managerial nomenclature in the early twentieth.

94. Gough, *Autobiography* (1845), 115. Reid quotes him, at an unstated date, as saying that he averaged 10,000 miles a year, giving an average of three hundred two-hour addresses each year, and written 1,500 letters per year (Reid, *Sketch of Life and Oratory of John B. Gough*, 55).

95. John Allen Krout, *The Origins of Prohibition* (New York: Alfred A. Knopf, 1925), 192.

96. Rand, *Knight*, 139–40.

97. Richard Menke, "Media in America, 1881: Garfield, Guiteau, Bell, Whitman," *Critical Inquiry* 31, no. 3 (2005): 660.

98. For an account of the affair, see Edward Van Every, *Sins of New York: As "Exposed" by the Police Gazette* (New York: Frederick A. Stokes, 1930), 52–60.

99. John B. Gough, *Autobiography and Personal Recollections* (San Francisco: Francis Dewing, 1870), 203–4.

100. John B. Gough, *Autobiography* (Boston: John B. Gough, 1845), 76–86.

101. Anonymous, *Goffiana: A Review of the Life of John B. Gough* (Boston: Ruggles, 1846), 8.

102. Hendler, "Bloated Bodies," 135.

103. Patent furniture was mechanized to move and adjust to human postures. See Sigfried Giedion, *Mechanization Takes Command: A Contribution to Anonymous History* (1948; Minneapolis: University of Minnesota Press, 2013).

104. Walter Benjamin, "The Work of Art in the Age of Its Technical Reproducibility" (2nd version), in *The Work of Art in the Age of Its Technical Reproducibility and Other Writings on Media*, ed. Michael W. Jennings, Brigid Doherty, and Thomas Y. Levin (Cambridge, Mass.: Belknap Press of Harvard University Press, 2008), 19–55.

105. Ibid., 31.

106. Augst, "Temperance, Mass Culture, and the Romance of Experience," 308.

107. Although she does not discuss collective formations, or engage Benjamin, Tamara Ketabgian reveals a nineteenth-century counterdiscourse that aligns affect with machine production. See *The Lives of Machines* (Ann Arbor: University of Michigan Press, 2010).

108. Kenneth Silverman, *Edgar A. Poe: Mournful and Never-Ending Remembrance* (New York: HarperCollins, 1991), 185.

109. On Poe's exclusion from F. O. Matthiessen's canon because of his antidemocratic views, see Betsy Erkkila, "Perverting the American Renaissance: Poe, Democracy, Critical Theory," in *Poe and the Remapping of Antebellum Print Culture*, ed. Jerome McGann and Gerald J. Kennedy (Baton Rouge: Louisiana University Press, 2012), 65–100.

110. Charles Baudelaire, "Edgar Allan Poe: His Life and Works," in *The Painter of Modern Life and Other Essays* (London: Phaidon, 1964), 89. Further citations are to this edition and appear in the text in parentheses.

111. Edgar Allan Poe, "The Imp of the Perverse," in *The Portable Edgar Allan Poe*, ed. J. Gerald Kennedy (London: Penguin, 2006), 205.

112. Edgar Allan Poe, "The Black Cat," in *Selected Tales* (Oxford: Oxford World's Classics, 1998), 232.

113. David Reynolds, "Poe's Art of Transformation: 'The Cask of Amontillado' in Its Cultural Context," in *The American Novel: New Essays on Poe's Major Tales*, ed. Kenneth Silverman (Cambridge: Cambridge University Press, 1993), 93–112.

114. See David S. Reynolds, *Beneath the American Renaissance: The Subversive Imagination in the Age of Emerson and Melville* (Oxford: Oxford University Press, 1988), 68.

115. Crowley, *Drunkard's Progress*, 29–30.

116. Thomas De Quincey, "National Temperance Movements," 1845, in *De Quincey's Collected Writings*, vol. 14, ed. David Masson (Edinburgh: Adam and Charles Black, 1890), 263–85.

117. Richard D. E. Burton, *Baudelaire and the Second Republic: Writing and Revolution* (Oxford: Clarendon, 1991), 268. My discussion is indebted to his.

118. Charles Baudelaire, *Les Fleurs du mal*, trans. Richard Howard (Boston: David R. Godine, 1982), 113.

119. Charles Baudelaire, *Artificial Paradises*, trans. Stacy Diamond (New York: Citadel, 1996), 70. Further citations are to this edition and appear in the text in parentheses.

120. On the analogy between intoxication and poetry, see E. S. Burt, "Baudelaire and Intoxicants," in *The Cambridge Companion to Baudelaire*, ed. Rosemary Lloyd (Cambridge: Cambridge University Press, 2005), 117–29; on the analogy in relation to allegory, see Virginia E. Swain, *Grotesque Figures: Baudelaire, Rousseau, and the Aesthetics of Modernity* (Baltimore: Johns Hopkins University Press, 2004).

121. Baudelaire, "To the Reader" in *Les Fleurs du mal*, 6.

122. Charles Baudelaire, *Paris Spleen: Little Poems in Prose*, trans. Keith Waldrop (Middletown, Conn.: Wesleyan University Press, 2009), 71.

123. Walter Benjamin, "Surrealism: The Last Snapshot of the European Intelligentsia," in *Selected Writings, vol. 2: 1927–1934*, trans. Rodney Livingstone et al. (Cambridge, Mass.: Belknap Press of Harvard University Press, 1999), 216. Further citations are to this edition and appear in the text in parentheses.

124. Walter Benjamin, "Hashish in Marseilles," in *On Hashish*, ed. Howard Eiland (Cambridge, Mass.: Belknap Press of Harvard University Press, 2006), 117–26.

125. Miriam Hansen, "Benjamin, Cinema, Experience: 'The Blue Flower in the Land of Technology,'" *New German Critique* no. 40 (1987): 191–92.

126. Walter Benjamin, *The Arcades Project*, trans. Howard Eiland and Kevin McLaughlin (Cambridge, Mass.: Belknap Press of Harvard University Press, 1999), 463, 474 (in Benjamin's convoluted citation system, N3,4 and N9a,7).

127. See also Benjamin's critical quotation of Engels in *The Arcades Project* rhapsodizing French wines and praising Parisians' unity of their "passion for enjoyment with the passion for historical action." Benjamin, *Arcades*, 704–5 [a4,1].

128. Miriam Hansen, "Benjamin and Cinema: Not a One-Way Street," *Critical Inquiry* 25, no. 2 (1999): 321.

2. TOBACCO PAPERS, HOLMES'S PIPE, CIGARETTE CARDS, AND INFORMATION ADDICTION

1. Arthur Conan Doyle, *The Penguin Complete Sherlock Holmes* (London: Penguin, 2009), 90. Further references are to this edition and are given after quotations in the text.

2. During the period of the Holmes oeuvre, cocaine and morphine went from unregulated to increasingly pathologized and criminalized substances, whereas tobacco became only more ubiquitous and normalized. Richard Davenport-Hines, *The Pursuit of Oblivion: A Global History of Narcotics* (New York: Norton, 2002), chaps. 7–8.

3. Ennis overturned the long-standing notion that William Gillette introduced the calabash in stage adaptations in 1901; Kuhn and Rosenblatt further traced its early appearances to comics of the 1920s and '30s. Robert S. Ennis, "The Great Calabash Question," *Baker Street Journal* 47, no. 2 (1997); Laura L. Kuhn, "The Great Calabash Question: A Possible Solution?" *Baker Street Journal* 47, no. 4 (1997): 43–45; and Albert A.M. Rosenblatt, "The Great Calabash Mystery" *Baker Street Journal* 48, no. 1 (1998).

4. Andrew William Chatto ("Joseph Fume"), *A Paper:—of Tobacco; Treating of the Rise, Progress, Pleasures, and Advantages of Smoking* (London: Chapman and Hill, 1839).

5. T. H. Roberts, ed., *The Cigarette* (London, 1898–1901).

6. Joseph Hatton, *Cigarette Papers for After-Dinner Smoking* (London: Hutchinson, 1892), 2.

7. Matthew Hilton, *Smoking in British Popular Culture, 1800–2000* (Manchester: Manchester University Press, 2000), 22.

8. On women's reading "addictions," see Kate Flint, *The Woman Reader, 1837–1911* (Oxford: Oxford University Press, 1995).

9. Reginald Pound, *Mirror of the Century: The Strand Magazine, 1891–1950* (Cranbury, N.J.: A. S. Barnes, 1966), 22, 32.

10. See Peter Bailey, *Popular Culture and Performance in the Victorian City* (Cambridge: Cambridge University Press, 1998), 17.

11. Pound, *Mirror*, 11.

12. Major collections of cigarette cards include the Arents Collection at the New York Public Library, part of which is digitized and can be viewed online; the Jay T. Last Collection, in the Huntington Library in San Marino, California; and the Edward Wharton-Tigar Collection, in the British Museum.

13. Anonymous, *Metamorphosis of Tobacco* (1602); James I, *Counterblaste to Tobacco* (Emmaus, Penn.: Rodale Press, 1954); Richard Braithwait, *The Smoaking Age* (London, 1617).

14. *The Life, Letters, and Writings of Charles Lamb*, vol. 1, ed. Percy Fitzgerald (London: W. W. Gibbings, 1892), 346.

15. Leigh Hunt, "Coffee-Houses and Smoking," in *The Wishing-Cap Papers* (Boston: Lee and Shepard, 1888), 255–56.

16. Ibid., 256.

17. Richard Sennett, *The Fall of Public Man* (New York: W. W. Norton, 1992), 217.

18. Anonymous, *Tobacco Talk and Smokers' Gossip* (London: George Redway, 1884); and Anonymous (Andrew Steinmetz), *The Smoker's Guide, Philosopher and Friend* (London: Hardwicke & Bogue, 1877).

19. Henry Dudeney, who edited the *Strand's* "Perplexities" puzzle column beginning in 1910, offered mathematical, visual puzzles involving matchsticks and cigarettes. See Henry Dudeney, *536 Puzzles and Curious Problems*, ed. Martin Gardner (Mineola, N.Y.: Dover, 2016).

20. F. W. Fairholt, *Tobacco: Its History and Associations* (London: Chapman and Hall, 1859), 137.

21. *Cope's Tobacco Plant* 1, no. 1 (1870): 12.

22. Huon Mallalieu, "Of Pipes, Putts, and Politics," *Country Life* 187 (1993): 48.

23. See A. V. Seaton, "Cope's and the Promotion of Tobacco in Victorian England," *Journal of Advertising History* 9 (1986): 5–26.

24. *Cope's Smoke-Room Booklets* (Liverpool: Cope's, 1889), no. 1; no page.

25. Seaton, "Cope's and the Promotion of Tobacco," 5; and Richard Altick, "Cope's Tobacco Plant: An Episode in Victorian Journalism" *Papers of the Bibliographic Society of America* 45 (1951): 333–50.

26. See Linda Austin, "Smoking, the Hack, and the General Equivalent," in *The New Economic Criticism*, ed. Martha Woodmansee and Mark Osteen (New York: Routledge, 1999), 330.

27. James Thomson, "Tobacco and Genius," in *Selections from Original Contributions by James Thomson to Cope's Tobacco Plant* (Liverpool: Cope's, 1893), 37.

28. Hilton, *Smoking in British Popular Culture*, 18–19.

29. Guy Thorne, *The Cigarette Smoker: Being the Terrible Case of Uether Kennedey* (London: Greening, 1902), 46.

30. Ibid., 99. A similar plotline resolves "The Adventure of the Speckled Band."

31. Ronald Thomas, *Detective Fiction and the Rise of Forensic Science* (Cambridge: Cambridge University Press, 2004), 1–20.

32. Garrett Stewart, *The Look of Reading: Book, Painting, Text* (Chicago: University of Chicago Press, 2006), 102.

33. Jonathan Crary, *Suspensions of Perception: Attention, Spectacle, and Modern Culture* (Cambridge, Mass.: MIT Press, 1999), 79.

34. "Hymn to St. Nicotine," *Cope's Tobacco Plant* 1 (1871): 250.

35. For more examples, see *Cope's Smoke Room Booklets* (Liverpool: Cope's, 1889–93); George Du Maurier's early sketches, reprinted throughout Felix Moscheles, *In Bohemia with Du Maurier* (New York: Harper and

Brothers, 1897), and the illustrations reproduced in Eugene Umberger, "In Praise of Lady Nicotine: A Bygone Era of Prose, Poetry . . . and Presentation," in *Smoke: A Global History of Smoking*, ed. Sander L. Gilman and Zhou Xun (London: Reaktion, 2004), 236–47.

36. Bret Harte, "Facts Concerning a Meerschaum," in *Stories and Poems and Other Uncollected Writings*, ed. Charles Meeker Kozlay (Boston: Houghton, Mifflin, 1914), 37, 42.

37. Oscar Wilde, *The Picture of Dorian Gray*, ed. Robert Mighall (London: Penguin, 2000), 43.

38. Isaac Hawkins Brown, "Pipe of Tobacco," in *The Cambridge Tart: Epigrammatic and Satirical-Poetic Effusions*, ed. Richard Gooch (London: James Smith, 1823), 176–84; and Robert Buchanan, "The Fleshly School of Poetry: Mr. D. G. Rossetti," *Contemporary Review* 18 (1871): 349.

39. Max Beerbohm, "Enoch Soames," in *The Incomparable Max: A Collection of Writings of Sir Max Beerbohm* (New York: Dodd and Mead, 1962), 184.

40. *The Works of William Cowper*, ed. by John S. Memes, 3 vols. (Edinburgh: Fraser, 1835), 3:381–83.

41. Andrew H. Miller, "The Specters of Dickens' Study," *Narrative* 5, no. 3 (1997): 323.

42. Dehn Gilmore reads Buss's painting as part of a broader trend valorizing Dickens's production of a gallery of types, which are associated with democratic consumption. See Dehn Gilmore, *The Victorian Novel and the Space of Art: Fictional Form on Display* (Cambridge: Cambridge University Press, 2014), 51.

43. Alison Byerly, *Are We There Yet? Virtual Travel and Victorian Realism* (Ann Arbor: University of Michigan Press, 2013), 194–97.

44. On shifts in the British economy at the end of the century, see Martin Wiener, *English Culture and the Decline of the Industrial Spirit, 1850–1980*, new ed. (Cambridge: Cambridge University Press, 2004). On cocaine and morphine as bourgeois work aids, see Susan Zieger, *Inventing the Addict: Drugs, Race, and Sexuality in Nineteenth-Century British and American Literature* (Amherst: University of Massachusetts Press, 2008), 98–125.

45. See Norma Clarke, "Strenuous Idleness," in *Manful Assertions: Masculinities in Britain since 1800*, ed. by Michael Roper (New York: Routledge, 1991), 25–43.

46. Edgar Allan Poe, "The Purloined Letter," in *Selected Tales* (Oxford: Oxford University Press, 2008), 249.

47. Wilkie Collins, *The Moonstone* (Peterborough, Ont.: Broadview, 1999), 374. For the social context of Blake's attempts to quit smoking to

please his fiancée, see Richard Altick, *The Presence of the Present* (Columbus: Ohio State University Press, 1991), 240–74.

48. For a reading of the story as an example of the "false beggar" narrative, see Audrey Jaffe, *Scenes of Sympathy: Identity and Representation in Victorian Fiction* (Ithaca, N.Y.: Cornell University Press, 2000), 47–76.

49. "A Day as a Professional Beggar," *Tit-Bits* 22 (January 17, 1891): 232.

50. Virginia Berridge and Griffith Edwards, *Opium and the People*, rev. ed. (London: Free Association Books, 1999), 200–202.

51. In this way, the story participates in the ideological purification Christopher Pittard ascribes to the early Holmes stories, and to the *Strand* more generally. See "'Cheap, Healthful Literature': *The Strand Magazine*, Fictions of Crime, and Purified Reading Communities" *Victorian Periodicals Review* 40, no. 1 (2007): 7.

52. See Dianne Maglio, "Luxuriant Crowns: Victorian Men's Smoking Caps," *Dress* 27 (2000): 9–17.

53. In its historical elision, tobacco functions differently here than in realist texts such as *Great Expectations*. See Elaine Freedgood, *The Ideas in Things: Fugitive Meaning in the Victorian Novel* (Chicago: University of Chicago Press, 2006).

54. Joseph Hatton, "A Day in a Tobacco Factory," *Cope's Smoke Room Booklets*, no. 14 (Liverpool: Cope's, 1893), 41–61; and F. Marion Crawford, *A Cigarette-Maker's Romance* (New York: Macmillan, 1894).

55. Hilton, *Smoking in British Popular Culture*, 83–84.

56. For a brilliant discussion of the figurative elision of Thomson's laboring body in his writings for Cope's, see Austin, "Smoking, the Hack, and the General Equivalent," 328–29.

57. Michael Saler describes Holmes in this way. See *As If: Modern Enchantment and the Literary Prehistory of Virtual Reality* (Oxford: Oxford University Press, 2012), 105–29.

58. John Tupper, "Smoke," *Germ* 4 (1849): 182. Accessed February 27, 2013 at http://www.rossettiarchive.org/docs/ap4.g415.1.4.rad.html#p183.

59. Saler documents the widespread belief that Holmes was not fictional. See *As If*, 106.

60. For these and other devices, see R. S. Pritchett, *Smokiana* (London: Bernard Quaritch, 1890).

61. Gordon Howsden, *Collecting Cigarette and Trade Cards* (London: New Cavendish Books, 1995), 28–29.

62. Amoret Scott and Christopher Scott, *Tobacco and the Collector* (London: Max Parrish, 1966), 171.

63. Maurice Rickards, *The Encyclopedia of Ephemera* (New York: Routledge, 2000), 96.

64. A. J. Cruse, *Cigarette Card Cavalcade* (London: Vawser and Wiles, 1948), 146.

65. Tobacco advertisements had represented Native Americans and African Americans, especially women, in similar ways since the seventeenth century. See Dolores Mitchell, "Images of Exotic Women in Turn-of-the-Century Tobacco Art," *Feminist Studies* 18, no. 2 (1992): 289–350.

66. Scott and Scott, *Tobacco and the Collector*, 169.

67. Edward Wharton Tigar, Foreword to Howsden, *Collecting Cigarette and Trade Cards*, 6.

68. Standish Meacham, *A Life Apart: The English Working Class, 1890–1914* (London: Thames and Hudson, 1977), 162.

69. Roy Genders, *A Guide to Collecting Trade and Cigarette Cards* (London: Pelham, 1975), 13.

70. Robert Roberts, *The Classic Slum: Salford Life in the First Quarter of the Century* (Manchester: Manchester University Press, 1971), 134–35.

71. Ibid.

72. Walter Benjamin, "Unpacking My Library," in *Illuminations* (New York: Shocken, 1968), 61.

73. Rickards, *Encyclopedia of Ephemera*, 96.

74. Walter Benjamin, "Eduard Fuchs, Collector and Historian," in *The Work of Art in the Age of Its Technological Reproducibility, and Other Writings on Media*, ed. Michael W. Jennings, Brigid Doherty, and Thomas Y. Levin (Cambridge, Mass.: Belknap Press of Harvard University Press, 2008), 132.

75. In this way, they shared this effect with similar trade cards that accompanied tea, another consumable habitually taken as a respite from work.

76. Wilde, *Picture of Dorian Gray*, 127.

77. Edward Bok, *Autobiography* (London: Thornton and Butterworth, 1921), 53–54.

78. George Orwell, *Dickens, Dali, and Others* (New York: Harcourt, Brace, Jovanovich, 1946), 69

79. Paul Schlicke, *Dickens and Popular Entertainment* (London: Allen and Unwin, 1985), 6–9.

80. Juliet John, *Dickens and Mass Culture* (Oxford: Oxford University Press, 2010), 164.

81. *The Sociable; or, A Thousand and One Home Amusements* (New York: Dick and Fitzgerald, 1858), 204.

82. Mary Dawson, *The Mary Dawson Game Book* (Philadelphia: David McKay, 1916), 516.

83. Mary White, *The Book of Games*, 9th ed. (New York: Scribner, 1898), 158.

84. Melanie Dawson, *Laboring to Play: Home Entertainment and the Spectacle of Middle-Class Cultural Life, 1850–1920* (Tuscaloosa: University of Alabama Press, 2005).

85. See Paul Schlicke, *Dickens and Popular Entertainment* (London: Allen and Unwin, 1985), 9.

86. See Alan Rauch, *Useful Knowledge: The Victorians, Morality, and the March of Intellect* (Durham, N.C.: Duke University Press, 2001), 22–59.

87. Margaret Oliphant, "The Byways of Literature: Reading for the Million," in *Victorian Print Media: A Reader*, ed. Andrew King and John Plunkett (Oxford: Oxford University Press, 2005), 198.

88. Richard Altick, *The English Common Reader: A Social History of the Mass Reading Public, 1800–1900* (Chicago: University of Chicago Press, 1957), 364.

89. Raymond Williams, *The Long Revolution* (1961; Cardigan: Parthian, 2011), 204.

90. Genders, *Guide to Collecting*, 21.

91. For an account of Sigmund Freud's nephew Edward Bernays's work on behalf of American tobacco, see Alan Brandt, "Engineering Consumer Confidence in the Twentieth Century," in Gilman and Xun, *Smoke*, 332–43.

92. Dorothy Bagnall, *Collecting Cigarette Cards and Other Trade Issues* (London: Arco, 1965), 25.

93. Ibid., 40.

3. INK, MASS CULTURE, AND THE UNCONSCIOUS

1. George Eliot, *Adam Bede*, ed. Margaret Reynolds (1859; London: Penguin, 2008), 9.

2. Harriet Martineau, *Eastern Life Present and Past* (London: Moxon, 1848), 2:140. Further references are to this edition and appear in the text in parentheses.

3. "Blot," n. 1. *OED*, 2nd online ed. Accessed 4/23/15.

4. Ezra Sampson, *Brief Remarker on the Ways of Man* (Hudson: Stone and Corss, 1818), 247.

5. Marshall McLuhan, *The Medium is the Massage* (New York: Random House, 1967), 48.

6. Isaac Taylor, *Scenes of British Wealth*. 2nd ed. (London: J. Harris, 1825), 150.

7. See, for example, Harry Howells Horton, *Birmingham: A Poem*, 2nd ed. (Birmingham: M. Billing, 1853), 152–67, and "Mr. Gillott and the Steel Pen Trade," *Practical Magazine* 1, no. 5 (1873): 321–25.

8. E. S. Dallas, "What May Come of the Exhibition," *Once a Week*, April 26, 1862, 492.

9. "The Making of a Pen," *Chambers's Journal of Popular Literature*, no. 473 (1863): 61.

10. "Steel Pens and Health," *Good Health* (June 1869): 47. Another wistful commentator lamented, "The poet now-a-days writes with a steel pen." "Steel Pens and Their Manufacture," *Illustrated Magazine of Art* 1 (1853): 23.

11. Henry James, *The Portrait of a Lady*, ed. Roger Luckhurst (1881; Oxford: Oxford World's Classics, 2009), 485.

12. See "Ode to My Grey Goose Quill," *Monthly Anthology and Boston Review* 9 (1810): 413; and Thomas Hood, "Ode to Perry, Inventor of the Steel Pen," in *The Humorous Poetry of the English Language, From Chaucer to Saxe*, ed. J. Parton, 7th ed. (New York: Mason, 1856), 426–31. See also James Howell, *Epistolae Ho-Elianae: Familiar Letters, Domestic and Foreign*, 7th ed. (London: Thomas Guy, 1705), 288; and Alexander Pope's *Essay on Man* (1734): "While man exclaims, 'See all Things for my Use!' / See Man for Mine, replies a pamper'd Goose!" (Dublin: Booksellers of London and Westminster, 1736), 18.

13. Dallas, "What May Come," 493.

14. "Ratcliff's Patent Inkstand," *Mechanics' Magazine*, no. 959 (1841): 497–98.

15. See respectively "Improved Inkstand," *Magazine of Science* 7 (1846): 101; *London Journal of Arts and Sciences* 21 (London: Newton, 1843): 336–40; and "Varieties," *Blackwood's Lady's Magazine* 14 (1843): 73.

16. Advertisement, *Publisher's Circular*, December 8, 1874, 1116.

17. Mihaly Csikszentmihalyi, *Flow: The Psychology of Optimal Experience* (New York: Harper and Row, 1990), 3.

18. S. T. Coleridge, "Substance of a Dialogue, With a Commentary on the Same," *Blackwood's Edinburgh Magazine* 10 (August–December 1821): 256.

19. Dallas, "What May Come," 493.

20. Washington Irving, "The Legend of Sleepy Hollow," in *The Complete Tales of Washington Irving*, ed. Charles Neider (1820; New York: Da Capo Press, 1975), 43.

21. Charles Dickens, *Bleak House*, ed. Nicola Bradbury (1854; London: Penguin, 1996), 60.

22. Lewis Carroll, *Alice's Adventures in Wonderland*. 1865. Reprinted in *The Annotated Alice: 150th Anniversary Deluxe Edition*, ed. Martin Gardner (New York: Norton, 2015), 134.

23. Frederick Cleaver, *Papers on Penmanship* (London: Pitman, 1886), 4.

24. Frederic Myers, *Lectures on Great Men* (London: Ballantyne, 1841), 2.

25. See Joe Nickell, *Pen, Ink, and Evidence* (Lexington: University of Kentucky Press, 1990), 37.

26. Adrian Johns, "Ink," in *Materials and Expertise in Early Modern Europe: Between Market and Laboratory*, ed. Ursula Klein and E. C. Spary (Chicago: University of Chicago Press, 2010), 107. On itinerant ink-sellers in the first part of the century, see Philip Hensher, *The Missing Ink: The Lost Art of Handwriting* (New York: Faber and Faber, 2012), 140–41.

27. Henry Frith, *Guide to the Study of Graphology, with an Explanation of Some of the Mysteries of Handwriting* (London: George Routledge, 1886), 57.

28. Louis Antoine Fauvelet de Bourrienne, *Memoirs of Napoleon Bonaparte* (London: Richard Bentley, 1836), 4:278.

29. *The Life of Beethoven*, vol., 2. ed. Alexander Wheelock Thayer; trans. Henry Edward Krehbiel (New York: Beethoven Association, 1921), 95. Alessandra Comini attests that later graphologists "have had a field day with Beethoven's handwriting." See *The Changing Image of Beethoven: A Study in Mythmaking* (Santa Fe, N.M.: Sunstone Press, 2008), 36. Illegible genius became a common trope. For example, the obscure U.S. education reformer Robert Hamilton Bishop wrote, "According to that standard that identifies genius with illegible handwriting . . . was undoubtedly one of the greatest geniuses of the age." William B. Sprague, *Annals of the American Pulpit* (New York: Robert Carter and Brothers, 1858), 4:325.

30. Thomas Moore, *Letters and Journals of Lord Byron* (Francfort: H. L. Brönner, 1830), 245–46.

31. George Gordon Byron, *Don Juan*, canto 3 (1821), in *The Works of Lord Byron*, vol. 9, ed. Thomas Moore (Boston: Francis A. Nicholls, 1900), 250. In another famous thrown-ink story, Thomas Carlyle described how Martin Luther hurled his inkstand at the devil, the ink spot enduring on the wall to symbolize the spiritual power of the word of God. See Thomas Carlyle, *On Heroes, Hero-Worship, and the Heroic in History* (London: Chapman and Hall, 1840), 164–65.

32. R. H. Super, *Trollope in the Post Office* (Ann Arbor: University of Michigan Press, 1981), 2.

33. See J. Hill and W. M. Brentford Butts, *An Analysis of Penmanship* (London: Seuter, 1821); Charles W. Smith, *How to Write a Good, Legible, and Fluent Hand* (London: Ward and Lock, 1858), 9; and B. F. Foster, *Penmanship: Theoretical and Practical* (London: Souter and Law, 1843), 24; on the tantalograph, see Tamara Plakins Thornton, *Handwriting in America: A Cultural History* (New Haven, Conn.: Yale University Press, 1996), 54–55.

34. Charles Lamb, "The Good Clerk," in *The Life and Works of Charles Lamb* (London: Macmillan, 1899), 5:290; and Edgar Allan Poe, *The Fall of the House of Usher and Other Writings*, ed. David Galloway (London: Penguin, 1867), 180–81.

35. Thomas Carlyle, *German Romance* (Edinburgh: Tait, 1827), 2:290. Further citations are to this edition and appear in parentheses in the text.

36. Sianne Ngai, *Our Aesthetic Categories: Zany, Cute, Interesting* (Cambridge, Mass.: Harvard University Press, 2012), 193. Further citations are to this edition and appear in parentheses in the text.

37. For an excellent account of the mechanization of handwriting in *Bleak House*, see Peter J. Capuano, *Changing Hands: Industry, Evolution, and the Reconfiguration of the Victorian Body* (Ann Arbor: University of Michigan Press, 2015), 185–213. For an important account of the novel's concern with textual and corporeal materiality, see Daniel Hack, *The Material Interests of the Victorian Novel* (Charlottesville: University of Virginia Press, 2005), chap. 2.

38. Herman Melville, *Billy Budd, Bartleby, and Other Stories*, ed. Peter Coviello (New York: Penguin, 2016), 25. Further citations are to this edition and appear in parentheses in the text.

39. On Turkey as a drunkard, see Hans Bergmann, *God in the Street: New York Writing from the Penny Press to Melville* (Philadelphia: Temple University Press, 1995), 161–62.

40. Thomas Augst, *The Clerk's Tale: Young Men and Moral Life in Nineteenth-Century America* (Chicago: University of Chicago Press, 2003), 233.

41. As Krook explains to Esther Summerson, "I have a turn for copying from memory, you see, miss, though I can neither read nor write" (Dickens, *Bleak House*, 76).

42. Anthony Trollope, "The Civil Service," *Dublin University Magazine* 46 (October 1855): 421.

43. On Romantic ideology as a reaction to mass print culture, see Raymond Williams, *Culture and Society, 1780–1950*, 2nd ed. (New York: Columbia University Press, 1983), 30–48.

44. Wilkie Collins, "The Unknown Public," *Household Words* 18, no. 439 (1858): 200.

45. In *The Mystery of Edwin Drood*, Edwin Drood plans to go to Egypt to work as an engineer; his fiancée Rosa, sick of their engagement, claims to be repulsed by Egypt. At the end of one conversation, she asks him what he sees in his hand, and when he professes to be flummoxed, she rejoins, "Why, I thought you Egyptian boys could look into a hand and see all sorts of phantoms? Can't you see a happy Future?" Charles Dickens, *The Mystery of Edwin Drood*, ed. David Paroissien (1871; London: Penguin, 2002), 35.

46. Edward William Lane, *Account of the Manners and Customs of the Ancient Egyptians*, reprinted from the 3rd ed. (1836; London: Ward, Lock, 1890), 254. Further references are to this edition and appear in parentheses in the text.

47. See, for example, George Nugent Grenville, *Lands, Classical and Sacred* (London: Charles Knight, 1846), 1:133–34; J. Bernard Burke, *Anecdotes of the Aristocracy*, 2nd series (London: Churton, 1850), 1:130; and "H.C.," "Indo-Mahomaden Folk-Lore," *Notes and Queries*, 3rd series, 11 (March 2, 1867): 180.

48. For an account of Egyptomania that draws on modern Egyptian material rather than the Western perspective only, see Elliott Colla, *Conflicted Antiquities: Egyptology, Egyptomania, Egyptian Modernity* (Durham, N.C.: Duke University Press, 2007).

49. A. C. Lindsay, *Letters on Egypt, Edom, and the Holy Land* (London: H. Colburn, 1838), 68.

50. John Gardner Wilkinson, *Modern Egypt and Thebes* (London: John Murray, 1843), 223.

51. Osmán was a Scot who had been taken prisoner in the failed British campaign at Alexandria in 1807, sold into slavery, and later, through the agency of Salt, was liberated, becoming an interpreter for the consulate and assuming the Muslim faith.

52. Grenville, *Lands, Classical and Sacred*, 1:140.

53. John Wilson, *Noctes Ambrosianae*, ed. R. S. Mackenzie (New York: Widdleton, 1872), 4:371.

54. Review of *Modern Egyptians*, *Quarterly Review* 59 (1837): 200. Further citations are to this edition and appear in the text in parentheses.

55. On "The Invisible Girl," see Steven Connor, *Dumbstruck: A Cultural History of Ventriloquism* (Oxford: Oxford University Press, 2000), 352–54. On phantasmagoria, see Marina Warner, *Phantasmagoria: Spirit Visions, Metaphors, and Media into the Twenty-First Century* (Oxford: Oxford University Press, 2006), 147–58. Joseph Faber's "Euphonia" appeared afterward, in the 1840s.

56. Neil Harris, *Humbug: The Art of P. T. Barnum* (Chicago: University of Chicago Press, 1981), 59–90.

57. David Brewster, *Letters on Natural Magic* (London: John Murray, 1864), 66.

58. Ibid., 68.

59. Helen Groth, *Moving Images: Nineteenth-Century Reading and Screen Practices* (Edinburgh: Edinburgh University Press, 2013), 79.

60. See Alexander Kinglake, *Eothen; or, Traces of Travel Brought Home from the East* (1844; London: J. M. Dent, 1908).

61. Patrick Brantlinger, *Bread and Circuses: Theories of Mass Culture as Social Decay* (Ithaca, N.Y.: Cornell University Press, 1983), 35.

62. Charles Musser, *The Emergence of Cinema: The American Screen to 1907* (New York: Scribner, 1990), 18.

63. Terry Castle, "Phantasmagoria: Spectral Technologies and the Metaphorics of Modern Reverie" *Critical Inquiry* 15, no. 1 (1988): 30.

64. Karl Marx, *The Eighteenth Brumaire of Louis Bonaparte* (1852), in *Karl Marx: Selected Writings*, ed. David McLellan (Oxford: Oxford University Press, 2000), 333.

65. Carlyle savaged the eighteenth-century magician and adventurer Cagliostro (Joseph Balsamo) for his deceptions cloaked in mysticism, demanding that his readers imagine how his form of theater acted "not only indirectly through the foolish senses of men, but directly on their Imagination." See Thomas Carlyle, *Critical and Miscellaneous Essays* (1839; New York: Scribner, 1872), 5:101.

66. Castle, "Phantasmagoria," 30.

67. Margaret Cohen, *Profane Illuminations: Walter Benjamin and the Paris of Surrealist Revolution* (Berkeley: University of California Press, 1993), 217–60.

68. See Walter Benjamin, "The Work of Art in the Age of Its Technical Reproducibility" (1936), in Walter Benjamin, *The Work of Art in the Age of Its Technological Reproducibility and Other Writings on Media*, ed. Michael Jennings, Brigid Doherty, and Thomas Y. Levin (Cambridge, Mass.: Harvard University Press, 2008), 19–55.

69. See Mary Louise Pratt, *Imperial Eyes: Travel Writing and Transculturation* (New York: Routledge, 1992). For more recent work, see *Imperial Optics*, ed. Martin Jay and Sumathi Ramaswamy (Durham, N.C.: Duke University Press, 2014).

70. Sigmund Freud, "The Uncanny" (1919). in *Literary Theory: An Anthology*, ed. Julie Rivkin and Michael Ryan, 2nd ed. (London: Blackwell, 2004), 418–430: 428–9.

71. Marianna Torgovnick, *Gone Primitive: Savage Intellects, Modern Lives* (Chicago: University of Chicago Press, 1991), 204.

72. G. H. Lewes, "Seeing Is Believing," *Blackwood's Edinburgh Magazine* 540, no. 88 (1860): 381.

73. Niklas Luhmann. *The Reality of the Mass Media*, trans. Kathleen Cross (1996; Stanford, Calif.: Stanford University Press, 2000), 83–84.

74. On this phrase and its queer grounding, see Eve Kosofsky Sedgwick, *Epistemology of the Closet* (Berkeley: University of California Press, 1990), 45.

75. Wilkie Collins, *The Moonstone* (1868), ed. Steve Farmer (Peterborough, Ont.: Broadview Press, 1999), 71. Further citations are to this edition and appear in the text in parentheses.

76. "On Writing Materials: No. VII: On Ink," *Saturday Magazine*, no. 407 (1838): 174.

77. See Marshall McLuhan, *Understanding Media: The Extensions of Man* (1964; Cambridge, Mass.: MIT Press, 1994), 41–47.

78. William Schmid's "Patent Detective Camera," introduced in 1883, was a wooden box with a shutter, viewfinder, and focusing dial; concealed within leather or even a brown paper bag, it resembled a parcel. See Colin Harding, "Camera Design: Portable Hand Cameras (1880–1900)," in *Encyclopedia of Nineteenth-Century Photography*, ed. John Hannavy (London: Routledge, 2013), 1:250.

79. Charles Dickens, "The Magic Crystal," *Household Words* 38 (14 December 1850), 137. The magician's name, Maghrab'ee, recalled Maugraby the Magician of *A Thousand and One Nights*, who kidnaps children and teaches them his Satanic sorcery. For the story of Maugraby, see Henry Weber, *Tales of the East* (Edinburgh: Ballantyne, 1812), 219–42. Weber notes that the name means "barbarous."

80. On telegraph boys, see Katie Hindmarch-Watson, "Male Prostitution and the London GPO: Telegraph Boys' 'Immorality' from Nationalization to the Cleveland Street Scandal," *Journal of British Studies* 51, no. 3 (2012): 594–617.

81. Luhmann, *Reality of the Mass Media*, 58.

82. On this discourse, see Kate Flint, *The Woman Reader, 1837–1914* (Oxford: Clarendon Press, 1993).

83. H. L. Mansel, "Sensation Novels," *Quarterly Review* 113 (1863): 481–514.

84. On this generic genealogy, see my "Opium, Alcohol, Tobacco: The Substances of Memory in *The Moonstone*," in *The Blackwell Companion to Sensation Fiction*, ed. Pamela Gilbert (Chichester: Blackwell, 2011), 208–19.

85. Alison Winter, *Mesmerized: Powers of Mind in Victorian Britain* (Chicago: University of Chicago Press, 1998), 326.

86. In this way, the formation may more closely resemble Freud's concept of the preconscious—stored information that is not repressed. See Sigmund Freud, "A Note on the Unconscious in Psychoanalysis" (1912), in *General Psychological Theory: Papers on Metapsychology* (New York: Touchstone, 1963), 33–40.

87. See Jenny Bourne-Taylor, *In the Secret Theatre of Home: Wilkie Collins, Sensation Narrative, and Nineteenth-Century Psychology* (London: Routledge, 1988), 174–206.

88. Edward Smedley, W. Cooke Taylor, Henry Edwards, and Elihu Rich, *Occult Sciences* (London: Richard Griffin, 1855), 321.

89. I draw the term "counterimperialism" from Ian Duncan, "*The Moonstone*, the Victorian Novel, and Imperialist Panic," *Modern Language Quarterly: A Journal of Literary History* 55, no. 3 (1994): 297–319.

90. See Jaya Mehta, "English Romance: Indian Violence," *Centennial Review* 39, no. 3 (1995): 644–47.

91. Wilkie Collins, "Magnetic Evenings at Home," *Leader* (January–April 1852). Accessed 3/22/15 at http://www.web40571.clarahost.co.uk/wilkie/etext/magnetictext.htm.

92. Geraldine Jewsbury, unsigned review, *Athenaeum* (July 25, 1868), 106; reprinted in *Moonstone*, ed. Farmer, 543–44.

93. Andrew Lang, *The Making of Religion*, 3rd ed. (London: Longmans, 1909), 83.

94. Anonymous (Ada Goodrich Freer), "Recent Experiments in Crystal-Vision," *Proceedings of the Society for Psychical Research*, part 14 (June 1889): 486–521; and "Miss X" (A. Goodrich Freer), *Essays in Psychical Research*, 2nd ed. (London: George Redway, 1899), 103–41.

95. On Goodrich Freer, see Roger Luckhurst, *The Invention of Telepathy* (Oxford: Oxford University Press, 2002), 130.

96. Goodrich Freer, *Essays*, 108.

97. F. W. H. Myers et al., *Proceedings of the Society for Psychical Research* 5 (London: Keegan, Paul, Trench, 1885): 524.

98. F. W. H Myers et al. *Proceedings of the Society for Psychical Research* 7 (London: Keegan, Paul Trench, 1892): 319.

99. Maurice Rickards, *The Encyclopedia of Ephemera* (New York: Routledge, 2000), 55.

100. *Standard's Dictionary of Advertising Blotting: A Book for Manufacturers, Selling Agents, and Principals* (Richmond, Va.: Standard Paper Manufacturing, 1922), 27.

101. Nickell, Pen, Ink, and Evidence, 62.

102. Sigmund Freud, "A Note upon the 'Mystic Writing Pad'" [1925]. From Freud, *General Psychological Theory: Papers on Metapsychology* (New York: Touchstone, 1963), 211–16.

103. Jacques Derrida, *Writing and Difference* (1978; Chicago: University of Chicago Press, 1993), 227. Further citations are to this text and appear in parentheses.

104. Kittler has noted Freud's aggressive lack of interest in the new media technologies of his era—the telephone, film, and phonograph. Just as he disdained mass media, so too did he eschew popular cultural referents in favor of classical, Renaissance, and Romantic myths, narratives, and tropes when delineating psychic structures. See Friedrich Kittler, "The World of the Symbolic—A World of the Machine," in *Literature Media Information Systems*, ed. John Johnson (Amsterdam: Overseas Publishers' Association, 1997), 135. See also Thomas Elsaesser, "Freud and the Technical Media: The Enduring Magic of the Wunderblock," in *Media Archaeology: Approaches,*

Applications, and Implications, ed. Erkki Huhtamo and Jussi Parikka (Berkeley: University of California Press, 2011), 95–115.

105. Alexander Cozens (1717–1786) was an earlier inkblot artist, but his practice belongs to an empirical tradition and a Lockean epistemology. See Charles A. Cramer, "Alexander Cozens's New Method: The Blot and General Nature," *Art Bulletin* 79. no. 1 (1997): 112–29. For the opposing idea, that Cozens's blots resemble marbling and thus anticipate nonrepresentational art, see Lothar Müller, *White Magic: The Age of Paper,* trans. Jessica Spengler (Cambridge: Polity Press, 2014), 119.

106. On Hugo's media, see Nathan Kernan, "Museum Reviews: Shadows of a Hand: The Drawings of Victor Hugo," *On Paper* 2, no. 6 (1998): 40.

107. Florian Rodari, "Victor Hugo, a Precursor a posteriori," in *Shadows of a Hand: The Drawings of Victor Hugo* (London: Holberton, 1998), 25.

108. Luc Sante, "The Octopus Bearing the Initials V H," in *Shadows of a Hand: The Drawings of Victor Hugo* (London: Holberton, 1998), 9.

109. Quoted in Jean Leymarie, *Victor Hugo and the Romantic Vision: Drawings and Watercolors* (New York: Jan Krugier Gallery, 1990), 13.

110. Justinus Kerner, preface to *Klecksographien* (1857; Berlin: Hofenberg, 2014), 6. Further references are to this edition and are cited in parentheses in the text.

111. Ruth McEnery Stuart and Albert Bigelow Paine, *Gobolinks; or, Shadow Pictures for Young and Old* (New York: Century, 1896), ix.

112. John Prosper Carmel, *Blottentots* (San Francisco: Paul Elder, 1907), 1.

113. For this point, I am indebted to Rachel Teukolsky.

114. Olga Rorschach, "Regarding/About the Life and Character (Personality) of Hermann Rorschach." A lecture given at a conference of the Swiss Society for Psychiatry, June 26, 1943, in Münsterlingen. Unpublished translation courtesy of Bianca Basten and James M. Wood.

115. Henri Ellenberger, "The Life and Work of Hermann Rorschach, 1884–1922," *Bulletin of the Menninger Clinic* 18, no. 5 (1954): 196.

116. Hermann Rorschach, *Psychodiagnostics,* trans. Paul Lemkau, ed. W. Morgenthaler (1922; Berne: Verlag Hans Huber, 1942), 87.

117. Ibid., 15.

118. Peter Galison, "Image of Self," in *Things That Talk: Object Lessons from Art and Science,* ed. Lorraine Daston (New York: Zone, 2004), 271.

119. Ernest G. Schachtel, *Experiential Foundations of Rorschach's Test* (New York: Basic, 1966), 22.

120. Tim Killick, *British Short Fiction in the Early Nineteenth Century: The Rise of the Tale* (Aldershot: Ashgate, 2008), 13.

121. Sigmund Freud, *Totem and Taboo,* ed. James Strachey (1913; New York: Norton, 1950), 77–81.

122. Lawrence K. Frank, *Projective Methods* (Springfield, Ill.: Charles Thomas, 1948), 47.

123. David Rapaport, Merton M. Gill, and Roy Schafer, *Diagnostic Psychological Testing*. 1948. Revised edition by Robert R. Holt (New York: International Universities Press, 1968), 225.

124. Benjamin, "The Work of Art in the Age of Its Technical Reproducibility," 31.

125. See Damion Searls, *The Inkblots: Hermann Rorschach, His Iconic Test, and the Power of Seeing* (New York: Crown, 2017), 144–46.

126. W. Morgenthaler, "The Struggle for the Publication of Psychodiagnostics." Originally published as "Der Kampf um das Erscheinen der Psychodiagnostik," in *Rorschachiana* 2 (1954): 255–70. Unpublished translation by Bianca Moehlmann and James M. Wood, and cited with their permission.

127. See Greg Siegel, *Forensic Media: Reconstructing Accidents in Accelerated Modernity* (Durham, N.C.: Duke University Press, 2014).

128. Schachtel, *Experiential Foundations*, 243.

129. Quoted in Pierre Pichot, "Centenary of the Birth of Hermann Rorschach," *Journal of Psychological Assessment* 48, no. 6 (1984): 593.

130. "Rorschach Test—Product Description." Accessed 9/6/16 at http://www.hogrefe.co.uk/rorschach-test-rors.html.

4. "DREAMING TRUE": PLAYBACK, IMMEDIACY, AND "DU MAURIERNESS"

1. Jonathan Crary, *Suspensions of Perception: Attention, Spectacle, and Modern Culture* (Cambridge: MIT Press, 1999), 30.

2. George Du Maurier, *Peter Ibbetson* (1891; London: Osgood, McIlvaine, 1892), Further citations are to this edition and appear in parentheses in the text.

3. Kittler and Huyssen each make this argument, distinguishing experimental modernist literature from popular genre fiction. Du Maurier's novels belong in between. See Friedrich Kittler, *Discourse Networks 1800/1900*, trans. Michael Metteer (Stanford, Calif.: Stanford University Press, 1992); and Andreas Huyssen, *After the Great Divide: Modernism, Mass Culture, Postmodernism* (Bloomington: Indiana University Press, 1987).

4. Richard Kelly, *The Art of George du Maurier* (Aldershot: Scolar Press, 1996), 16.

5. John Carey, *The Intellectuals and the Masses: Pride and Prejudice among the Literary Intelligentsia, 1880–1939* (London: Faber and Faber, 1992), 6.

6. Henry Copley Greene, "George du Maurier, the Writer," *Harvard Monthly* 19, no. 2 (1894): 49.

7. David Harvey, *Paris: Capital of Modernity* (London: Routledge, 2005), 10.

8. On Haussmannization as radical break, see Harvey and to a lesser extent, Priscilla Parkhurst Ferguson, *Paris as Revolution: Writing the Nineteenth-Century City* (Berkeley: University of California Press, 1994); for arguments that emphasize his continuity with earlier urban plans and realities, see Nicholas Papayanis, *Planning Paris before Haussmann* (Baltimore: Johns Hopkins University Press, 2004), and Vanessa Schwartz, *Spectacular Realities: Early Mass Culture in Fin-de-siècle Paris* (Berkeley: University of California Press, 1998).

9. On "Haussmannize," see Ferguson, *Paris as Revolution*, 118.

10. "Notable Recent Novels," *Atlantic Monthly* 80, no. 482 (1897): 851; Hélène Cixous, *Philippines*, trans. Laurent Milesi (Cambridge: Polity, 2011), 27.

11. Henry James, "George du Maurier," *Harper's New Monthly Magazine* 95, no. 568 (1897): 606, 604.

12. John Masefield, "Introduction to *Peter Ibbetson* and *Trilby*," in *Novels of George Du Maurier* (London: Pilot Press and Peter Davies, 1947), ix. J. M. Barrie's Peter Pan would take his first name, via Du Maurier's young grandson Peter Llewellyn Davies, from *Peter Ibbetson*.

13. C. C. Hoyer Millar, *George du Maurier and Others* (London: Cassell, 1937), 132–33. Mott also lists *Peter Ibbetson* as a "better seller" in the United States, meaning that it did not reach the "best seller" status of total sales equal to one percent of the population. Frank Luther Mott, *Golden Multitudes: The Story of Best-Sellers in the United States* (New York: Macmillan, 1947).

14. John N. Raphael, *Peter Ibbetson: A Play in Four Acts* (New York: Samuel French, 1915).

15. Quoted in Michael Richardson, *Surrealism and Cinema* (New York: Berg, 2006), 64.

16. Jill Galvan, *The Sympathetic Medium: Feminine Channeling, the Occult, and Communication Technologies, 1859–1919* (Ithaca, N.Y.: Cornell University Press, 2010), 126–34; and Nicholas Daly, *Modernism, Romance and the Fin de Siècle: Popular Fiction and British Culture, 1880–1914* (Cambridge: Cambridge University Press, 1999), 158–61.

17. Thomas Richards links this intensification to a second phase of commodification following the Crystal Palace Exhibition, related to the Golden Jubilee of 1887, and giving rise to new imperial and gendered meanings; in the U.S. context, Susan Harris Smith and Melanie Dawson evoke the confluence of a rising middle class, desire for national culture, heightened imperialism, and a self-conscious rhetoric of technological and social novelty in the expansion of commodity culture. See Thomas Richards, *The Commodity Culture of Victorian Britain: Advertising and Spectacle,*

1851–1914 (Stanford, Calif.: Stanford University Press, 1990); and Susan Harris Smith and Melanie Dawson, *The American 1890s: A Cultural Reader* (Durham, N.C.: Duke University Press, 2000).

18. J. L. Gilder and J. B. Gilder, eds., *Trilbyana: The Rise and Progress of a Popular Novel* (New York: Critic Co., 1895), 25–26.

19. See Jonathan Freedman, "Mania and the Middlebrow: The Case of *Trilby*," in *Lyrical Symbols and Narrative Transformations: Essays in Honor of Ralph Freedman*, ed. Kathleen L. Komar and Ross Shideler (Columbia, S.C.: Camden House, 1989), 149–69; and Barbara Hochman, *Getting at the Author: Reimagining Books and Reading in the Age of American Realism* (Amherst: University of Massachusetts Press, 2001).

20. James, "George du Maurier," 595.

21. Critics such as Robert Patten and Andy Williams have demonstrated how the literary form of *The Pickwick Papers* was shaped by its commercial context; however, they have not analyzed the ancillary Pickwick merchandise such as cigars, canes, and coats. See Robert Patten, "Serialized Retrospection in *The Pickwick Papers*," in *Literature in the Marketplace: Nineteenth-Century British Publishing and Reading Practices*, ed. John O. Jordan and Robert Patten (Cambridge: Cambridge University Press, 1995), 123–42; and Andy Williams, "Advertising and Fiction in *The Pickwick Papers*," *Victorian Literature and Culture* 38, no. 2 (2010): 319–35. Whereas Pickwick consumer items disseminated a popular aesthetic, those associated with Du Maurier were more clearly middlebrow: Trilby sausage and ice cream purchases were driven by a desire for a Bohemian-inflected, high bourgeois European culture.

22. Emily Jenkins, "*Trilby*: Fads, Photographers, and 'Over-Perfect' Feet," *Book History* 1 (1998): 226.

23. Jonathan Crary, *24/7: Late Capitalism and the Ends of Sleep* (London: Verso, 2013), 10–11.

24. Du Maurier also drew a cartoon in which the Ramsgate camera obscura eye captures a young man proposing to his sweetheart. See "Where Ignorance Is Bliss" (1868) in Kelly, *Art of George du Maurier*, 45.

25. S. T. Coleridge, *The Works of Samuel Taylor Coleridge, Prose and Verse, Complete in One Volume* (Philadelphia: Crissy and Markley, 1853), 54, 218.

26. S. T. Coleridge, *Biographia Literaria* (London: Rest, Penner, 1817), 1:115.

27. Thomas De Quincey, *Confessions of an English Opium-Eater*, ed. Grevel Lindop (1821; Oxford: Oxford World Classics, 1985), 69.

28. E. S. Dallas, *The Gay Science* (London: Chapman and Hall, 1866), 1:213.

29. W. B. Carpenter, *Principles of Mental Physiology* (1874; New York: Appleton, 1883), 436.

30. For a recent account of the cultural significance of dreaming in Victorian Britain, see Natalya Lusty and Helen Groth, *Dreams and Modernity: A Cultural History* (London: Routledge, 2013).

31. Robert Macnish, *The Philosophy of Sleep* (1830; Glasgow: M'Phun, 1838), 48.

32. Henry Holland, *Chapters on Mental Physiology* (London: Longman Brown Green, 1852), 94.

33. Henri Ellenberger, *The Discovery of the Unconscious: The History and Evolution of Dynamic Psychiatry* (New York: Basic Books, 1970), 306.

34. James Sully, "The Dream as Revelation," *Fortnightly Review* 59 (1893): 365.

35. Ellenberger, *Discovery of the Unconscious*, 306–7.

36. Hervey de Saint-Denys, *Dreams and How to Guide Them*, ed. and trans. Morton Schatzman (London: Duckworth, 1982), 39; further citations are to this edition and appear in parentheses in the text.

37. Mark Twain, *Old Times on the Mississippi* (Toronto: Belford, 1876), 149–57.

38. See Daniel Cavicchi, *Listening and Longing: Music Lovers in the Age of Barnum* (Middletown, Conn.: Wesleyan University Press, 2011).

39. See Fiona Coll, "'Just a Singing Machine': The Making of an Automaton in George du Maurier's *Trilby*," *University of Toronto Quarterly* 79, no. 2 (2010): 742–63.

40. Carole Marvin, *When Old Technologies Were New* (Oxford: Oxford University Press, 1988), 212–13.

41. Ibid., 109–51.

42. T. Martin Wood, *George Du Maurier: The Satirist of the Victorians* (New York: McBride, Nast, 1913), 46.

43. Walter Pater, *The Renaissance* (1873; Oxford: Oxford University Press, 1998), 153.

44. John Picker, *Victorian Soundscapes* (Oxford: Oxford University Press, 2003), 111.

45. Jonathan Sterne, *The Audible Past: Cultural Origins of Sound Reproduction* (Durham, N.C.: Duke University Press, 2003), 204.

46. Picker, *Victorian Soundscapes*, 116.

47. "George du Maurier," *Critic*, no. 765 (1896): 223.

48. On this aspect of the train's cultural significance, see Wolfgang Schivelbusch, *The Railway Journey: The Industrialization of Space and Time* (Berkeley: University of California Press, 1987), 113–28.

49. Ivan Kreilkamp, *Voice and the Victorian Storyteller* (Cambridge: Cambridge University Press, 2005), 187.

50. Bernard Stiegler, "Memory," in *Critical Terms for Media Studies*, ed. W. J. T. Mitchell and Mark B. N. Hansen (Chicago: University of Chicago Press, 2010), 80.

51. Nicholas Dames, *Amnesiac Selves: Nostalgia, Forgetting, and British Fiction, 1810–1870* (Oxford: Oxford University Press, 2001).

52. Marcel Proust, *Swann's Way*, trans. Lydia Davis (New York: Penguin, 2003), 47.

53. Sara Danius, *The Senses of Modernism: Technology, Perception, Aesthetics* (Ithaca, N.Y.: Cornell University Press, 2002).

54. Walter Benjamin, "On Some Motifs in Baudelaire," 1938, in *Illuminations*, trans. Harry Zohn (New York: Schocken, 1968), 186–87.

55. Marshall McLuhan, *Understanding Media: The Extensions of Man: The Critical Edition* (Corte Madura, Calif.: Gingko Press, 2003), 47.

56. Susan Buck-Morss, "Aesthetics and Anaesthetics: Walter Benjamin's Artwork Essay Reconsidered," *October* 62 (Autumn 1992): 18.

57. Benjamin, "On Some Motifs," 160–61.

58. See, for example, Ronald R. Thomas, *Dreams of Authority: Freud and the Fictions of the Unconscious* (Ithaca, N.Y.: Cornell University Press, 1990).

59. More radical readings in performance studies construe all presence as presence effects. See *Archaeologies of Presence: Art, Performance, and the Persistence of Being*, ed. Gabriella Giannachi, Nick Kaye, and Michael Shanks (New York: Routledge, 2012).

60. Andrew King and John Plunkett, *Victorian Print Media: A Reader* (Oxford: Oxford University Press, 2005), 1.

61. See, for example, Verity Hunt's reading of his cartoon "The Telephonoscope." Verity Hunt, "Electric Leisure: Late Nineteenth-Century Dreams of Remote Viewing by Telectroscope," *Journal of Literature and Science* 7, no. 1 (2014): 59–60.

62. George Du Maurier, *Trilby* (1894; Oxford: Oxford University Press, 1998), 194–5. Further citations are to this edition, in parentheses in the text.

63. Elaine Freedgood, *The Ideas in Things: Fugitive Meaning in the Victorian Novel* (Chicago: University of Chicago Press, 2006).

64. Richards, *Commodity Culture*, 7.

65. Joseph Bristow, "'Dirty Pleasure': *Trilby*'s Filth," in *Filth: Dirt, Disgust, and Modern Life*, ed. William A. Cohen and Ryan Johnson (Minneapolis: University of Minnesota Press, 2005), 175.

66. Jill Matus accordingly finds trauma to be a later development in the history of psychology. See Jill Matus, *Shock, Memory, and the Unconscious in Victorian Fiction* (Cambridge: Cambridge University Press, 2009).

67. This aspect of the novel resembles the consumption of panoramas, a popular contemporaneous entertainment. See Peter Otto, "Artificial Environments, Virtual Realities, and the Cultivation of Propensity in the London Colosseum," in *Virtual Victorians: Networks, Connections, Technologies*, ed. Andrew Stauffer and Veronica Alfano (London: Palgrave Macmillan, 2015), 167–87.

68. Leonée Ormond, *George Du Maurier* (Pittsburgh: University of Pittsburgh Press, 1969), 20.

69. George Du Maurier, *The Martian* (New York: Harper and Brothers, 1896), 61. Further citations are to this edition and appear in the text in parentheses.

70. Ferguson, *Paris as Revolution*, 25.

71. For an excellent alternative reading of this passage in the context of late Victorian theories of ancestral memory, see Athena Vrettos, "'Little Bags of Remembrance': Du Maurier's *Peter Ibbetson* and Victorian Theories of Ancestral Memory," *Romanticism and Victorianism on the Net* 53 (February 2009).

72. Richards, *Commodity Culture*, 90.

73. Ormond, *George Du Maurier*, 67–68. Other details of Du Maurier's life are drawn from this standard biography.

74. Sianne Ngai, *Ugly Feelings* (Cambridge, Mass.: Harvard University Press, 2005), 91. Ngai describes the racialized aspects of animatedness in U.S. culture from *Uncle Tom's Cabin* through the Fox Claymation television show *The PJs*. Du Maurier's aesthetic by contrast is markedly white and eugenic.

75. James, "George du Maurier." 606.

76. David Kunzle, *The History of the Comic Strip: The Nineteenth Century* (Berkeley: University of California Press, 1990), 5.

77. George Du Maurier, *Social and Pictorial Satire* (London: Harper & Brothers, 1898), 139–41.

78. Charles Baudelaire, *The Painter of Modern Life and Other Essays*, trans. Jonathan Mayne (London: Phaidon, 1995), 3.

79. Kelly, *Art of George du Maurier*, 13.

80. Gerry Beegan, *The Mass Image: A Social History of Photomechanical Reproduction in Victorian London* (Basingstoke: Palgrave Macmillan, 2008), 18.

81. This joke can also be read against Du Maurier, who, throughout his oeuvre, drew the same idealized female face and figure, producing the modern type he satirized.

82. Daly, *Modernism, Romance*, 158–59.

83. See Leah Price, *How to Do Things with Books in Victorian Britain* (Princeton, N.J.: Princeton University Press, 2012), 45–71.

84. Du Maurier even writes the duchess into *Trilby*, as a society acquaintance of Little Billee who reminds him of his lost love; he posits the two as cousins "(though on the wrong side of the blanket)." See Du Maurier, *Trilby*, 273.

85. Kelly, *Art of George du Maurier*, 28.

86. For her punning play with the word, see Cixous, *Philippines*, 19–26.

87. Michael Atkinson, "Between Worlds," *Film Comment* 29, no. 4 (1993): 78.

88. Henry Hathaway, *Peter Ibbetson* (Paramount, 1935).

89. Rachel Bowlby, *Just Looking: Consumer Culture in Dreiser, Gissing and Zola* (New York: Methuen, 1985), 8.

90. Ormond, *George Du Maurier*, 429.

91. Du Maurier, *Social and Pictorial Satire*, 139–41.

92. T. J. Clark, *The Painting of Modern Life: Paris in the Art of Manet and His Followers*. Revised edition (Princeton, N.J.: Princeton University Press, 1999), 237.

93. Ormond, *George Du Maurier*, 491.

5. "A FORM OF REVERIE, A MALADY OF DREAMING": *DORIAN GRAY*, PERSONALITY, AND MASS CULTURE

1. Oscar Wilde, *The Picture of Dorian Gray*, ed. Robert Mighall (New York: Penguin, 2003), 121. Further citations are to this edition and appear in parentheses.

2. Nancy Armstrong, *Fiction in the Age of Photography: The Legacy of British Realism* (Cambridge, Mass.: Harvard University Press, 1999), 24. See also Audrey Jaffe, "Embodying Culture: Dorian's Wish," in *Aesthetic Subjects*, ed. Pamela R. Matthews and David McWhirter (Minneapolis: University of Minnesota Press, 2003), 295–312.

3. Jaffe, "Embodying Culture."

4. Walter Benjamin, "The Work of Art in the Age of Its Technical Reproducibility: Second Version," in *The Work of Art in the Age of Its Technical Reproducibility and Other Writings on Media*, ed. Michael Jennings, Brigid Doherty, and Thomas Y. Levin (Cambridge, Mass.: Belknap Press of Harvard University Press, 2008), 19–55.

5. Niklas Luhmann, *The Reality of the Mass Media*, trans. Kathleen Cross (1996; Stanford, Calif.: Stanford University Press, 2000), 47. Further citations are to this edition and are made parenthetically in the text.

6. On this point, see Regenia Gagnier, *Idylls of the Marketplace* (Stanford, Calif.: Stanford University Press, 1986), 98.

7. See, for example, Daniel A. Novak, *Realism, Photography, and Nineteenth-Century Fiction* (Cambridge: Cambridge University Press, 2008),

118–45; and Ronald Thomas, "Poison Books and Moving Pictures: Vulgarity in *The Picture of Dorian Gray*," in *Victorian Vulgarity: Taste in Verbal and Visual Culture*, ed. Susan David Bernstein and Elsie B. Michie (Farnham: Ashgate, 2009), 185–200.

8. Eve Kosofsky Sedgwick, *Epistemology of the Closet* (Berkeley: University of California Press, 1990), 160, 186–87. Further citations are to this edition and appear in the text parenthetically.

9. John Locke, *Essay concerning Human Understanding*, ed. Roger Woolhouse (1689; London: Penguin, 1998).

10. Jean-Jacques Rousseau, *Reveries of the Solitary Walker*, ed. Russell Goulbourne (Oxford: Oxford World's Classics, 2011).

11. Erasmus Darwin, *Zoonomia; or, The Laws of Organic Life.* 3rd U.S. ed. (1794; Boston: Thomas and Andrews, 1809), 174.

12. Thomas McFarland, *Romanticism and the Heritage of Rousseau* (Oxford: Clarendon Press, 1995), 61.

13. On Rousseau's solipsism, see Jean Starobinski, *Jean-Jacques Rousseau: Transparency and Obstruction*, trans. Arthur Goldhammer (Chicago: University of Chicago Press, 1988), 352.

14. Michael Davis, *The Autobiography of Philosophy: Rousseau's* The Reveries of the Solitary Walker (Lanham, Md.: Rowan and Littlefield, 1999), 180.

15. Paul Ponder, *Noctes Atticae; or, Reveries in a Garret* (London: Longman, 1825).

16. Benjamin, "Work of Art," 34.

17. Oscar Wilde, "A Few Maxims and Phrases for the Instruction of the Over-Educated," 1894, in *Collins Complete Works of Oscar Wilde: Centenary Edition* (Glasgow: HarperCollins, 1999), 1242.

18. G. H. Lewes, *The Physiology of Common Life* (1860; New York: Appleton, 1875), 2:311.

19. Elizabeth S. Goodstein, *Experience without Qualities: Boredom and Modernity* (Stanford, Calif.: Stanford University Press, 2004), 188.

20. Gustave Flaubert, *Madame Bovary*, trans. Margaret Mauldon (1857; Oxford: Oxford World's Classics, 2004), 32.

21. Jeff Nunokawa, *Tame Passions of Wilde: The Styles of Manageable Desire* (Princeton, N.J.: Princeton University Press, 2003), 71–89.

22. Walter Pater, *The Renaissance: Studies in Art and Poetry*, ed. Adam Phillips (Oxford: Oxford University Press, 1985), 152. Further citations are to this edition and appear in parentheses.

23. Kate Hext, *Walter Pater: Individualism and Aesthetic Philosophy* (Edinburgh: Edinburgh University Press, 2013), 12.

24. For a discussion of Aestheticism's relationship to commodification and advertising, see Jonathan Freedman, *Professions of Taste: Henry James,*

British Aestheticism, and Commodity Culture (Stanford, Calif.: Stanford University Press, 1989).

25. *Oxford English Dictionary*, 2nd online ed.

26. Armstrong, *Fiction in the Age of Photography*, 159–60.

27. Oscar Wilde, "The Decay of Lying," in *The Complete Works of Oscar Wilde, Vol. 4: Criticism*, ed. Josephine Guy (Oxford: Oxford University Press, 2007), 93.

28. Oscar Wilde, "The Critic as Artist," in *Collins Complete Works of Oscar Wilde: Centenary Edition* (Glasgow: HarperCollins, 1999), 1134–35.

29. See Talia Schaffer, *Forgotten Female Aesthetes: Literary Culture in Late-Victorian England* (Charlottesville: University of Virginia Press, 2000), chap. 1.

30. Talia Schaffer, *Novel Craft: Victorian Domestic Handicraft and Nineteenth-Century Fiction* (Oxford: Oxford University Press, 2014), 16.

31. Leah Price, *How to Do Things with Books in Victorian Britain* (Princeton, N.J.: Princeton University Press, 2012).

32. Nicholas Frankel, *Oscar Wilde's Decorated Books* (Ann Arbor: University of Michigan Press, 2000), 149.

33. Joseph Bristow, Introduction to *The Complete Words of Oscar Wilde*, vol. 3 (Oxford: Oxford University Press, 2005), xi–lxviii.

34. See Nicholas Frankel, *The Picture of Dorian Gray: An Annotated, Uncensored Edition* (Cambridge, Mass.: Belknap Press of Harvard University Press,, 2011), 194–95.

35. William Seabrook, *No Hiding Place: An Autobiography* (Philadelphia: J. B. Lippincott, 1942), 187.

36. Gagnier, *Idylls of the Marketplace*, 65–66; Schaffer, *Forgotten Female Aesthetes*, 50. Youngkin has recently complicated this correlation. See Molly Youngkin, "The Aesthetic Character of Oscar Wilde's *The Woman's World*," in *Wilde Discoveries: Traditions, Histories, Archives*, ed. Joseph Bristow (Toronto: University of Toronto Press, 2013), 121–142.

37. Frankel, *Annotated, Uncensored Edition*, 198n29.

38. Laurel Brake, *Subjugated Knowledges: Journalism, Gender, and Literature* (New York: New York University Press, 1994), 132–33.

39. Walter Benjamin, *The Arcades Project*, trans. Howard Eiland and Kevin McLaughlin (Cambridge, Mass.: Belknap Press of Harvard University Press, 1999), 69.

40. Oscar Wilde, "The Truth of Masks: A Note on Illusion," in *The Complete Works of Oscar Wilde*, vol. 4, ed. Josephine Guy (Oxford: Oxford University Press, 2007), 207–28.

41. See, for example, Herbert Maxwell, "The Craving for Fiction," *Nineteenth Century* 33 (1893): 1046–61.

42. See Kelly J. Mays, "The Disease of Reading and Victorian Periodicals," in *Literature in the Marketplace*, ed. John Jordan and Robert Patten (Cambridge: Cambridge University Press, 1995), 165–94; and Kate Flint, *The Woman Reader, 1837–1914* (Oxford: Oxford University Press, 1993).

43. Garrett Stewart, *The Look of Reading: Book, Painting, Text* (Chicago: University of Chicago Press, 2006), 32.

44. Carol Armstrong, *Manet Manette* (New Haven, Conn.: Yale University Press, 2002), 244–50.

45. Kathryn Brown, *Women Readers in French Painting, 1870–1890: A Space for the Imagination* (Farnham: Ashgate, 2012), 37.

46. Wilde, "Decay of Lying," 93.

47. Stewart, *Look of Reading*, 101.

48. See Stefan Bollmann, *Reading Women* (London: Merrell, 2005), 86.

49. Stewart, *Look of Reading*, 42.

50. Wilde, "Critic as Artist," 1115.

51. The quotation from the letter to Alma Schindler shown in the epigraph is from Karen Monson, *Alma Mahler: Muse to Genius* (Boston: Houghton Mifflin, 1983), 40–41.

52. Georg Simmel, "The Metropolis and Mental Life," 1903, in *On Individuality and Social Forms*, ed. Donald N. Levine (Chicago: University of Chicago Press, 1972), 336.

53. *OED*, 3rd online ed.

54. Quoted in David Higgins, *Romantic Genius and the Literary Magazine: Biography, Celebrity, Politics* (New York: Routledge, 2005), 46.

55. David Higgins, *Romantic Genius and the Literary Magazine: Biography, Celebrity, Politics* (New York: Routledge, 2005), 46.

56. G. E. Berrios, "European Views on Personality Disorders: A Conceptual History," *Comprehensive Psychiatry* 34, no. 1 (1993): 17–18.

57. On the concept of character, see Stefan Collini, "The Idea of Character in Victorian Political Thought," *Transactions of the Royal Historical Society*, 5th series, vol. 35 (1985): 29–50.

58. Lynn M. Voskuil, *Acting Naturally: Victorian Theatricality and Authenticity* (Charlottesville: University of Virginia Press, 2004), 204.

59. Oscar Wilde, "The Soul of Man under Socialism," in *Collins Complete Works of Oscar Wilde: Centenary Edition* (Glasgow: HarperCollins, 1999), 1179.

60. Wilde, "Critic as Artist," 1131–32.

61. Teresa Brennan, *The Transmission of Affect* (Ithaca, N.Y. Cornell University Press, 2004), 3.

62. Freedman, *Professions of Taste*, 43.

63. Performance tends to resist definition. Here, as in chapters 1 and 2, I draw primarily on Jon Mackenzie's *Perform or Else*, which situates perfor-

mance at the crux of cultural and technological demands within modern economies. I am also drawing very generally on queer theory's appropriation of performativity from speech act theory and application to gendered and other social expectations. See Mackenzie, *Perform or Else: From Discipline to Performance* (New York: Routledge, 2001); and Judith Butler, *Gender Trouble: Feminism and the Subversion of Identity* (New York: Routledge, 1990), chap. 3, sec. 4.

64. Paul Fortunato, *Modernist Aesthetics and Consumer Culture in the Writings of Oscar Wilde* (New York: Routledge, 2007), 124–25.

65. See Neil Hultgren, "Oscar Wilde's Poetic Injustice in *The Picture of Dorian Gray*," in *Wilde Discoveries: Traditions, Histories, Archives*, ed. Joseph Bristow (Toronto: University of Toronto Press/Clark Memorial Library, 2013), 212–30.

66. On gay men's adoption of female star personas at the turn of the century, see George Chauncey, *Gay New York: Gender, Urban Culture, and the Making of the Gay Male World, 1890–1940* (New York: Basic Books, 1994), 50–51.

67. Thomas, "Poison Books and Moving Pictures," 194.

68. On this point, see Jaffe, "Embodying Culture," 306–7.

69. See also Armstrong, *Fiction in the Age of Photography*, 159–60.

70. Wilde, "Decay of Lying," 91.

71. For Baudelaire's definition, see "The Painter of Modern Life," 1863, in *The Painter of Modern Life and Other Essays*, ed. and trans. Jonathan Mayne (London: Phaidon, 1995), 3.

72. Rachel Bowlby, *Shopping with Freud* (New York: Routledge, 1993), 22.

73. Charles Bernheimer, "Unknowing Decadence," in *Perennial Decay: On the Aesthetics and Politics of Decadence*, ed. Liz Constable, Matthew Potolsky, and Dennis Denisoff (Philadelphia: University of Pennsylvania Press, 1999), 60.

74. Walter Benjamin, "Surrealism: The Last Snapshot of the European Intelligentsia," in *Selected Writings*, vol. 2: *1927–1934*. Trans. Rodney Livingstone et al. (Cambridge, Mass.: Belknap Press of Harvard University Press, 1999), 216.

75. See, for example, Gustave Le Bon, *The Crowd: A Study of the Popular Mind*, 2nd ed. (New York: Macmillan, 1897), 10–11; and Gabriel Tarde, *The Laws of Imitation*, trans. Elsie Clews Parsons (New York: Henry Holt, 1903), 76–77.

76. George W. S. Trow, Foreword to *Infotainment* by Alan Belcher et al. (New York: Berg, 1985), 3.

77. Barbara Leckie, "The Novel and Censorship in Late-Victorian England," in *The Oxford Handbook of the Victorian Novel*, ed. Lisa Rodensky (Oxford: Oxford University Press, 2013), 172–74.

78. Freedman, *Professions of Taste*, 181–82.

79. See Amy Milne-Smith, *London Clubland: A Cultural History of Gender and Class in Late-Victorian Britain* (Basingstoke: Palgrave-Macmillan, 2011), chap. 6.

80. Lee Edelman, *Homographesis: Essays in Gay Literary and Cultural Theory* (New York: Routledge, 1994), 9–10.

81. Ibid., 10.

82. See Frankel, "Textual Introduction," to *The Picture of Dorian Gray: An Annotated, Uncensored Edition*, 40–42. See also Josephine Guy and Ian Small, *Oscar Wilde's Profession: Writing and the Culture Industry in the Late Nineteenth Century* (Oxford: Oxford University Press, 2000), 234.

83. Ibid., 172.

84. Brake, *Subjugated Knowledges*, 129.

85. Nicholas Frankel, *Masking the Text: Essays on Literature & Mediation in the 1890s* (High Wycombe: Rivendale Press, 2009), 22–23.

86. H. Montgomery Hyde, *The Trials of Oscar Wilde* (New York: Dover, 1962), 112.

87. See Ed Cohen, *Talk on the Wilde Side* (New York: Routledge, 1993). See also Foucault's famous definition: "The nineteenth-century homosexual became a *personage*, a past, a case history, and a childhood, in addition to being a type of life, a life form, and a morphology." Michel Foucault, *History of Sexuality*, vol. 1 (1978; New York: Vintage, 1994), 43; my emphasis.

CONCLUSION: UNKNOWN PUBLICS

1. Wilkie Collins, "The Unknown Public," *Household Words*, 18, no. 439 (1858): 217. Further citations are to this edition and appear in the text in parentheses.

2. Susanna Paasonen, Ken Hills, and Michael Petit, "Introduction: Networks of Transmission: Intensity, Sensation, Value," in *Networked Affect*, ed. Paasonen et al. (Cambridge, Mass.: MIT Press, 2015), 10.

3. Ibid., 2.

4. On Google's reactivation of "nineteenth-century ideas about an infinite census of things," see John Durham Peters, *The Marvelous Clouds: Toward a Philosophy of Elemental Media* (Chicago: University of Chicago Press, 2015), 351.

5. See, for example, Tamara Ketabgian, *The Lives of Machines: The Industrial Imaginary in Victorian Literature and Culture* (Ann Arbor: University of Michigan Press, 2011).

6. N. Katherine Hayles, *How We Became Posthuman: Virtual Bodies in Cybernetics, Literature, and Informatics* (Chicago: University of Chicago Press, 1999), 2.

7. See Wendy Hui Kyong Chun, *Programmed Visions: Software and Memory* (Cambridge, Mass.: MIT Press, 2011), 98. Further citations are to this edition and are found in the text in parentheses.

8. On vidding, see Alexis Lothian, "A Different Kind of Love Song: Vidding Fandom's Undercommons," *Cinema Journal* 54, no. 3 (2015): 138–45; on isolating tracks, see James Tobias, "Isolated Tracks and Media Clouds," *Music, Sound, and the Moving Image* 9, no. 2 (2015): 101–14; on cosplay, see Joel Gn, "Queer Simulations: The Practice, Performance, and Pleasure of Cosplay," *Continuum: Journal of Media and Cultural Studies* 25, no. 4 (2011), 583–93.

9. Alan Liu, *The Laws of Cool: Knowledge Work and the Culture of Information* (Chicago: University of Chicago Press, 2004), 237.

10. Charles Baudelaire, *The Painter of Modern Life and Other Essays*, trans. Jonathan Mayne (London: Phaidon, 1995), 29.

11. Sarah Banet-Weiser, *Authentic^{TM}: The Politics of Ambivalence in Brand Culture* (New York: New York University Press, 2012), 19.

Google reverse a perfume

Why should it always
be that weak cut inspired
by strong? Maybe the other
way around.

→ Add to sketch

ephemera unique as

— like hourour's weird works
perfume left in Dorian Gray

✱